GOVERNMENT PROCUREMENT SPECIALISTS

Presents

The Beginners Guide to Government Contracting

RESOURCES FOR THE

U.S. Government Contractor

Published by lulu.com

Order more copies from: http://www.lulu.com/content/1074028

ISBN-13: 978-1-4303-1204-8
ISBN-10: 1-4303-1204-1

Table of Contents

Introduction

A brief overview

Would you like to have a customer whose budget exceeds $250 Billion a year for goods and services? You can have that customer. The United States Federal Government is the largest purchaser of goods and services in the world. Each year, the Government issues contracts totaling more than $250 Billion for pencils, furniture, computer equipment, landscape services, janitorial services, security guard services, consultant services, etc., etc., etc. Even projects as large as construction of the Space Shuttle are performed by private industry contractors.

The desire to decrease the size of our Federal Government has increased the need for contractors dramatically. All you need to join the thousands of contractors presently selling their products and services to the Government is information and the desire to succeed. With The Beginner's Guide to Government Contracting, you now have the information you need to reach your personal and business goals of financial success.

QUICK START

The first thing you should do on your road to success in Government contracting, is locate the agencies requesting your goods or services. Normally, when the Government needs a product or service, the contracting agency involved will issue a written Request for Proposals (RFP) or Invitation for Bids (IFB). IFBs are used in sealed bidding purchases, while RFPs involve awards to be made following negotiation. Requests for Quotations (RFQs) and other solicitations are also used on a limited basis. RFQs are used for soliciting small items or limited services. As a general rule, all Government solicitations are available to anyone that requests a copy, free of charge.

To find these opportunities, you should start with the FedBizOpps.gov. It is the single government point-of-entry (GPE) for Federal government procurement opportunities over $25,000. Government buyers are able to publicize their business opportunities by posting information directly to FedBizOpps via the Internet. Through one portal - FedBizOpps (FBO) - commercial vendors seeking Federal markets for their products and services can search, monitor and retrieve opportunities solicited by the entire Federal contracting community.

The fastest and least expensive way to keep track of the daily offering of solicitations is online. The FedBizOpps is available, free of charge, on the World Wide Web at: http://www.fedbizopps.gov/.

SAMPLE FEDBIZOPPS NOTICE

The following is a notice as it was published in the FedBizOpps

Description

The US Army Contracting Agency Capital District Contracting Center, Ft Belvoir VA intends to issue a solicitation by 22 Feb 07 for Janitorial Services at Ft Myer, Virginia. Services required shall include but not limited to management, supervision, transportation, labor, materials, supplies, equipment to include planning, scheduling, coordinating, and performing a full range of custodial services post wide at Fort Myer Virginia. Custodial services shall be in accordance with the requirements defined in the Performance Work Statement (PWS). The proposed solicitation is total 8(a) set aside. Prospective offerors must be registered at DOD Central Contractor Register and must be 8(a) certified in order to be awarded a resultant contract from this solicitation.   Interested sources are responsible for frequent review to the ASFI or FedBizOpps websites for any changes or update to the solicitation after issuance to keep current on amendment or changes thereto.   No paper copy will be issued to this solicitation.   The solicitation will be posted at the ASFI or FedBizOpps website https://acquisition.army.mil/asfi

OTHER SOURCES

If you can supply a variety of products or services, you should also check other sources of information on Government purchasing. This way, there will be less chance of overlooking potential opportunities. Helpful sources are the:

U.S. Government Purchasing and Sales Directory:

This SBA publication is a comprehensive guide to the Government's (both civilian and military) purchasing and sales activities. The directory lists products and services bought by the Government and indicates which agencies buy them and the proper purchasing offices to be contacted by potential suppliers. Copies may be purchased from the Superintendent of Documents, U.S. Government Printing Office, Washington, D.C. 20402. Stock Number 378-8310-82-13.

Business Service Centers of the General Services Administration:

The GSA acts as a purchasing agency for numerous items of equipment and supplies, as well as services used by Federal agencies. You can find out about items bought by GSA by writing to or visiting the nearest GSA Business Service Center. These offices are located in Atlanta, GA; Boston, MA; Chicago, IL; Fort Worth, TX; Denver, CO; Kansas City, MO; Los Angeles and San Francisco, CA; Philadelphia, PA; New York, NY; and Washington, D.C.

HOW TO GET ON SOLICITATION MAILING LISTS

After determining which agencies procure the items or services your company can supply, you should ask them for the forms needed to place your company's name on their solicitation mailing lists. In answer to your request, the purchasing office will send a "Solicitation Mailing List Application, Standard Form 129".

If the agency does not include a buying list, or if the buying list they send does not include the exact products or services you can supply, you should attach a separate sheet to the SF 129 showing:

- The specific name of each product or service you offer;

- Additional items or services you could provide the purchasing agency other than those already listed; and

- Any item or service you have supplied in the past under Government contracts.

- Each product or service listed in the attached sheet should be fully described, and, if possible, you should indicate the Government specification number for each item.

Once you are on an agency's list, you will be notified every time they need a product or service you provide. When you receive IFBs or RFPs from a purchasing agency that has you on their list, you should always either submit an offer or notify the purchasing office that you are unable to bid on the particular item or service requested, but wish to remain on the active list for future purchases. Otherwise, you may be dropped from their list and miss future opportunities.

SPECIFICATIONS AND STANDARDS

All published Government specifications and standards for items or services purchased by military and civilian departments and agencies may be obtained from the following locations:

- Federal Specifications and Standards and Commercial Item Descriptions - Nearest Business Service Center of the General Services Administration or the Federal Specifications Distribution Center, Federal Supply Service, GSA, 7th & "D" Streets, S.W., Washington, D.C. 20407; and

- Military Specifications - Commanding Officer, Naval Publications and Forms Center, 5801 Tabor Avenue, Philadelphia, PA 19120.

Copies of specifications and standards needed by businesses for Government bidding and contracting purposes are available without charge. But, there will be a charge for large quantities or complete libraries, and copies wanted by individuals or organizations not directly involved in Government bidding or contracting.

RESPONDING TO RFPS AND IFBS

Note

For the purposes of this book, IFBs and RFQs will be treated in the same manner. There is little difference in them.

Preparing a bid is much easier than writing a proposal. Normally, a bid prepared in response to an IFB, only contains price information. However, a proposal written in response to an RFP, is usually made up of multiple volumes and always requires some type of technical explanation, making it much more difficult to complete.

Before preparing an offer, study the specifications closely, to be sure that all requirements of the solicitation can be met by your company. Particular attention should be given to the instructions to Offerors, evaluation factors and conditions of purchase, delivery and payment.

When determining the amount of the offer, your company should include all costs of material, labor, overhead, packaging, and transportation. Also, you should be sure to comply with such important provisions of the solicitation as submitting the required number of copies, mailing the offer in sufficient time to reach the purchasing office before the closing date, acknowledging all amendments and properly tagging, marking, and mailing any required samples well in advance of the opening date.

If you want to change or withdraw a bid you submitted in response to an IFB, you may send a letter or telegram to this effect to the purchasing office that received it. However, the notification must reach the office prior to the time set for the bid opening or your submission will remain in the contract competition.

When preparing a proposal on a negotiated procurement, the same care should be taken as with a sealed bid. Some people will tell you that the negotiated purchase procedure is more flexible than the sealed bid procedure, thereby giving you an opportunity to seek modification. And, this is true. But, you should not use this as an excuse to procrastinate. Do your homework up-front and never rely on making changes to your proposal later. The Contracting Officer has the right to make award with no discussions at all. Negotiation is an option with RFPs, not the only way it can be done.

If the contracting officer decides to negotiate on your proposal, a complete cost analysis may be required. This means you should be prepared to support your original quotation with facts and figures. Try to avoid the dangerous practice of pulling a bid price out of the air. You should prepare cost spreadsheets for each bid you submit *before* the bid is submitted.

AFTER YOU DOWNLOAD YOUR FIRST SOLICITATION

Before you respond to your first solicitation, there are some things you can do to get ahead of the game.

Find Your SIC Code:

The Standard Industrial Classification Code is used by the Government and private industry to identify the type of service or products provided by a company. You can find the SIC code for your company by looking through the list included in Chapter 13 of this book.

Join PASS:

PASS is the Procurement Automated Source System that provides a central referral system for small businesses interested in selling to the Government. Call the PASS hotline at 1-800-231-7277 and join today; its free.

Other free assistance sources are listed on the following pages (see also: Chapters 6 & 7 about the SBA).

ASSISTANCE SOURCES FOR ALL 50 STATES: PTACS AND SBDCS

The following consists of a selected list of Procurement Technical Assistance Centers (PTACs) that provide assistance to DoD contractors and Small Business Development Centers (SBDCs) that provide management assistance to small business owners.

Alabama PTACs

University of Alabama at Birmingham
1717 11th Avenue South,
Suite 419
Birmingham, AL 35294-4410
Charles A. Hopson
205-934-7260

Alabama SBDCs

University of Alabama
Birmingham, AL 35294
205-934-7260

Alaska PTACs

PTAC
430 West 7th Avenue
Suite 100
Anchorage, AK 99501
Ron Hadden
907-274-7232

Alaska SBDCs

University of Alaska
Anchorage, AK 99501
907-274-7232

Arizona PTACs

National Ctr. For American Indian
Enterprise Development (AIED)
953 E. Juanita Avenue
Mesa, AZ 85204
Anson J. Arviso
602-545-1298

Aptan, Inc.
1435 North Hayden Road
Scottsdale, AZ 85257
Paul R. Roddy
602-945-5452

Arizona SBDCs

Maricopa County Community College
Tempe, AZ 85281
602-731-8720

Arkansas PTACs

Board of Trustees, University of
Arkansas
Cooperative Extension Service
P.). Box 391
Little Rock, AR 72203
Toni Tosch
501-337-5045

Arkansas SBDCs

University of Arkansas
Little Rock, AR 72201
501-324-9043

California PTACs

Merced County Dept of Economic and
Strategic Development
California Central Valley Contract
Procurement Center
1632 N. Street
Merced, CA 95340

Inland Empire Economic Partnership
SBDC
2002 Iowa Ave., Suite 110
Riverside, CA 92507
Teri Ooms
909-781-2345

Riverside Community College District
4800 Magnolia Ave.
Riverside, CA 92506
Gail Zwart
909-222-8094

San Diego Incubator Corporation
Contracting Opportunities Center
3350 Market Street
San Diego, CA 92102
Charles P. Waldrop
619-595-7055

West Valley-Mission
Community College District
14000 Fruitdale Ave.
Saratoga, CA 95070
Fred Prochaska
408-741-2190

California SBDCs

California Trade & Commerce Agency
Sacramento, CA 95814
916-324-5068

Colorado PTACs

PTAC
Denver, CO 80202
303-892-3840

Colorado SBDCs

Office of Business Development
Denver, CO 80202
303-892-3809

Connecticut PTACs

Southeast Area Technical
Development Center
(SEATECH)
1084 Shennecossett Road
Groton, CT 06340
Melody J. Sacatos
203-449-8777

Connecticut SBDCs

University of Connecticut
Storrs, CT 06269-5094
203-486-4135

Delaware PTACs

Delaware State University School of
Business and Economics
1200 North DuPont Highway
Onike Sawyer
302-739-5146

District of Columbia PTACs

N/A

District of Columbia SBDCs

Howard University
Washington, DC 20059
202-806-1550

Florida PTACs

University of West Florida
Florida PTAC Program
11000 University Parkway
Pensacola, FL 32514
Laura Subel
904-444-2066

Florida SBDCs

University of West Florida
Pensacola, FL 32501

Georgia PTACs

Georgia Tech Research Corporation
Georgia Institute of Technology
400 Tenth St. CRB RM 246
Atlanta, GA 30332
Zack Osborne
912-953-1460

Center for PTA
Columbus College
4225 University Avenue
Columbus, GA 31907
Robert Walsh
706-649-1092

Georgia SBDCs

University of Georgia
Athens, GA 30602-5412
706-542-6762

Hawaii PTACs

COC of Hawaii
1132 Bishop Street, Ste 200
Honolulu, HI 96813
James H. Proctor, Jr.
808-544-4301

Hawaii SBDCs

University of Hawaii at Hilo
Hilo, HI 96720-4091
808-933-3515

Idaho PTACs

Idaho Department of Commerce
State of Idaho
700 West State Street

Boise, ID 83703
Larry Demirelli
208-334-2470

Idaho SBDCs

Boise State University
Boise, ID 83725
208-385-1640

Illinois PTACS

State of Illinois
IL Dept of Commerce & Community
Affairs
620 E. Adams Street, 3rd Floor
Springfield, IL 62701
Lois Vanmeter
217-785-6310

Latin American Chamber of
Commerce
The Chicago PAC
2539 N. Kedzie Ave., Ste. 11
D. Lorenzo Padron
312-252-5211

Illinois SBDCs

Department of Commerce &
Community Affairs
Springfield, IL 62701
207-524-5856

Indiana PTACs

ISBD Corp
Government Marketing Assistance
Group
One North Capitol Ave. Suite 1275
Indianapolis, IN 46204-2026
A. David Schaaf
317-264-5600

Partners in Contracting Corporation
PTA CTR
3510 Calumet, Suite 2B
Hammond, IN 46320
Linnea Hokanson
219-932-7811

Indiana SBDCs

Economic Development Council
Indianapolis, IN 46204-2248
317-264-6871

Iowa PTACs

State of Iowa
Iowa Department of Economic
Development
200 East Grand Avenue
Des Moines, IA 50309
Bruce Coney
515-242-4888

Iowa SBDCs

Iowa State University
Ames, IA 50014
515-292-6351

Kansas PTACs

N/A

Kansas SBDCs

Wichita State University
Wichita, KS 67208-0148
316-689-3193

Kentucky PTACs

KY Cabinet for Economic
Development
Dept. Of Community Development
500 Mero St, 22nd Floor,
Capital Plaza Tower

Frankfort, KY 40601
James A. Kurz
800-838-3266

Kentucky SBDCs

University of Kentucky
Lexington, KY 40506-0034

Louisiana PTACs

Louisiana Productivity Center
University of Southwester Louisiana
P.O. Box 44172
Lafayette, LA 70504
Stephen A. Killingsworth
318-482-6767

Louisiana Government Procurement
Center
Shreveport Chamber of Commerce
P.O. Box 20074
Shreveport, LA 71120
Sherrie B. Mullins
318-677-2530

Louisiana SBDCs

Northeast Louisiana University
Monroe, LA 71209-6435
318-342-1224

Maine PTACs

Eastern Development Corporation
Market Development Center
One Cumberland PL, Suite 300
Bangor, ME 04401
Conley Salyer
800-955-6549

Maine SBDCs

University of Southern Maine
Portland, ME 04101
207-780-4420

Maryland PTACs

Tri-County Council for Western
Maryland
111 S. George Street
Cumberland, MD 21502
Michael J. Wagoner

Maryland SBDCs

Department of Economic &
Employment Development
Baltimore, MD 21202
410-333-6995

Massachusetts PTACs

PTAC - Massachusetts Office of
Business Development
Lowell, MA
508-657-8600

Massachusetts SBDCs

University of Massachusetts
Amherst, MA 01003
413-545-6301

Michigan PTACs

Genessee County Metropolitan
Planning Commission
PTA Center
1101 Beach Street, Room 223
Flint, MI 48502
Cindy Bruett
810-257-3010

Jackson Alliance for Business
Development
PTA Center
133 West Michigan Avenue
Jackson, MI 49201

Pennie Kay Southwell
Northeast Michigan Consortium
20709 State Street
P.O. Box 711
Onaway, MI 49765
Denise Hoffmeyer
517-733-8548

Saginaw Future, Inc.
Procurement Technical Assistance
Center
301 East Genessee, 3rd Floor
Saginaw, MI 49765
Delena Spates-Allem
517-754-8222

Downriver Community Conference
Economic Development
15100 Northline
Southgate, MI 48195
Paula Boase
313-281-0700, ext 190

Northwest Michigan Council of
Governments
Procurement Technical Assistance
Center
P.O. Box 506
Traverse City, MI 49685
James F. Haslinger
616-929-5036

Southwest MI Technical Assistance
COE Council Inc.
100 West Michigan, Suite 294
Kalamazoo, MI 49007
Sandra Ledbetter
616-342-0000

Schoolcraft College
18600 Haggerty Road
Livonia, MI 48152-2696
313-462-4438

Marquette County Economic
Development Corp.
Upper Peninsula PTAC
198 Airport Road
Negaunee, MI 49866
Martin L. Tremethick
906-475-4121

Thumb Area Consortium CGA
3270 Wilson Street
Marlette, MI* 48453
Thomas Young
517-635-3561

W. Central Michigan Empl & Training
Consort
PTAC
110 Elm Street
Big Rapids, MI 49307
John Calabrese
616-796-4891

Warren, Center Line, Sterling Heights
Chamber of Commerce
30500 Van Dyke, Suite 118
Warren, MI 48093
Janet Masi
810-751-3939

Michigan SBDCs

Wayne State University
Detroit, MI 48202
313-577-4848

Minnesota PTACs

Minnesota Project Innovation
Government Marketing Assistance
111 Third Avenue, Suite 100
Minneapolis, MN 55401

Minnesota SBDCs

Department of Trade and Economic
Development
St. Paul, MN 55101
612-297-5770

Mississippi PTACs

Mississippi Contract Procurement
Center, Inc.
1636 Pops Ferry Road
Biloxi, MS 39532
Ed Baca
601-396-1288

Mississippi SBDCs

University of Mississippi
University, MS 38677
601-232-5001

Missouri PTACs

Curators of the University of Missouri
University Extension
310 Jesse Hall
Columbia, MO 65211
Morris Hudson
314-882-0344

Missouri Southern State College
3950 East Newman Road
Joplin, MO 64801
Guy Thomas
417-625-3001

Missouri SBDCs

University of Missouri
Columbia, MO 65211
314-882-0344

Montana PTACs

High Plains Development Authority
2800 Terminal Dr. Suite 209
P.O. Box 2568
Great Falls, MT 59404
Karl J. Dehn
406-454-1934

Montana Tradeport Authority
2722 Third Ave. No., Suite 300W
Billings, MT 59101
Maureen Jewell
406-256-6871

Montana SBDCs

Department of Commerce
Helena, MT 59620
406-444-4780

Nebraska PTACs

University of Nebraska at Omaha
Business Development Center
1313 Farnam-on-the-Mall, Suite 132
Omaha, NE 68182
Leon Milobar
402-595-2381

Nebraska SBDCs

University of Nebraska at Omaha
Omaha, NE 68182
402-554-2521

Nevada PTACs

State of Nevada Commission on
Economic Development
Capitol Complex
Carson City, NV 89710

Nevada SBDCs

University of Nevada in Reno
Reno, NV 89557
702-784-1717

New Hampshire PTACs

State of New Hampshire Office of
Business & Industrial Development
172 Pembroke Road, P.O. Box 1856
Concord, NH 03302
603-271-2591

New Hampshire SBDCs

University of New Hampshire
Durham, NH 03824
603-862-2200

New Jersey PTACs

Foundation at New Jersey Institute of
Technology
PTA Center
University Heights
Newark, NJ 07102
John McKenna
201-596-3105

Union County Development
Corporation
PTA Program
1085 Morris Ave., Suite 531
Lib Hall
John Fedkenheuer
908-527-1166

New Jersey SBDCs

Rutgers University
Newark, NJ 07102
201-648-5950

New Mexico PTACs

State of New Mexico General
Services Department
Procure Assist Program
1100 St. Francis Dr. RM 2006
Santa Fe, NM 87502
Rita Cordova
505-827-0425

New Mexico SBDCs

Santa Fe Community College
Santa Fe, NM 87502
505-438-1362

New York PTACs

Cattaraugus County Department of
Economic Development, Plan & Tour
303 Court Street
Little Valley, NY 14755
Thomas Livak
716-938-9111

Long Island Development Corporation
PTA Program
255 Glen Cove Road
Carle Place, NY 11514
Sol Soskin
516-741-5690

New York City Department of
Business Services
Procurement Outreach Program
110 William Street, 2nd Floor
New York, NY 14785
Gordon Richards
212-513-6472

Rockland Economic Development
Procurement
One Blue Hill Plaza, Suite 812
Pearl River, NY 10965
Holly Freedman
914-735-7040

South Bronx Overall Economic
Development Corporation
Procurement
370 E. 149th St.
Bronx, NY 10455
Patricia Finn
718-292-3113

New York SBDCs

State University of New York
Albany, NY 12246
518-443-5398

North Carolina PTACs

University of North Carolina at Chapel
Hill
Small Business and Technical
Development Center
Room 300 Bynum Hall
Chapel Hill, NC 25799
Michael Seibert
919-571-4154

North Carolina SBDCs

University of North Carolina
Raleigh, NC 27612
919-571-4154

North Dakota PTACs

University of North Dakota
ND Small Business Development
Center
P.O. Box 7308
Grand Forks, ND 58202
Eric Nelson
701-237-9678

North Dakota SBDCs

University of North Dakota
Grand Forks, ND 58202
701-7777-3700

Ohio PTACs

Toledo-Lucas County Public Library
325 North Michigan Street
Toledo, OH 43624
Galen Avery
419-259-5244

Central State University
Ohio Procurement & Tech Assistance
Center
100 Jenkins Hall
Wilberforce, OH 45384
James H. Sangster
513-376-6660

Mahoning Valley Economic
Development Corporation
Mahoning Valley Technical
Procurement Center.
4319 Belmont Ave.
Youngstown, OH 44505
Greater Cleveland Growth
Association
Cleveland Area Dev. Corporation
200 Tower City Center 50 Public
Square
Cleveland, OH 44113
James A. Werleg
216-621-3300 x 280

Greater Columbus Chamber of
Commerce
CGMAP
37 North High Street
Columbus, OH 43215
Burt Schildhouse
614-335-6952

Lawrence Economic Dev. Corporation
Procurement Outreach Center
101 Sand & Solida Rd.
P.O. Box 488
South Point, OH 45680
Kay A. Richmond
614-894-3838

North Central Ohio Procurement
Technical Assistance
Terra Community College
1220 Cedar Street
Fremont, OH 43420
Ronda Gooden
419-332-1002

Improvement Corporation of Lake
County Ohio
Northeast Ohio Government Contract
Assistance Center
7750 Clocktower Drive
Kirtland, OH 44094
Virginia E. Mullenax
216-951-8488

University of Cincinnati Government
Marketing Assistance Program
111 Edison Drive
Cincinnati, OH 45216
Nancy Rogers
]513-948-2083

Ohio SBDCs

Department of Development
Columbus, OH 43216
614-466-2711

Oklahoma PTACs

Tribal Government Institute
111 N. Peters Suite 400
Norman, OK 73069
Roy Robert Gann, Jr.
405-329-5542

Oklahoma Department of Vocational
& Technical Education
OK Bid Assistance Network
1500 W. Seventh Ave.
Stillwater, OK 74074
C.L. Vache
405-743-5571

Oklahoma SBDCs

SE Oklahoma State University
Durant, OK 74701
405-924-0277

Oregon PTACs

Government Contract Acq. Program
99 West 10th Ave. Suite 337-B
Eugene, OR 97401
503-344-3537

Oregon SBDCs

Lane Community College
Eugene, OR 97401
503-726-2250

Pennsylvania PTACs

Southern Alleghenies Planning &
Development Commission
PTA State of PA
541-949-6528

Mon-Valley Renaissance
California University of PA
Govt. Agency Coordination Office
250 University Office
California, PA 15419
Joseph E. Hopkins
412-938-5881

Indiana University of Pennsylvania
College of Business
650 S. 13th Street
Robertshaw Bldg. Room 10
Indiana, PA 15705

Johnstown Area Regional Industries
Defense Procurement Assistance
Cntr.
111 Market Street
Johnstown, PA 15901
Robert J. Murphy
814-539-4951

NW PA Regional Planning and
Development Commission
614 Eleventh Street
Franklin, PA 16323
814-437-3024

Private Industry Cncil Westmoreland/
Fayette, Inc.
PTAC
531 South Main Street
Greensburg, PA 15601
Charles R. Burtyk
412-836-2600

SEDA - Council of Governments
RR 1, Box 372
Lewisburg, PA 17837
A. Lawrence Barletta
717-524-4491

University of Pennsylvania-Wharton
SE-PA PTAP
Philadelphia, PA 19104
Charles L. Rech
215-898-1219

Southwest Pennsylvania Regional
Development Council, Inc.
SW PA Local Development District
The Waterforn, 200 First Ave.
Pittsburgh, PA 15222
William J. Dugan
412-391-5590

Economic Development Council of
Northeast PA
Local Development District
1151 Oak Street

Pittston, PA 18640
David Kern
717-655-5581

North Central PA Regional Planning
and Development Commission
P.O. Box 488, 651 Montmorenci Ave.
Ridgway, PA 18848
Northern Tier Regional Planning and
Development Commission
Economic/Community Development
507 Main Street
Towanda, PA 18867
Leo Miller
717-265-9103

West Chester University Center for
the Study of Connectivity and
Databases
Elsie O. Bull Center
West Chester, PA 19383
Susan Hart
610-436-3337

Pennsylvania SBDCs

University of Pennsylvania
Philadelphia, PA 19104
215-898-1219

Rhode Island PTACs

Rhode Island Department of
Economic Development
7 Jackson Walkway
Providence, RI 02903
Daniel E. Lilly, Jr.
401-277-2601

Rhode Island SBDCs

Bryant College
Smithfield, RI 02917
401-232-6111

South Carolina PTACs

College of Business Administration
Frank L. Roddey SBDC of SC
University of South Carolina
Columbia, SC 29208
John M. Lenti
803-777-4907

South Carolina SBDCs

University of South Carolina
Columbia, SC 29201
803-777-4907

South Dakota PTACs

University of South Dakota
414 East Clark Patterson 118
Vermillion, SD 57069
Kareen H. Dougherty
605-367-5252

South Dakota SBDCs

University of South Dakota
Vermillion, SD 57069
605-367-5757

Tennessee PTACs

University of Tennessee
Center for Industrial Services
226 Capitol Boulevard, Bldg, suite
606
Nashville, TN 37219
Becky Peterson
615-532-4906

Tennessee SBDCs

University of Memphis
Memphis, TN 38152
901-678-2500

Texas PTACs

Panhandle Regional Planning
Commission
Economic Development Unit
P.O. Box 9257
Amarillo, TX 79105
Doug Nelson
806-372-3381

University of Texas at Arlington
Automation and Robotics Research
Institute
Office of the President
Box 19125
Arlington, TX 79105
Rogerio Flores
817-794-5978

University of Texas at Brownsville
Center for Business and Economic
Dev.
1600 East Elizabeth Street
Brownsville, TX 78250
Rosalie O. Manzano
210-548-8713

Greater Corpus Christi Business
Alliance
Small Business Development Center
1201 North Shoreline
Corpus Christi, TX 78401
Melissa Garrett
512-881-1831

El Paso Resource Development
P.O. Box 20500
El Paso, TX 79998
Mary Lou Cummings
915-594-2283

University of Houston/TIPS
1100 Louisiana, Suite 500
Houston, TX 77002
Jacqueline Taylor
Texas Technical University

College of Business Administration
2579 South Loop 289
Lubbock, TX 79423
Otilo Castellano
806-745-1637

Angelina College Procurement
Assistance Center
P.O. Box 1768
Lufkin, TX 75902
Glenn E. Harris
409-639-3678

Northeast Texas Community College
East Texas PTA Program
P.O. Box 1307
Mt. Pleasant, TX 75456
Dr. Charles Welch
903-572-1911

San Antonio Procurement Outreach
Program
Economic Development Department
P.O. Box 839966
Terri L. Williams
210-207-3910

Texas SBDCs

Dallas Community College
Dallas, TX 75215
214-565-5831

University of Houston
Houston, TX 77002
713-752-8404

Texas Tech University
Lubbock, TX 79423
806-745-1637

University of Texas at San Antonio
San Antonio, TX 78212
210-558-2450

Utah PTACs

Utah Department of Community &
Economic Development
Utah Procurement Outreach Program
324 South State St, Suite 504
Salt Lake City, UT 84111
Johnny C. Bryan
801-538-8791

Utah SBDCs

University of Utah
Salt Lake City, UT 84101
801-581-7905

Vermont PTACs

State of Vermont Department of
Economic Development
109 State Street
Montpelier, VT 05609
Greg Lawson
802-828-3221

Vermont SBDCs

Vermont Technical College
Randolph Center, VT 05060
802-728-9101

Virginia PTACs

Crater Planning District Commission
Procurement Assistance Center
1964 Wakefield Street
P.O. Box 1808
Petersburg, VA 23805
Dennis Morris
804-861-1667

George Mason University
Entrepreneurship Center
4400 University Drive
Fairfax, VA 22030

Southwest Virginia Community
College
Economic Development Division
P.O. Box SVCC
Richlands, VA 24641
Glenda D. Calver
703-964-7334

Virginia SBDCs

Dpt of Economic Development
Richmond, VA 23219
804-371-8253

Washington PTACs

Economic Development Council of
Snohomish County
917 134th St. SW Suite 103
Everett, WA 98204
Teena M. Kennedy
206-743-4567

Washington SBDCs

Washington State University
Pullman, WA 99164
509-335-1576

West Virginia PTACs

Mid-Ohio Valley Regional Council
PTA CTR
P.O. Box 247
Parkersburg, WV 26102
Belinda Sheridan
304-295-8714

Regional Contracting Assistance
Center
1116 Smith Street, Suite 202
Charleston, WV 25301
Frank Giglio
304-344-2546

West Virginia SBDCs

Office of Community and Industrial Dev.
Charleston, WV 25301
304-558-2960

Wisconsin PTACs

Madison Area Technical College
Small Business PTA
211 North Carrol Street
Madison, WI 53703
Ralph Steckman
608-258-2330

Wisconsin Procurement Institute
840 Lake Avenue
Racine, WI 53403
Mary M. Frey
Wisconsin SBDCs

University of Wisconsin
Madison, WI 53706
608-263-7794

Wyoming PTACs

N/A
Wyoming SBDCs

University of Wyoming
Laramie, WY 82071

DEFENSE CONTRACT MANAGEMENT DISTRICTS (DCMDS) AND DEFENSE CONTRACT MANAGEMENT AREA OPERATIONS (DCMAOS)

These offices, part of the Defense Logistics Agency, have small business specialists assigned to them to respond to inquiries and assist potential small business contractors.

DCMD South
805 Walker Street
Marietta, GA 30060-2789
Telephone: (404) 590-6196
  (800) 331-6415
  (800) 551-7801 (Georgia only)
FAX (404) 590-2612

DCMAO Atlanta
805 Walker Street
Marietta, GA 30060-2789
Telephone: (404) 590-6187
FAX (404) 590-2110

DCMAO Dallas
1200 Main Street, Room 640
PO Box 50500
Dallas, TX 75202-4399
Telephone: (214) 670-9205
  (800) 255-8574
FAX (214) 573-2182

DCMAO Birmingham
2121 8th Avenue, N., Suite 104
Birmingham, AL 35203-2376
Telephone: (205) 226-4304
FAX (205) 251-5325

DCMAO Orlando
3555 Maguire Blvd.
Orlando, FL 32803-3726
Telephone: (407) 228-5113/5260
FAX (407) 228-5312

DCMAO San Antonio
15 E. Houston Street
PO Box 1040
San Antonio, TX 78294-1040
Telephone: (210) 229-4650
FAX (210) 229-6092

DCMAO Baltimore
200 Towsontown Blvd., W.
Towson, MD 21204-5299
Telephone: (410) 339-4809
FAX (410) 339-4990

DCMD Northeast
495 Summer Street, 8th Floor
Boston, MA 02210-2184
Telephone: (617) 753-4317/4318
(800) 321-1861
FAX (617) 753-3174

DCMAO Boston
495 Summer Street
Boston, MA 02210-2184
Telephone: (617) 753-4108/4109
FAX (617) 753-4005

DCMAO Garden City
605 Stewart Avenue
Garden City, Long Island, NY 11530-4761
Telephone: (516) 228-5722
FAX (516) 228-5938

DCMAO Stratford
550 Main Street
Stratford, CT 06497-7574
Telephone: (203) 385-4418
FAX (203) 385-4357

DCMAO Hartford
130 Darlin Street
E. Hartford, CT 06108-3234
Telephone: (203) 291-7715
FAX (203) 291-7992

DCMAO New York
Ft. Wadsworth
Staten Island, NY 10305
Telephone: (718) 390-1016
FAX (718) 390-1020

DCMAO Indianapolis
Building 1
Fort Benjamin Harrison, IN
46249-5701
Telephone: (317) 542-2015/2347
FAX (317) 542-2348

DCMAO Dayton
Gentile Station
1001 Hamilton Street
Dayton, OH 45444-5300
Telephone: (513) 296-5150
FAX (513) 296-5577

DCMAO Syracuse
615 Erie Blvd., W.
Syracuse, NY 13204-2408
Telephone: (315) 448-7897
FAX (315) 448-7914

DCMAO Grand Rapids
Riverview Center Building
678 Front Street, N.W.
Grand Rapids, MI 49504-5352
Telephone: (616) 456-2620/2971
FAX (616) 456-2646

DCMAO Detroit
905 McNamara Federal Building
477 Michigan Avenue
Detroit, MI 48226-2506
Telephone: (313) 226-5180
FAX (313) 226-5250

DCMAO Philadelphia
2800 S. 20th Street
PO Box 7699
Philadelphia, PA 19101-7478
Telephone: (215) 737-5818
FAX (215) 737-7046

DCMAO Reading
1125 Berkshire Blvd., Suite 160
Wyomissing, PA 19610-12494
Telephone: (610) 320-5012
FAX (610) 320-5075

DCMAO Pittsburgh
1629 William Moorhead Federal
Building
1000 Liberty Avenue
Pittsburgh, PA 15222-4190
Telephone: (412) 644-5926
FAX (412) 644-5907

DCMAO Springfield
955 S. Springfield Avenue
Springfield, NJ 07081-3170
Telephone: (201) 564-7204
FAX (201) 467-5232

DCMAO Cleveland
1240 E. 9th Street
Cleveland, OH 44199-2064
Telephone: (216) 522-5446
FAX (216) 522-5387

DCMD West
222 N. Sepulveda Blvd.
El Segundo, CA 90245-4394
Telephone:
(800) 624-7372
(800) 233-6521 (California only)
FAX (310) 335-4443

DCMAO Chicago
O'Hare International Airport
PO Box 66911
Chicago, IL 60666-0911
Telephone: (312) 825-5210
(800) 637-3848
FAX (617) 451-4005

DCMAO San Diego
7675 Dagget Street
Suite 200
San Diego, CA 92111-2241
Telephone: (619) 637-4922
FAX (619) 495-7660

DCMAO Denver
Orchard Place 2, Suite 200
5975 Greenwood Plaza Blvd.
Englewood, CO 80110-4715
Telephone: (303) 843-4381
(800) 722-8975
FAX (303) 843-4334

DCMAO San Francisco
1265 Borregas Avenue
Sunnyvale, CA 94089
Telephone: (408) 541-7041/7042
FAX (408) 541-7084

DCMAO Santa Ana
34 Civic Center Plaza
PO Box C-12700
Santa Ana, CA 92712-2700
Telephone: (714) 836-2912, x661
FAX (714) 836-2358

DCMAO St. Louis
1222 Spruce Street
St. Louis, MO 63103-2811
Telephone: (314) 331-5392
(800) 325-3419
FAX (314) 325-3419

DCMAO Van Nuys
6230 Van Nuys Blvd.
Van Nuys, CA 91401-2713
Telephone: (818) 904-6158
FAX (818) 904-6499

DCMAO Seattle
3009 112th Avenue, N.E., Suite 200
Bellevue, WA 98004-8019
Telephone: (206) 889-7317/7318
FAX (206) 889-7252

DCMAO Twin Cities
3001 Metro Drive, Suite 200
Bloomington, MN 55425-1573
Telephone: (612) 335-2003
FAX (612) 335-2054

DCMAO Wichita
U.S. Courthouse, Suite D-34
401 N. Market Street
Wichita, KS 67202-2095
Telephone: (316) 269-7137/7048
FAX (316) 269-7152

DCMAO Phoenix
The Monroe School Building
215 N. 7th Street
Phoenix, AZ 85034-1012

The IFB

I n many instances, IFBs contain nothing more than a description of the service or product the Government is requesting and forms you must complete. These forms tell the Contracting Officer what you will charge for your service or product and provide general information on your company. On rare occasions, the Contracting Officer may ask for additional information, such as information on your existing contracts and past performance history or the Quality Control Plan you will use in performance of the contract. But, these requests are uncommon.

After reviewing the solicitation, you may have questions. These questions should be submitted in writing to the person listed in block 10 of the Solicitation, Offer and Award (Standard Form 33) or in block 7 of the Solicitation/Contract/Order For Commercial Items (Standard Form 1449) provided with the solicitation.

If your questions are fairly simple, you should call the Contracting Officer or the Contract Specialist to ask your questions. Many people in procurement will help you with your problems over the telephone. Important or complex questions are submitted in writing to prevent one person or company from getting information that other companies competing in the procurement don't have. These questions are answered in writing and submitted to everyone that requested the solicitation. This prevents the company that asked the questions from gaining an unfair advantage over other companies competing for the contract.

Your written questions should be submitted to the Government as soon as possible. The Government often has a cut-off date for receiving them. If your questions are not received by the cut-off date, they may not get answered.

AMENDMENTS

Many times after a solicitation has been issued, the Government issues Amendments to answer questions or make changes to the original solicitation. A summary description of the modifications made to the original solicitation is contained on the Amendment of Solicitation/Modification of Contract (Standard Form 30) issued with the Amendment.

Always check block 11 of the Standard Form 30, shown in Figure 1, to see if the due date for the submission of your bid has been extended. Sometimes, the Government will give you extra time to complete your response if they make changes to the original solicitation.

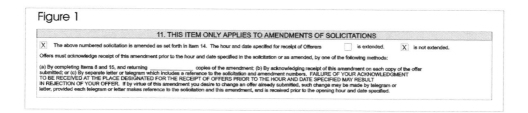

Figure 1

Note

All of the forms discussed in this Chapter are applicable to RFPs (discussed later). Amendments also apply to RFPs in the same way they apply to IFBs.

Bid Preparation

T
o assist you in evaluating an IFB, I will walk you through an Invitation for Bids to provide real estate property closing services. This solicitation follows the Uniform Contract Format required by the Federal Acquisition Regulations and should be similar to any IFB or RFP you choose to evaluate.

Bid Sticker (OF-17):

There is an Official Form 17 or "Bid Sticker." This sticker is sometimes included with the IFB and is red in color. It should be completed and attached to the outside, lower left corner of the envelope you use to send your bid to the Contracting Officer, as shown in Figure 2 below. This ensures that the mailroom of the Government agency knows that there is a bid in the package and gets it to the Contracting Officer quickly.

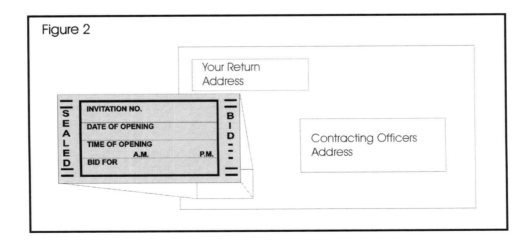

Figure 2

Section A (SF 33):

The first page of our sample IFB is the Solicitation, Offer and Award or Standard Form 33 (SF 33) you saw at the end of the previous Chapter. You must complete the "OFFER" section of this form, shown in Figure 3 below, and submitted the completed SF33 with the rest of your bid package.

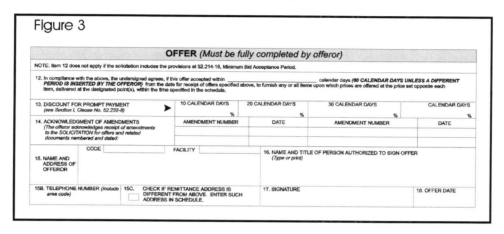

Figure 3

Section B: Section B of the IFB contains price forms you must submit with your bid to tell the Government how much you will charge for your product or service. In our example, this section explains that the Government is requesting a price to perform real estate closing services for one base year and four option years. The bidder must submit a price for the base year and each of the four option years or the bid will be considered non-responsive and excluded from the competition.

Section C: of the IFB describes the work to be performed on this contract. You should review this section of the IFB carefully. Make sure your company is capable of providing the product or performing the work requested before submitting your bid.

Section D: Section D of the IFB sets out requirements for packaging and marking. This section describes the way information and products will be shipped to the Government. Normally, you will be required to pay all shipping and postage cost for sending products and/or reports to the purchasing agency. Remember to include these cost when you complete Section B above.

Section E: Section E of the IFB sets out the Government inspection and acceptance procedures for your products or services. Inspections are performed by the Government Technical Representative (GTR) or the Contracting Officer's Technical Representative (COTR). These specialists are assigned to inspect your work or product because of their knowledge in that particular area. In our example, the GTR would be a person experienced in real estate closings.

Section F: of the IFB sets out the delivery and performance requirements of the contract. In our example, delivery orders can be issued for a period of twelve (12) months from the effective date of the contract. If any options to extend the term of the contract are exercised, the ordering period will extend through the end date of the options. Any and all real estate closings assigned to the contractor prior to expiration of the contract performance period must be completed by the contractor within 60 calendar days of contract expiration.

> **Note**
>
> You will often find Federal Acquisition Regulation (FAR) clauses incorporated by reference in these sections. You can look these FAR clauses up on the World Wide Web at the sites listed in Chapter 16.

Section G: of the IFB sets out contract administration data. In this section, the Government often sets out the personnel positions they feel are essential to the performance of work on the contract. In our example, this would be the closing agents. Prior to assigning any new closing agents to work on the contract, the contractor would be required to get permission from the Contracting Officer.

This section may also set out the procedures for submission of vouchers and how payments will be made to your company. In our example, payment for all services will be made at the time of the property sales closing from the sales proceeds.

Section H: of the IFB sets out special contract requirements. You should always read this section of the IFB carefully. You will find bonding requirements and any requirements that are unique to the type of IFB you are reviewing. In our example, one of the unique requirements is the creation of a non-interest bearing escrow account for the deposit of earnest money, loan proceeds, and purchaser's funds presented at closing.

Section I: of the IFB sets out a variety of contract clauses. Again, many of these are incorporated by reference to specific Federal Acquisition Regulations clauses. This Section may also set out the type of contract to be awarded from this particular IFB. In our example, the contract will be an Indefinite Quantity Contract. Delivery under this contract will only be performed when the contractor receives a specific Work Order from the Contracting Officer.

<u>Section J:</u> sets out the list of attachments to the IFB. In our example, the attachments include a Sales Contract, Settlement Statement, Sample Deed and other forms the Government wants the Contractor to complete in performance of the contract.

<u>Section K:</u> of the IFB is the Representations, Certifications and Other Statements of Offerors that must be completed and returned with your bid.

<u>Section L:</u> of the IFB contains instructions for preparation of your response to the IFB. You should review this section of the IFB carefully. In our example, the following instructions are given:

Each bid submitted must include:

1)   The Standard Form 33, Solicitation, Offer and Award

     a.   Complete Blocks 13 through 18 as required. If no prompt payment discount is offered, Block 13 should be left blank.

     b.   Include your DUNS number in block 15 after the term "DUNS"

     c.   You must sign Block 17

2)   The Standard Form 30, Amendment of Solicitation (if issued).

Note

All amendments, if issued, must be acknowledged as stated in Block 11 of the Standard for 30 or in Block 14 of the SF 33, Solicitation, Offer and Award, as shown in Figure 4 below.

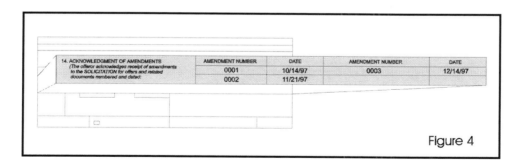

Figure 4

Note

If there are more than four amendments, you can attach a continuation page to the SF33 that shows the other amendment numbers and the date they were issued.

3)   A completed Section B.

4)   A completed Section G.

   a.   In this section, you must list all Key Personnel and submit a resume on each. Use extra sheets as necessary.

   b.   You must include the name of the supervisor under which the contract work will be performed.

5)   A completed Section K.

6)   To the outside of the bid envelope, attach the Bid Sticker

In order for the bid to be considered responsive, it must be accompanied by all material listed above.

Section M: Section M of the IFB contains the evaluation factors for award. In our example, award of the contract will be made to the *responsible* bidder submitting the lowest *responsive* bid. The words "responsible" and "responsive" in this sentence are very important. This contract will be awarded to a company that has submitted the lowest bid price AND

1)   Can prove they are capable of performing the work; and

2)   Have properly completed all of the forms and other requirements set out in the IFB.

Sample Spreadsheets

In order to complete Section B, you should prepare spreadsheets for every bid you submit to the Government. These spreadsheets should include considerations for all expenditures you will incur in contract performance. The following is an example of a spreadsheet used to calculate price for a grounds maintenance contract.

Note

The following is an example of a spreadsheet used to calculate price for a grounds maintenance contract. It is included to show you the cost elements that should be considered when determining the price to be submitted in response to any solicitation.

FACILITY:	SAMPLE AFB		CONTRACTOR:	SAMPLE MAINTENANCE SERVICES
RFP #:	Fxxxx-96-R-0006		CONTACT:	Mr. Sample
LATEST REV:			PHONE#:	(555) 555-5555
LOCATION:	STATE		ADDRESS:	5000 Anywhere DR Anywhere, USA
CONTRACTING OFFICER:	Ms. Smith			
LABOR RELATED STATISTICS:				
ANNUAL HOURS AVAILABLE:	2,080			
VACATION HOURS:	80			
HOLIDAY HOURS:	80			
TOTAL LOSS LABOR HOURS:	160			
ANNUAL PRODUCTIVE HRS PER EMPLOYEE:	1,920			
HEALTH & WELFARE	$0.055			
STATE REQUIRED INSURANCE PER MO	$10.11			
GENERAL PUBLIC LIABILITY	1.50%			
WORKMAN'S COMPENSATION	7.62%			
PAYROLL TAX RATES:	FICA	FUTA	SUTA	Medicare
LIMIT	60,600	7,000	7,000	no limit
RATE	6.20%	0.80%	2.70%	1.45%
max	3,757	56	189	
INFLATION FACTORS:				
BASE YEAR	01 APR 97 - 31 MAR 98			
OPTION YEAR 1	01 APR 98 - 31 MAR 99			
OPTION YEAR 2	01 APR 99 - 31 MAR 00			
OPTION YEAR 3	01 APR 00 - 31 MAR 01			
OPTION YEAR 4	01 APR 01 - 31 MAR 02			

Fxxxx-96-R-0006	STATE			Gross		Total		Total	
				Labor		Gross	Gross	Labor	Prod
	No.	Hourly	Annualized	Hours	Manning	Labor	Labor	Loss	Labor
	Months	Rate	Salary	Per-Man	FTE's	Hours	Cost	Hours	Hours
Labor Category	1	2	3	4	5	6	7	8	9
--------	------	------	-------	-------	------	-------	------	-------	------
Project Manager	12	19.00	39,520	2,080	1.00	2,080	39,520	160	1,920
Ass't Project Manager/	12	17.50	36,400	2,080	1.00	2,080	36,400	160	1,920
Administrator/	12	11.00	22,880	2,080	1.00	2,080	22,880	160	1,920
Maintenance Mechanic	12	13.96	29,037	2,080	1.00	2,080	29,037	160	1,920
Tractor Operator	12	10.71	22,277	2,080	4.00	8,320	89,107	640	7,680
Laborer	12	9.33	19,406	2,080	19.00	39,520	368,722	3,040	36,480
--------	------	------	-------	-------	------	-------	------	-------	------
TOTALS			169,520	12,480	27.00	56,160	585,666	4,320	51,840

Prod	Wkrs				STATE		STATE	STATE	Total	
Labor	Comp	Wkrs	6.20%	0.80%	2.70%	1.45%	$159.14	$10.11	Payroll	
Costs	Rate	Comp	FICA	FUTA	SUTA	Medicare	Health Ins	TDI Ins	Tax/WC	Uniforms
10	11	12	13	14	15	16	17	18	19	18
--------	-----	-------	-------	-------	-----	-------	--------	-------	------	------
36,480	7.62%	3,011	2,450	56	189	573	1,910	121	8,311	0
33,600	7.62%	2,774	2,257	56	189	528	1,910	121	7,834	
21,120	7.62%	1,743	1,419	56	189	332	1,910	121	5,770	
26,803	7.62%	2,213	1,800	56	189	421	1,910	121	6,710	
82,253	7.62%	6,790	5,525	224	756	1,292	7,639	485	22,711	0
340,358	7.62%	28,097	22,861	1,064	3,591	5,346	36,284	2,305	99,548	0
--------	-----	-------	-------	-------	-----	-------	--------	-------	------	------
540,614		44,628	36,311	1,512	5,103	8,492	51,561	3,276	150,883	0

Vacation	Health	General	Total	Total
And	and	Public	Fringe	Labor &
Holidays	Welfare	Liability	Benefits	Fringes
20	21	22	23	24
-------	------	------	------	--------
3,040	114	593	12,058	48,538
2,800	114	546	11,295	44,895
1,760	114	343	7,987	29,107
2,234	114	436	9,493	36,297
6,854	458	1,337	31,359	113,612
28,363	2,174	5,531	135,615	475,974
-------	------	------	------	--------
45,051	3,089	8,785	207,808	748,423

EQUIPMENT COST

	QUAN	UNIT	UNIT COST	TOTAL COST	Value after 5 Yrs	Accumulated Depreciation
Jacobsen HR-5111	3	EA	45206	135618	33904.5	101713.5
Jacobsen HR-15	1	EA	64960	64960	16240	48720
Jacobsen Turfcat	2	EA	18783	37566	391.5	28174.5
Jacobsen 720E Sweeper	2	EA	14940	29880	7470	22410
Smithco Spray Star	2	EA	16695	33390	8347.5	25042.5
Blowers	10	EA	250	2500	0	2500
AeroKing Aerator	1	EA	5179	5179	1294.75	3884.25
John Deere Tractor	1	EA	30000	30000	7500	22500
Shindiawa T-20 String Trimmers	22	EA	300	6600	0	6600
Water Cannon	12	EA	1400	16800	0	16800
Water Cannon, small	12	EA	150	1800	0	1800
GMC Pickup Trucks	6	EA	23000	138000	34500	103500
Pipes	1200	FT	8	9600	0	9600
Fire Hoses	6000	FT	4.5	27000	0	27000
Hand Rakes	15	EA	12	180	0	180
Gas Cans, half gal.	12	EA	6.25	75	0	75
Fertilizer Spreader	1	EA	300	300	0	300
Fertilizer Spreader, 300 gal.	1	EA	4600	4600	0	4600
Shed	1	EA	450	450	0	450
Trailer	2	EA	4500	9000	2250	6750
Water Hose	1000	FT	0.23	230	0	230
Gas Can, 5 gal.	2	EA	30	60	0	60
				--------		--------
				553788		432889.75

SUMMARY SHEET

Cost Category		Base Year	Option Year 1	Option Year 2	Option Year 3	Option Year 4		Total
Direct Labor		748422.52	748422.52	748422.52	748,423	748,423		3,742,113
Other Direct Costs								
Equipment		136757.6	136757.6	136,758	136,758	136,758		683,788
Maintenance		5000	5000	5000	5,000	5,000		25,000
Misc. Materials (Incl Fertilizer)		30000	30000	30000	30,000	30,000		150,000
Uniforms		2500	2500	2500	2,500	2,500		12,500
Fuel		40000	40000	40000	40,000	40,000		200,000
	Total Other Direct Costs	214257.6	214257.6	214257.6	214,258	214,258		1,071,288
General & Admin.	9%	86641.211	86641.211	86641.211	86,641	86,641		433,206
Fee/Profiit	8%	77014.41	77014.41	77014.41	77,014	77,014		385,072
		========	========	=======	========	========		========
Total		1126335.7	1126335.7	1126335.7	1,126,336	1,126,336		5,631,679
Material Cost		21332	21332	21332	21,332	21,332		106,660
		--------	--------	--------	--------	--------		--------
Sub Total		1147667.7	1147667.7	1147667.7	$1,147,668	$1,147,668		$5,738,339
State General Excise Tax	4.17%	47857.745	47857.745	47857.745	47,858	47,858		239,289
		========	========	=======	========	========		========
		1195525.5	1195525.5	1195525.5	$1,195,525	$1,195,525		$5,977,627
Reimbursed Material Cost		21332	21332	21332	21,332	21,332		106,660
		========	========	=======	========	========		========
Grand Total		1174193.5	1174193.5	1174193.5	$1,174,193	$1,174,193		$5,870,967

Invitation For Bids Checklist:

To ensure that you are submitting a compliant bid to the Government, it is always best to work from a checklist. The checklist on the following page is an example.

INVITATION FOR BIDS CHECKLIST

Solicitation No. _____   Due Date _____

- [ ] Order Solicitation
- [ ] Study Solicitation, giving particular attention to Sections, "L", "M" and "C"

[ ] Yes [ ] No Are any bonds required

[ ] Yes [ ] No Are there any materials that must be submitted early

[ ] Yes [ ] No Can your company provide the requested product or service

- [ ] Prepare any questions you have for the Contracting Officer
- [ ] Mail your written questions or call the Contracting Officer with oral questions
- [ ] Mark your calendar with the due date for the bid
- [ ] Prepare spreadsheets to determine your cost and the bid price you will submit
- [ ] Prepare any additional information required, i.e. Past Performance, QC Plan
- [ ] Complete Section "B" of the IFB
- [ ] Complete Section "K" of the IFB
- [ ] Complete the SF 33, SF 1449 or other cover page

[ ] Yes [ ] No Have you acknowledged all amendments

- [ ] Prepare Cover Letter and Proprietary Statement

[ ] Yes [ ] No Have you signed all required documents, SF 33, Section "K", etc.

- [ ] Assemble all required copies and make a copy for yourself
- [ ] Prepare bid for shipment to the Government
- [ ] Secure the OF 17 "Bid Sticker" to the outside of your bid package
- [ ] Ship to the Government in time to ensure delivery by the due date

Notes: _____

_____

_____

The RFP

A Request for Proposals (RFP) is the most complex solicitation issued by the Government and is normally used to solicit services. It can range from twenty pages to thousands of pages in length, depending on the complexity of the services being requested. Section "L" of the solicitation will tell you the required format for the proposal being requested by the Government.

Most RFPs require a minimum of two proposal volumes: a cost volume that contains the prices you will be charging for your services and a technical volume that discusses the way your services will be performed. The cost volume is prepared in much the same manner as an IFB, described in Chapter 2. The technical volume can be assembled in a three-ring binder as shown in Figure 5.

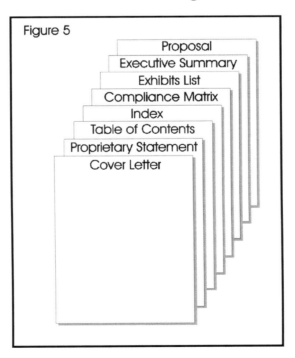

Figure 5

- Proposal
- Executive Summary
- Exhibits List
- Compliance Matrix
- Index
- Table of Contents
- Proprietary Statement
- Cover Letter

Each volume should be in a separate three-ring binder. This makes it easy to send change pages to the Government, if they are requested.

Sometimes, Section "L" of the solicitation sets out specific document format instructions, such as type size (no smaller than 10 point), line spacing (no less than 1.5), margins (no less than one inch), etc. When they do this, there is usually a page limit imposed on the technical volume. If you complete the technical volume and discover that it is longer than the page limit imposed by Section "L" of the solicitation, you can try formatting the proposal in two columns. Before you do this, make sure that the instructions do not require the proposal to be in single column format. I have been able to get thirty or forty percent more information in a proposal by using two-column format on some occasions.

COVER LETTER:

Your cover letter should be printed on company letterhead and signed by an officer of your company. A copy of this letter should be included at the beginning of every volume submitted with your proposal package. An example of the type of letter normally used follows:

Date
Name of Government Agency Address of Government Agency
Attn: Name of Contracting Officer
Reference: Solicitation No. 263-98-R-XXXX

Dear Ms. Smith,

I am pleased to submit this proposal for [state the type of service to be provided]. We at [Company Name] view this contract as a partnership between the Government and our company. At [Company Name], we are proud of our reputation as a responsive provider of high quality service. We will be a valuable member of your team.

The content of this proposal adheres to the format defined in the RFP and addresses the evaluation areas specified in the solicitation package. We take no exceptions or deviations to the requirements of the solicitation or the proposed contract. The proposal is fully compliant with all instructions.

Thank you for the opportunity to participate in this effort. If we can be of any assistance, please contact us. We look forward to hearing from you and taking part in the next stage of this procurement.

This letter states that you have adhered to the requirements of the solicitation and that you are not taking exception to the requirements. Solicitations often require that you make these statements in your cover letter, even though they sound redundant.

PROPRIETARY STATEMENT:

The Freedom of Information Act is discussed in Chapter 9. In order to protect your company's business information from discovery under this Act, you should include a Proprietary Statement with every Bid and/or Proposal you submit. The following is the language used in most statements. It can be included as a footer to your cover letter or as a separate page. When you prepare your proposal, add a footer that includes the words "USE OR DISCLOSURE OF DATE CONTAINED ON THIS PAGE IS SUBJECT TO THE RESTRICTION ON THE TITLE PAGE OF THIS PROPOSAL OR QUOTATION" at the bottom of every page of the proposal.

This Proposal, furnished in response to solicitation No. XXXX02-98-R-XXXX, contains proprietary and/or privileged or confidential commercial or financial information. This information is maintained in confidence in the course of the offeror's business and is not otherwise publicly available. The offeror submits this information to the Government in confidence and understands that it is received with that intent. This information shall not be released or disclosed outside the Government under the Freedom of Information Act (5 U.S.C. 552) or under any circumstances.

This data, furnished in connection with solicitation No. XXXX02-98-R-XXXX, shall not be disclosed outside the Government and shall not be duplicated, used or disclosed in whole or in part for any purpose other than to evaluate the proposal; provided that if a contract is awarded to this Offeror as a result of or in connection with the submission of this data, the Government's right to use information contained, subject to this restriction, is identified on sheets marked: "USE OR DISCLOSURE OF DATA CONTAINED ON THIS PAGE IS SUBJECT TO THE RESTRICTION ON THE TITLE PAGE OF THIS PROPOSAL OR QUOTATION."

TABLE OF CONTENTS

The Table of Contents should be prepared using tabs that can be purchased in any office supply store. There should be one tab for every n.0 section of the proposal. In the "Sample Outline" section of this Chapter, there would be five tabs required, as seen in Figure 6 on the following page.

Past Performance

Demonstrated Understanding of the Scope of Work

Personnel Qualifications/Experience

Management Approach

Subcontracting Plan

INDEX

Even though this portion of your technical volume will be called an Index, it would be more technically correct to call it a Table of Contents. An Index is normally prepared in alphabetical order, but the index used in proposals is prepared in chronological order as shown in the example below for a HUD Real Estate Asset Management solicitation.

Since the tabs you use in the volume come with a printed sheet that calls itself a Table of Contents, you title this as an index to eliminate any confusion. It should show all section headings listed in your outline and give the page where each section begins

COMPLIANCE MATRIX

A Compliance Matrix is rarely required by a solicitation, but you should include one with your Technical Proposal to assist the evaluators. Many evaluators start the proposal evaluation process with your proposal in one hand and a checklist in the other. This checklist sets out all aspects of the solicitation that must be covered in the proposal. Your Compliance Matrix shows the Government where your proposal satisfies the requirements of sections "C", "L" and "M" of the solicitation. An example of a Compliance Matrix is shown on the next page. It makes it easy for the evaluators to find the items on their checklist in your proposal.

Compliance Matrix		RFP# NRC-R-XXXX		
RFP SECTION	PROPOSAL SECTION	DESCRIPTION	PAGE
C.1.3	2.0	DEMONSTRATED UNDERSTANDING OF THE SCOPE OF WORK	17
C.1.3.1	2.1	ANALYSIS, REVIEW, MAINTENANCE AND UPDATE OF CONFIGURATION MANAGEMENT PLAN AND STANDARD AND SPECIALIZED OPERATING PROCEDURES	19
C.1.3.2	2.2	OPERATION OF NRC'S COMPUTER FACILITY	23
C.1.3.2.1	2.2.1	General Computer Facilities Operation	24
C.1.3.2.2	2.2.2	Specialized Systems	28
C.1.3.2.2.1	2.2.2.1	Payroll System Operation	29
C.1.3.2.2.2	2.2.2.2	Emergency Response Data System (ERDS) Operation	33
C.1.3.2.2.3	2.2.2.3	Nuclear Documents System (NUDOCS) Operation	37
C.1.3.2.2.4	2.2.2.4	Personnel System	41
C.1.3.3	2.3	CLEANING OF COMPUTER EQUIPMENT	47
C.1.3.4	2.4	PERSONNEL REQUIREMENTS	53
C.1.3.5	2.5	TRAINING REQUIREMENTS	56
L.8(e)1	1.0	PAST PERFORMANCE	1
L.8(e)2	2.0	DEMONSTRATED UNDERSTANDING OF THE SCOPE OF WORK	17
L.8(e)2	2.6	POTENTIAL PROBLEM AREAS AND APPROACH TO RESOLUTION	61
L.8(e)3	3.0	PERSONNEL QUALIFICATIONS/EXPERIENCE	64
L.8(e)4	4.0	MANAGEMENT APPROACH	67
L.8(e)4.a	4.1	MANAGEMENT APPROACH TO CONTRACT IMPLEMENTATION	71
L.8(e)4.a.i	4.1.1	Proposed Management Techniques for Contract Administration	74
L.8(e)4.a.ii	4.1.2	Procedures to Provide Ongoing and Backup Support to Avoid System Interruptions	93
L.8(e)4.aii	4.1.3	Training Plan to Keep Personnel Up-To-Date With New Hardware/Software Features	97
L.8(e)5	5.0	SUBCONTRACTING PLAN	106
M.2.1	1.0	PAST PERFORMANCE	1
M.2.2	2.0	DEMONSTRATED UNDERSTANDING OF THE SCOPE OF WORK	17
M.2.3	3.0	PERSONNEL QUALIFICATIONS/EXPERIENCE	64
M.2.4	4.0	MANAGEMENT APPROACH	67

You will notice that some sections of the proposal satisfy more than one requirement of the solicitation. For instance, Section 3.0 of the proposal satisfies the requirements of Sections L.8(e)3 and M.2.3 of the solicitation. This is because Section "L" of the solicitation tells you the format of your proposal and Section "M" tells you the level of importance the Government will give this information. By setting up your Compliance Matrix in this format, the evaluator can find the information he is seeking from any section of the solicitation.

EXHIBITS LIST

Your Exhibits List should show the name and page number of each exhibit included in your proposal. These exhibits should include your Corporate Organization Chart, Project Organization Chart and other graphical representations prepared to enhance the understanding of your technical volume.

EXECUTIVE SUMMARY

There are two schools of thought about Executive Summaries. Some people believe that you should prepare the summary before you start the proposal. Others believe that the summary should be the last thing you write. I believe that you should prepare the Executive Summary last. The outline, explained later in this Chapter, will be the first thing prepared. Use the Executive Summary to make sure that you have followed your outline properly.

You should include an Executive Summary with each proposal you submit to the Government. This summary of your proposal should be designed to give the evaluator a "quick view" of what he will see in the proposal itself.

Sample Executive Summary

Company, is pleased to submit this proposal in response to RFP DADA10-97-R-XXXX for Hospital Housekeeping Services.

EXPERIENCE

Company is a service-based diversified corporation that competes on a national basis as a prime contractor to the United States government, as well as to the commercial sector.

At Company we foster an environment that encourages innovation and rewards employees who contribute to our performance success. We create the value we seek by managing our operations to achieve total quality in everything we do. To us, total quality is doing the right things right the first time. We manage our business, make decisions, and allocate resources on the basis of whether actions will increase our value to the customer. Our commitment is to keep value enhancement the key priority of this enterprise and provide quality service into the future.

ORGANIZATION

Company's proposed management approach incorporates into the project all of the elements needed to produce the highest quality and schedule control. We provide full program planning for effective resource utilization and compliance with our training, as well as safety and contingency plans.

We will establish, document, and maintain effective and economical standard inspection requirements. The inspection requirements will provide control for the prevention of discrepancies and for timely, positive corrective action.

APPROACH TO MISSION SUCCESS

The Company approach to succeeding in this endeavor is founded on three basic elements:

1. **Proven Expertise in Fulfilling Service Contracts** - Critical to providing quality services immediately and sustaining them throughout the contract

2. **Management Systems** - Application of proven automated cost and project control systems to deliver the best quality services at the most effective prices

3. **Company Commitment** - Contract oversight in daily project implementation is critical and responsiveness to changing situations and emergencies is required.

Application of these factors to our approach is demonstrated throughout this proposal and will continue in the Pre-award Survey.

However, they are of particular importance in the following areas:

Project Phase-In - Because of our technical expertise and project management experience, we will be able to provide a seamless transfer of responsibilities from the incumbent to our staff. There will be no interruption in, or detraction from, ongoing operations during the phase-in period. Our Corporate staff is dedicated to customer service. Company representatives will arrive immediately after contract award and thoroughly review all systems and services for efficiency.

Management Controls - Through application and refinement on numerous contracts, Company has developed policies and procedures that ensure prompt and efficient contract management

Quality Control - We are particularly dedicated to Total Quality Management (TQM) and have adopted Corporate wide systems to ensure all services are of the highest quality

Company hires only top quality personnel at all levels and ensures that they have the skills and material to successfully undertake their specific project assignments. We continue this philosophy down to the project level through an ongoing effort to hire only the most qualified personnel.

UNDERSTANDING SOLICITATION REQUIREMENTS

Part I of our proposal contains the administrative and pricing data set forth in the solicitation.

Part II of our proposal provides information pertaining to our past and present performance. We have included specific contracts that directly relate to the services to be provided under this contract. We have also provided a certification of experience as required by the solicitation.

Part III of our proposal will be conducted orally by our proposed Project Manager on the date and at the time specified by the Contracting Officer.

Our proposal is complete and comprehensive; it addresses all of the elements required in the solicitation. Presented in the format required by the RFP, this proposal conclusively demonstrates:

An understanding of the solicitation requirements

A dedication to quality and safety at every level that will ensure the performance you and our corporate heritage demand

A realistic approach to pricing

OPERATING AND MANAGEMENT PHILOSOPHY

We will be dedicated to the mission of your facility, not merely the satisfaction of minimal contract requirements.

To this end, our Project Manager has the authority to call upon the full resources of Company, to ensure desired performance. Our Corporate management staff will provide support functions and technical assistance as necessary, but will not interfere in, or dictate, day-to-day operations. This structure equips the Project Manager with all of the tools required to ensure project performance and quality.

In addition to our management processes, our personnel policies are similarly directed by this philosophy. Salaries and benefits at all levels are fair, competitive, and aimed at attracting and retaining quality, experienced personnel. We seek to avoid turnover in order to maximize our capability to maintain peak performance on all projects at all times. Every person on this contract will play an active role in the continuous improvement of our service.

FINAL STATEMENT

In this Project, the organizational and individual commitments of our staff of managerial and operational personnel are the basis for the strength of our team. Our commitment to excellence is reflected in this proposal and will be reflected in our performance as the selected contractor.

Our past performance and excellent reputation will once again serve the U.S. Government, our most valued customer.

Chapter

5

Proidosal Preparation

W̲hen responding to an RFP, the first thing you should do is prepare an outline. This outline should conform to the solicitation and be used to prepare your proposal.

The following outline structure is commonly used in proposals:

1.0	**ALL CAPS, BOLD UNDERLINE**
1.1	**ALL CAPS, BOLD**
1.1.1	**Initial Caps, Bold, Underline**
1.1.1.1	**Initial Caps, Bold**
1.1.1.1.1	Initial Caps

You will often see this structure in the solicitation you receive. If you use this structure in preparation of your proposal, it will be easier for the evaluation board to follow. That is your goal: to make it as easy on the Government to evaluate your proposal as possible

SAMPLE OUTLINE

The following outline was prepared for a solicitation received from the Nuclear Regulatory Commission (NRC). The solicitation was requesting complete operation services for the NRC Computer Facilities.

1.0 **PAST PERFORMANCE** (L.8(e)1) (M.2.1)

2.0 **DEMONSTRATED UNDERSTANDING OF THE SCOPE OF WORK** (L.8(e)2) (M.2.2) (C.1.3)

2.1 **ANALYSIS, REVIEW, MAINTENANCE AND UPDATE OF CONFIGURATION MANAGEMENT PLAN AND STANDARD AND SPECIALIZED OPERATING PROCEDURES** (C.1.3.1)

2.2 **OPERATION OF NRC'S COMPUTER FACILITY** (C.1.3.2)

2.2.1 **General Computer Facilities Operation** (C.1.3.2.1)

2.2.2 **Specialized Systems** (C.1.3.2.2)

2.2.2.1 **Payroll System Operation** (C.1.3.2.2.1)

2.2.2.2 **Emergency Response Data System (ERDS) Operation** (C.1.3.2.2.2)

2.2.2.3 **Nuclear Documents System (NUDOCS) Operation** (C.1.3.2.2.3)

2.2.2.4 **Personnel System** (C.1.3.2.2.4)

2.3 **CLEANING OF COMPUTER EQUIPMENT** (C.1.3.3)

2.4 **PERSONNEL REQUIREMENTS** (C.1.3.4)

2.5 **TRAINING REQUIREMENTS** (C.1.3.5)

2.6 **POTENTIAL PROBLEM AREAS AND APPROACH TO RESOLUTION** (L.8(e)2)

3.0 **PERSONNEL QUALIFICATIONS/EXPERIENCE** (L.8(e)3) (M.2.3)

3.1 **PERSONNEL RESUMES**

4.0 **MANAGEMENT APPROACH** (L.8(e)4) (M.2.4)

4.1 **MANAGEMENT APPROACH TO IMPLEMENTATION** (L.8(e)4.a)

4.1.1 **Proposed Management Techniques for Contract Administration** (L.8(e)4.a.i)

4.1.2 **Procedures to Provide Ongoing and Backup Support to Avoid System Interruptions** (L.8(e)4.a.ii)

4.1.3 **Training Plan to Keep Personnel Up-To-Date With New**

As I discussed earlier, you should prepare an index from the outline and include it with the technical volume of your proposal after the proposal is completed. This serves more than one purpose. It makes you go back through the technical volume and ensure that all aspects of the outline have been covered, and it assists the evaluation committee in their evaluation of your proposal.

At the end of each entry of the outline/index, you see references to specific sections of the solicitation [(L.8(e)2) (M.2.2) (C.1.3), etc.]. This tells the Government what requirements of sections "L", "M" and "C" of the solicitation this section of the proposal is satisfying, making it easier for the evaluators to find the required information.

QUALITY CONTROL

The Government invariably requests a Quality Control Plan in their RFPs. They consider quality to be one of their highest priorities. Their primary source of quality measurement comes from the principals of Total Quality Management (TQM).

Total Quality Management involves the planning and implementation of strategies designed to improve personal and professional development, interpersonal relations, managerial effectiveness and organizational productivity. It fosters the belief that understanding the employee's perspective leads to loyalty and credibility.

The basis of total quality is continuous improvement. No person or Company should be content to stay where they are, no matter how successful they seem to be. Very few people or companies could be content with the status quo if they were regularly receiving accurate feedback on their performance. Total quality is an expression of the need for continuous improvement in four areas: 1) personal and professional development; 2) interpersonal relations; 3) managerial effectiveness; and 4) organizational productivity.

Personal and Professional Development

Your personnel are the keys to total quality. The TQM approach often requires personal change - not personnel changes. W. Edwards Deming has said that about 90 percent of the problems in organizations are general problems (bad systems); only about ten percent are specific problems with people. Many managers misinterpret this information, supposing that if they correct the structure and systems, the problems with people will go away. The reverse is actually true: if you correct the personnel problem first, the other problems will go away.

Interpersonal

Total quality on an interpersonal level means making a constant effort to enhance the emotional aspects of your personnel. It is continually building good will and negotiating in good faith. If you create an expectation of continuous service improvement but fail to deliver on that expectation, you send the wrong message to your personnel and your clients. A corporate culture, like the human body, is an ecosystem of interdependent relationships, and these must be balanced and based on trust to achieve quality

Managerial

Managerial quality is basically nurturing quality performance and partnership agreements: making sure they are "in sync" with what is happening inside that person and what is happening inside your business. People must know that they are being managed by principles and entitled to due process. If you want to influence and empower people, you must first recognize that they are resourceful and have vast untapped capability and potential.

Organizational

This requires a feedback system on what your customers, employees, suppliers, distributors, and other parties want and expect. There is a place for competition, but it is not in areas where you need to cooperate. The key to total quality is to listen to personnel and clients, to seek first to understand, then to be understanding.

> **Note**
>
> When you are preparing your Quality Control Plan, keep in mind that the Government wants to make sure you will be watching the quality of the service you provide. Tell them that you understand the principals of Total Quality Management and make sure that your plan includes checklists for each service function.

MANAGEMENT PLAN

Your management plan should give the Government a clear understanding of the way you intend to perform the contract. One of the most effective ways to do this is by including a Project Organization Chart. A sample chart is included on the following page.

Project Orginiization Chart

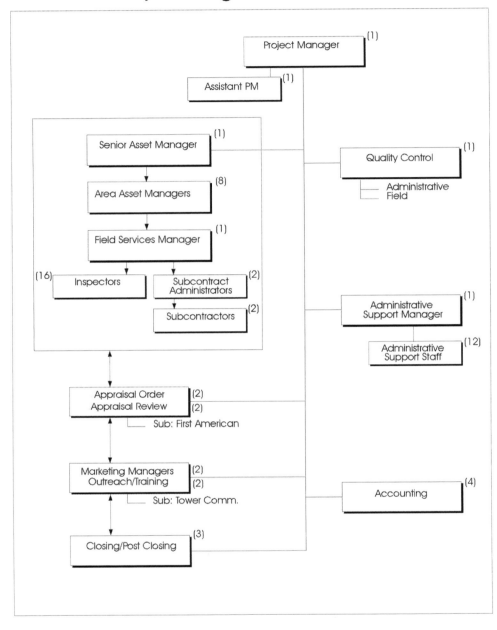

Chapter 6

The SBA

T he U.S. Small Business Administration (SBA) was created in 1953 as an independent agency of the Federal Government to aid, counsel, assist and protect the interests of small business concerns, to preserve free competitive enterprise, and to maintain and strengthen the overall economy of our nation. The SBA's vision revolves around two principles: customer-driven outreach and quality-focused management. They are determined to reach out to small businesses in an unprecedented way, to listen to their needs, to report these needs back to the President, and to suggest appropriate initiatives to help small businesses

SBA CUSTOMER SERVICE STANDARDS

As one of their first initiatives, President Clinton and Vice President Gore challenged their administration to "reinvent" the SBA, to create an agency that not only works better, but is smaller and costs less. The best possible customer service is a key element of reinventing Government, and the SBA is committed to providing quality service at all of their service delivery points and to all their customers -- small businesses, lenders, resource partners, among others. Specifically, the SBA is committed to the following principles:

- Providing prompt, courteous and accurate responses to requests for information received by telephone, in writing or in person;

- Continuing to look for cost-effective and user-friendly ways to make information easily accessible to the small business community;

- Continuing to streamline and reinvent processes to make conducting business with the SBA easier for both their resource partners and small business owners;

- Providing the small business owner with specialized technical assistance through a variety of programs in a variety of locations;

- Continuing to work to relieve the regulatory burden on small business; and

- Continuing to facilitate and strengthen working relationships between small contractors and federal procuring agencies.

The SBA provides financial assistance in the form of loan guaranties rather than direct loans. They do not provide grants to start or expand a business.

SBA PROFILE

Information for each program is broken down into four categories:

- "Program" lists each SBA program by name;

- "Function" summarizes the purpose of the program;

- "Customer" identifies the customer(s) served by the program; and

- "Delivered through" identifies the means through which SBA delivers the program.

A list of SBA offices is at the end of this chapter. Telephone numbers can be found under "U.S. Government" in those locations or by calling the SBA Answer Desk: (800) 8-ASK-SBA. To send a fax to the SBA, dial (202) 205-7064. For the hearing impaired, the TDD number is (704) 344-6640.

SBA OnLine electronic bulletin board - modem and computer required:
   (800) 697-4636 (limited access)
   (900) 463-4636 (full access)
   (202) 401-9600 (D.C. metro area)

Internet using uniform resource locators (URLs)
   SBA Home Page: http://www.sba.gov
   SBA gopher: gopher://gopher.sba.gov
   File transfer protocol: ftp://ftp.sba.gov
   Telnet: telnet://sbaonline.sba.gov
   U.S. Business Advisor: http://www.business.gov

LENDING

Program: 7(a) Loan Guaranty

Function: Section 7(a) of the Small Business Act authorizes the SBA to guarantee loans to small businesses that cannot obtain financing on reasonable terms through normal lending channels. The SBA basic guaranty program generally is used to fund the varied long-term needs of small businesses. The program is designed to promote small business formation and growth by guaranteeing long-term loans to qualified firms. Loans are available for many business purposes, such as real estate, expansion, equipment, working capital or inventory. The SBA can guarantee 75 percent of the loan amount up to $750,000. For loans of $100,000 or less, the guaranty rate is 80 percent. The interest rate is not to exceed 2.75 over the prime lending rate. Maturities are up to 10 years for working capital and up to 25 years for fixed assets.

Customer: Small businesses

Delivered through: Commercial lending institutions

Program: Low Documentation Loan (LowDoc), a 7(a) Loan Program

Function: The purpose of this program is to reduce the paperwork involved in loan requests of $100,000 or less. Under LowDoc, the SBA uses a one-page application and relies on the strength of the individual applicant's character and credit history. The applicant must first satisfy all of the lender's requirements. The lender may then request a LowDoc guaranty.

Customer: Small businesses

Delivered through: Commercial lending institutions

Program: CAPLines, a 7(a) Loan Program

Function: CAPLines (replaces GreenLine) finances small businesses' short-term, cyclical working-capital needs. Under CAPLines, there are five distinct short-term working capital loans: the Seasonal, Contract, Builder's, Standard Asset-Based, and Small Asset-Based lines. For the most part, the SBA regulations governing the 7(a) Program also govern this program. Under CAPLines, SBA generally can guarantee up to $750,000.

Customer: Small businesses

Delivered through: Commercial lending institutions

Program: FA$TRAK, a 7(a) Loan Program

Function: A new loan program being piloted with selected banks nationwide, FA$TRAK encourages lenders to make more small loans to the small business community. Participating banks are permitted to use their own documentation and procedures to approve, service and liquidate loans of up to $100,000. In return, the SBA agrees to guarantee up to 50 percent of each loan.

Customer: Small businesses

Delivered through: Commercial lending institutions

Program: Women's Prequalification Pilot Loan, a 7(a) Loan Program

Function: This pilot loan program enables the SBA to prequalify a guaranty for loan applications of $250,000 or less before the business owner goes to a bank. The program focuses on an applicant's character, credit, experience and reliability rather than assets. Designated independent loan packagers work with a business owner to review and strengthen her loan application. The review is based on key financial ratios as well as credit history, business history and the loan-request terms. This program is available in a limited number of locations.

Customer: Women-owned small businesses

Delivered through: Commercial lending institutions, nonprofit intermediaries such as small business development centers (SBDCs) and certified development companies (CDCs)

Program: Minority Prequalification Loan, a 7(a) Loan Program

Function: This pilot program assists qualified minority-owned, for-profit companies. Companies can receive an SBA pre-approval for a 7(a) loan guaranty. This program is available in a limited number of locations.

Customer: Small disadvantaged businesses, low-income individuals

Delivered through: SBA-designated, non-profit intermediaries

Program: Defense Loan and Technical Assistance (DELTA), a 7(a) Loan Program

Function: DELTA provides both financial and technical assistance to help defense-dependent small firms adversely affected by defense cuts diversify into the commercial market. Loans must be used to retain jobs of defense workers, create new jobs in impacted communities, or to modernize or expand in order to remain in the national technical and industrial base. DELTA uses 7(a) (maximum total loan $1.25 million) and/or 504 (maximum guaranteed debenture $1 million). The SBA also will leverage federal, state and private-sector resources to provide a full range of management and technical assistance.

Customer: Defense-dependent small firms adversely impacted by defense cuts

Delivered through: SBA district offices, resource partners

Program: Export Working Capital Program (EWCP), a 7(a) Loan Program

Function: Replaces the Export Revolving Line of Credit Program. Under the EWCP, the SBA guarantees up to 75 percent of a secured loan (80 percent on loans of $100,000 or less) or $750,000, whichever is less. Loan maturities may be for up to three years with annual renewals. Loans can be for single or multiple export sales and can be extended for pre-shipment working capital and post-shipment exposure coverage or a combination of the two. Proceeds can only be used to finance export transactions.

Customer: Export-ready small businesses

Delivered through: Commercial lending institutions

Program: International Trade Loan (ITL), a 7(a) Loan Program

Function: The ITL offers long-term financing to small businesses engaged or preparing to engage in international trade, as well as those businesses adversely affected by import competition. The SBA can guarantee up to $1.25 million for a combination of fixed-asset financing and working capital. The working capital portion cannot exceed $750,000.

Customer: Export-ready small businesses

Delivered through: Commercial lending institutions

Program: 7(m) MicroLoan

Function: Under this pilot program, short-term loans of up to $25,000 are made to small businesses for the purchase of machinery and equipment, furniture and fixtures, inventory, supplies, and working capital. Proceeds cannot be used to pay existing debts. These loans are made through SBA-approved nonprofit groups, that also provide counseling and educational assistance. This program is available at a limited number of locations.

Customer: Small businesses needing small-scale financing and technical assistance for start-up or expansion, intermediaries.

Delivered through: Intermediary lenders (nonprofit organizations with experience in lending and technical assistance)

Program: 504 Certified Development Companies

Function: Through certified development companies (CDCs), the 504 CDC provides long-term, fixed-rate financing to small businesses to acquire real estate, machinery and equipment for expansion of business or modernizing facilities. Typically, 504 loan proceeds are provided as follows: 50 percent by an unguaranteed bank loan, 40 percent by an SBA-guaranteed debenture, and 10 percent by the small business customer. The maximum SBA debenture is $1 million. DELTA funding is also available under this program.

Customer: Small businesses

Delivered through: Certified development companies (private nonprofit corporations set up to contribute to the economic development of its community or region)

Program: Certified and Preferred Lenders

Function: The most active and expert lenders qualify for the SBA's Certified and Preferred Lenders Program. Certified lenders receive a partial delegation of authority to approve loans. Preferred lenders enjoy full delegation of lending authority. A listing of participants in the Certified and Preferred Lenders Program is available from SBA district offices.

Customer: Borrowers and financial institutions participating in SBA-guaranteed lending programs

Delivered through: Lenders

INVESTMENT

Program: Small Business Investment Companies (SBICs)

Function: The SBA licenses private venture-capital firms - small business investment companies - and supplements their capital with U.S. Government-guaranteed debentures or participating securities. SBICs make equity investments and long-term loans to small businesses.

Customer: Small businesses

Delivered through: SBICs (approximately 270 active SBICs)

Program: Main Street Investment

Function: Main Street Investment is a public/private partnership between the SBA and state governments to make capital more available to lenders who, in turn, make loans to small businesses. Participating states invest tax revenues in community banks that agree to make LowDoc loans.

Customer: Community banks, small businesses

Delivered through: Community banks

SURETY BONDS

Program: Surety Bond Program

Function: By law, prime contractors to the Federal Government must post surety bonds on federal construction projects valued at $100,000 or more. Many states, counties, municipalities, and private-sector projects and subcontracts also require surety bonds. The SBA can guarantee bid, performance and payment bonds for contracts up to $1.25 million for eligible small businesses that cannot obtain surety bonds through regular commercial channels. The SBA's guaranty goes to the surety company, and contractors must apply through a surety bonding agent.

Customer: Small construction and service contractors; surety and insurance companies, their agents; federal and state agencies; state insurance departments; federal, state and other procurement officials

Delivered through: Surety and insurance companies and their agents

International Trade

Program: U.S. Export Assistance Centers (USEACs)

Function: These one-stop shops combine the trade-promotion and export-finance resources of the SBA, the U.S. Department of Commerce, and the Export-Import Bank. They are designed to improve delivery of services to small and medium sized businesses. The USEACs also work closely with other federal, state and local trade partners in the local communities.

Customer: Export-willing and export-ready small businesses

Delivered through: SBA, Export-Import Bank, U.S. Department of Commerce, Agency for International Development (AID), individual states

Program: Small Business Automated Trade Locator System (SBAtlas)

Function: This computer database system provides key market data to exporters. SBAtlas generates two types of reports: product-specific and country-specific.

Customer: Export-willing and export-ready small businesses

Delivered through: SBA, SBDCs, SCORE

Program: Export Legal Assistance Network (ELAN)

Function: ELAN provides initial, free legal consultations to small business exporters. Under an agreement among the SBA, the U.S. Department of Commerce, and the Federal Bar Association, experienced trade attorneys volunteer their time to answer exporters' legal questions.

Customer: Export-willing and export-ready small businesses

Delivered through: SBA, U.S. Department of Commerce, Federal Bar Association

DISASTER ASSISTANCE

> **Note**
>
> The SBA Disaster Assistance Program is the primary federally funded disaster-assistance loan program for funding long-range recovery for private-sector, nonagricultural disaster victims. Eligibility is based on financial criteria. Interest rates fluctuate according to statutory formulas. There is a lower rate, not to exceed 4 percent, available to applicants without credit available elsewhere and a higher interest rate, not to exceed 8 percent, for those with credit available elsewhere. In addition to presidential declarations, the program handles disaster loans when a declaration is made by the SBA Administrator. There are three disaster loan programs: physical disaster loans to businesses of any size, economic injury loans to small businesses without credit available elsewhere, and loans for homes and personal property.

Program: Physical Disaster Business Loans

Function: Loans are available for uninsured losses up to $1.5 million to qualified applicant businesses of any size to repair or replace business property to pre-disaster conditions. Loans may be used to replace or repair equipment, fixtures and inventory and to make leasehold improvements.

Customer: Large and small businesses, nonprofit organizations

Delivered through: Disaster area offices, disaster assistance centers, disaster-specific hotline number

Program: Economic Injury Disaster Loans (EIDLs)

Function: Loans are available, up to $1.5 million, for businesses that sustain economic injury as a direct result of a disaster. These working capital loans are made to help businesses pay ordinary and necessary operating expenses that would have been payable barring disaster.

> **Note**
>
> Maximum loan amount is $1.5 million for EIDL and physical disaster business loans combined, unless the business meets the criteria for a major source of employment (MSE).

Customer: Small businesses without credit elsewhere available

Delivered through: Disaster area offices, disaster assistance centers, disaster-specific hotline number

Program: Loans for Major Source of Employment (MSE)

Function: The $1.5 million limit may be waived for businesses that employ 250 or more people in an affected area.

Customer: Businesses -- large and small, nonprofit organizations

Delivered through: Disaster area offices, disaster assistance centers, disaster-specific hotline number.

Program: Real Property

Function: Loans are available to qualified homeowners for uninsured losses up to $200,000 to repair or restore a primary residence to pre-disaster condition. Homeowners may apply for an additional 20 percent for disaster mitigation. This is the major long-term recovery program for individual disaster losses.

Customer: Individuals

Delivered through: Disaster area offices, disaster assistance centers, disaster-specific hotlines

Program: Personal Property

Function: Loans are available to qualified homeowner and renter applicants for uninsured losses up to $40,000 to repair or replace personal property such as clothing, furniture, cars, etc. This loan is not intended to replace extraordinarily expensive or irreplaceable items such as antiques, pleasure crafts and recreational vehicles, fur coats, etc.

Customer: Individuals

Delivered through: Disaster area offices, disaster assistance centers, disaster-specific hotline number

FEDERAL PROCUREMENT

Program: Breakout Procurement
Function: This program promotes, influences and enhances the breakout of historically sole-source contracts for full and open competition.

Customer: Federal procuring agencies

Delivered through: SBA breakout procurement center representatives (Breakout PCRs)

Program: Prime Contracting
Function: This program increases small business opportunities in the federal acquisition process through initiation of small business set-asides, identification of new small business sources, counseling of small businesses on doing business with the Government, and assessment of compliance with the Small Business Act through surveillance reviews.

Customer: Small businesses, other Government agencies

Delivered through: SBA procurement center representatives (PCRs)

Program: Subcontracting
Function: This program ensures that small business receives the maximum practical opportunity to participate in federal contracts as subcontractors and suppliers.

Customer: Large and small contractors, other Government agencies

Delivered through: SBA commercial market representatives (CMRs)

Program: Certificate of Competency (CoC)

Function: Helps small businesses to secure Government contracts by providing an appeal process to low-bidder businesses denied Government contracts for a perceived lack of ability to satisfactorily perform.

Customer: Small businesses that have been denied Government contracts for perceived lack of ability

Delivered through: SBA field industrial and financial specialists

Program: Women-Owned Business Procurement

Function: A multifaceted, pilot program aimed at teaching women to market to the Government.

Customer: Women-owned businesses

Delivered through: Office of Government Contracting

Program: Procurement Automated Source System (PASS)

Function: PASS is a computerized database of small businesses nationwide that are interested in federal procurement opportunities. Information on each company includes a summary of capabilities, ownership and qualifications.

Customer: Small businesses that are interested in federal procurement opportunities, federal and large prime contractors

Delivered through: SBA contractor and PASS specialists

MINORITY ENTERPRISE DEVELOPMENT

Program: 8(a) Small Disadvantaged Business Development

Function: The MED office utilizes SBA's Section 8(a) contracting authority to provide business development assistance to minority-owned and other disadvantaged-owned firms through federal procurement opportunities.

Customer: Small socially and economically disadvantaged businesses

Delivered through:Contracting officers, SBA, Office of Small Disadvantaged Business Utilization (OSDBU)

Program: 7(j) Management and Technical Assistance

Function: Under Section 7(j) of the Small Business Act, the MED office enhances business development assistance by entering into grants and cooperative agreements with service providers to provide targeted assistance in accounting, marketing and proposal/bid preparation. (The SBA does not provide grants to start or expand a business.) Industry-specific technical assistance and entrepreneurial training also are available.

Customer: Small disadvantaged businesses, low-income individuals, firms in either labor-surplus areas or areas with a high proportion of low-income individuals

Delivered through: 7(j) Program providers of management and technical assistance (including small businesses, and minority and other educational institutions), SBA

NATIVE AMERICAN AFFAIRS

Program: Native American Affairs
Function: The SBA's Office of Native American Affairs (ONAA) develops initiatives that ensure native individuals have access to business-development resources, training and services in their communities. The ONAA's main focus is economic development and job creation through small business ownership and education. The ONAA works with individual and tribally owned organizations; other federal, state and local agencies; nonprofit organizations; and national Native American organizations.

Customer: American Indians, Alaska Natives and Native Hawaiians

Delivered through: SBA field offices, small business development centers, and reservation-based tribal business information centers (TBICs)

BUSINESS COUNSELING AND TRAINING

Program: Small Business Development Centers (SBDCs)
Function: Administered by the SBA, the SBDC Program provides management assistance to current and prospective small business owners. SBDCs offer one-stop assistance by providing a wide variety of information and guidance. The program is a cooperative effort of the private sector, the educational community, and federal, state and local governments. Its purpose is to enhance economic development by providing management and technical assistance to small businesses.

Customer: Small businesses, small business start-ups

Delivered through: Universities, colleges, state government, private sector (57 SBDCs, 950 service locations)

Program: Business Information Centers (BICs)

Function: The SBA's technology toolbox, the business information center, provides the latest in high-tech hardware, software and telecommunications to help small businesses get started and grow strong. BIC counseling and training are provided by SCORE.

Customer: Small businesses

Delivered through: In some locations, private sector co-sponsors and SCORE (29 BICs in service, 40 BICs to be in service by end of FY 97)

Program: Service Corps of Retired Executives (SCORE)

Function: SCORE is a program sponsored by the SBA that matches volunteers with small businesses that need expert advice. Volunteers, whose collective experience spans the full range of American enterprise, share their management and technical expertise with present and prospective owners/managers of small businesses.

Customer: Small businesses, start-ups, pre-business start-ups.

Delivered through: Local SCORE chapters (nearly 12,400 members, 383 chapters, 400 other locations)

RESEARCH AND DEVELOPMENT

Research and Development programs are administered by the Office of Technology.

Program: Small Business Innovation Research (SBIR)

Function: Under the SBIR Program, small businesses propose innovative ideas in competition for Phase I and Phase II awards -- representing specific R&D needs of the federal participating agencies -- that will result in commercialization of the effort at the Phase III level. More than 4,000 SBIR awards totaling nearly $700 million were made in FY94.

Customer: Innovative small businesses that are interested in competing for federal R&D awards.

Delivered through: 11 federal agencies with $100 million in extramural R&D budgets that participate in the SBIR Program

Program: Small Business Technology Transfer (STTR)

Function: This pilot program requires each small firm competing for an R&D project to collaborate with a nonprofit research institution. It is a joint venture from the initial submission of the proposal to the completion of the designated effort.

Customer: Small innovative R&D firms

Delivered through: Five federal agencies with extramural research and R&D budgets of $1 billion: Departments of Defense, Energy, Health & Human Services; NASA and the National Science Foundation

Program: Small Business Research, R&D Goading

Function: This program measures and reports the amount of federal funding for research and R&D (excluding the amounts for SBIR and STTR) awarded to small business concerns each year by the major research and R&D federal agencies.

Customer: Small business concerns that compete for federal R&D awards

Delivered through: 18 federal agencies with annual R&D budgets in excess of $20 million

WOMEN'S BUSINESS OWNERSHIP

Program: Women's Demonstration Program

Function: Provides women with long-term training and counseling in all aspects of owning or managing a business, including financial, management, marketing and technical assistance, and procurement training.

Customer: Women-owned small businesses

Delivered through: 54 women's business centers in 28 states and Washington, D.C.

Program: Women's Network for Entrepreneurial Training (WENT)

Function: In a year-long, one-on-one program, established women business owners (WBS) serve as mentors, passing on knowledge, skills and support to WBS who are ready to expand their businesses. The WENT Round table provides mentoring and support for women business owners in a group setting. Sponsors include small business development centers, local business leaders, Government representatives and SCORE.

Customer: Women-owned small businesses

Delivered through: SBA field offices, women's business and professional organizations, SBDCs, women's demonstration sites, SCORE

VETERANS AFFAIRS

Program: Veterans' Entrepreneurial Training (VET)
Function: The VET Program provides long-term (up to 12 months), in-depth business training to veterans.

Customer: U.S. Veterans

Delivered through: SBA grant recipients and their subcontractors

Program: Business Opportunity Conferences
Function: This training helps veteran-owned companies and firms impacted by military downsizing sell to Government agencies and prime contractors.

Customer: U.S. Veteran-owned Government contractors

Delivered through: Department of Veterans Affairs

Program: Transition Assistance Program (TAP)
Function: Through this nationwide program, the SBA assists all military personnel about to be discharged. The SBA provides in-depth business assistance and guidance to those who wish to become entrepreneurs.

Customer: U.S. Veterans, active-duty personnel

Delivered through: Department of Labor, Department of Defense (includes individual armed services), SBA field offices

Program: Technology Transfer Conferences
Function: In a new initiative, the Office of Veterans Affairs is facilitating and coordinating technology transfer conferences with 10 small business development centers. These conferences provide assistance to defense-dependent firms adversely affected by reductions in defense spending and non-defense-dependent small firms interested in buying or selling technology.

Customer: High-tech, veteran-owned small businesses and defense-dependent and non-defense-dependent small firms

Delivered through: Office of Veterans Affairs and SBDCs

EMPOWERMENT ZONES/ENTERPRISE COMMUNITIES

Program: One-Stop Capital Shops (OSCSs)

Function: The one-stop capital shop is the SBA's contribution to the Empowerment Zones/Enterprise Communities Program, an initiative headed by HUD and USDA. The EZ/EC Program targets resources to a small number of distressed communities. Located in designated empowerment zones or enterprise communities, the shops will be managed by local nonprofit community-development entities and will centralize access to a full range of SBA lending programs and technical assistance. Business information centers, located within the OSCSs, will offer the latest high-tech hardware, software, interactive videos and telecommunications to access market research databases, individual planning and spreadsheets, and other tools for the small business owner.

Customer: Would-be entrepreneurs and small businesses-especially in the designated EZ/EC where the OSCS is located

Delivered through: Primary: Nine nonprofit economic/business development organizations located in selected EZs or ECs; Secondary: SBA 7(a) lenders and 7(m) micro-lenders, SBICs, CDCs, SCORE, SBDCs

BUSINESS INFORMATION SERVICES

Program: Answer Desk

Function: The Answer Desk, established in 1983, is a nationwide, toll-free information center that helps callers with questions and problems about starting and running businesses. Service is provided through a computerized telephone message system augmented by staff counselors. It is available 24 hours a day, seven days a week, with counselors available Monday through Friday, 9 a.m. to 5 p.m. Eastern Time.

Customer: General public

Delivered through: Toll-free telephone number: (800) 8-ASK-SBA

Program: Publications

Function: The SBA produces and maintains a library of management-assistance publications, videos and computer programs. These are available by mail to SBA customers for a nominal fee (to defray reproduction and shipping costs). A complete listing of these products can be found in the Resource Directory for Small Business Management. SBA field offices also offer free publications that describe SBA programs and services.

Customer: General public, small businesses, libraries, universities

Delivered through: SBA, SBA OnLine, SCORE, SBDCs, chambers of commerce, libraries, consumer information centers, etc.

Program: SBA OnLine

Function: SBA OnLine is a computer-based electronic bulletin board providing fast and easy help to the small business community. Operating 23 hours a day, SBA OnLine gets relevant and current information to the public as quickly as possible. Services on-line include SBA publications, access to SBA programs and services, points of contact, calendars of local events, on-line training, access to other federal on-line services, data from other agencies, electronic mail, Internet mail, information exchange by special-interest groups, and downloadable files.

Customer: General public
Delivered through: Limited access: (800) 697-4636
Full access: (900) 463-4636
D.C. metro area: (202) 401-9600
SBA Home Page: http://www.sba.gov/
SBA gopher: gopher://gopher.sba.gov
File transfer protocol: ftp://ftp.sba.gov
Telnet: telnet://sbaonline.sba.gov
U.S. Business Advisor: http://www.business.gov

Program: U.S. Business Advisor

Function: When it is completed, this World Wide Web site will be a one-stop electronic link to all the business information and services the Government provides. With the U.S. Business Advisor, small businesses will no longer have to contact dozens of agencies and departments to access applicable laws and regulations, or figure out on their own how to comply. They will be able to download business forms and conduct a myriad of other business transactions. The U.S. Business Advisor is still under development and is currently on the World Wide Web in a beta version. You are welcome to participate in this development through a feedback mechanism at the web site.

Customer: General Public

Delivered through: http://www.business.gov/

ADVOCACY

Program: Office of Interagency Affairs

Function: Oversees enforcement of the Regulatory Flexibility Act. Analyzes current small business issues and develops policy options. Prepares testimony for use before Congress and regulatory bodies. Served as policy resource for the 1995 White House Conference on Small Business. Currently implementing the recommendations resulting from the conference.

Customer: Small businesses, regulatory agencies, Congress

Delivered through: Regulatory agencies, Congress, trade associations

Program: Office of Economic Research

Function: Produces the annual report to Congress, "The State of Small Business: A Report of the President." Oversees research contracting program. Compiles and interprets statistics on small businesses according to size, industry and geographic distribution.

Customer: Small businesses, Congress, media, academic institutions, Government agencies, foreign governments

Delivered through: White House, federal agencies, Congress, state and local governments, media and independent researchers

Office: Office of Information

Function: Publishes technical books and economic reports. Publicizes and disseminates small business issues, statistics and advocacy publications. Prepares printed materials for Office of Advocacy-sponsored conferences. Provides public information and outreach to support SBA and Office of Advocacy functions.

Customer: Small businesses, Congress, state legislatures, media, Government agencies, economic-research organizations

Office: Regional Advocates

Function: Regional advocates serve as the SBA chief counsel's direct link to local communities and help identify new problems and issues of small businesses. They monitor the impact of federal and state regulations and policies on communities within their regions. They also work with state officials to develop policy and legislation that shape an environment in which small companies can prosper and grow.

Customer: Local business, owners, state and local government agencies and legislatures

SBA's Service Structure

<u>Office: Regions</u>

Function: SBA regional offices:

- Implement the four goals of the Administrator in the region -- to act as the Administrator's eyes and ears in the small business community, to reinvigorate the SBA and increase its efficiency, to help relieve the credit crunch, and to eliminate unnecessary paperwork;

- Work with district offices, resource partners, advisory councils, and state and local leaders to accomplish agency goals and initiatives and foster economic development in the region;

- Ensure that SBA products and services are delivered in a cohesive and consistent manner; and

- Educate SBA customers on the major issues affecting small business.

- Customer: District offices, small businesses, surety bond applicants

<u>Office: Districts</u>

Function: SBA district offices:

- Are the point of delivery for most SBA programs and services;

- Work to accomplish the SBA mission by providing quality service to the small business community; and

- Work with SBA resource partners, other partners and intermediaries to accomplish the SBA mission.

Customer: Small businesses, SBA branch offices, local communities

Delivered through: Each district office's individualized list of resources, partners and intermediaries

Chapter 7

Government Contracting and the SBA

G overnment purchasing installations buying items or services offered by small firms work closely with SBA when seeking small business suppliers. If your company supplies one item or just a few products or services, the SBA field office representative can tell you which agencies purchase those particular products or services. Other sources of information regarding multiple items can be found in chapter 1.

Names and addresses of prospective military and civilian customers are also available through SBA's field offices. When requesting information on the location and names of possible customers, you must give SBA complete information on the line of products or services you can supply.

PRIME CONTRACTING ASSISTANCE

Prime contracting concerns itself with the relationship between Federal buying agencies and companies directly responsible for providing the supplies or services needed by the Government.

In fiscal year 1994, Federal agencies collectively purchased a total of $170 billion worth of supplies and services, of which $ 42.3 billion was awarded to small business as prime contracts. Much of this small business prime contracting occurs without intervention by SBA because:

- A small business wins the award in head-to-head competition resulting from responses to an "Invitation for Bids" (IFB) with other businesses both large and small; or

- A small business is judged to have the best proposal in response to a "Request for Proposals" (RFP) and successfully negotiates a contract with the agency.

A buying activity, determining on its own that there will be adequate small business competition and award will be at a fair and reasonable price, can set-aside a procurement for exclusive small business participation.

SBA, however, continually tries to increase both the dollar value and percentage of total awards to small businesses principally through the work of its procurement center representatives (PCRs) stationed at selected military and civilian locations where there are major buying programs. There are two types of PCRs, traditional (TPCR) and breakout (BPCR), whose duties are different but complementary.

TPCRs have many challenging tasks in support of SBA's procurement assistance mission, but most of their time is spent on the prime contracting program. TPCRs operate under provisions of the Federal Acquisition Regulation (FAR) and other directives, and are in the review cycle of the requirement packages (describing what the agency wants) as they are being processed by the contracting officer. The agencies are required to submit to the TPCR, for independent review, all requirements that are valued at more than the simplified acquisition threshold and that are not to be processed as small business set-asides restricted to competition among small businesses only.

In reviewing the requirement, the TPCR attempts to obtain a small business set-aside, i.e., restricts the acquisition to small business firms. The FAR states that small business set-asides are mandatory when a determination is reached that there is reasonable expectation that offers will be obtained from at least two responsible small business concerns so that awards will be made at fair market prices. When the TPCR recommends a small business set-aside that is then rejected by the contracting officer, the TPCR may appeal the decision. This appeal may go all the way to the head of the department involved. Many times, the TPCR is sustained on an appeal and the acquisition is set aside.

If set-aside criteria cannot be met, then the TPCR attempts to provide competent small business sources to ensure the widest possible small business participation in the acquisition. These sources can come from activity files, from other PCRs or from SBA's Procurement Automated Source System. Purchasing agencies will send copies of the solicitation to these additional sources upon request of the TPCR.

While reviewing requirement packages, the TPCR is constantly on the lookout for provisions or procedures that may inhibit, restrict or discourage small business firms from submitting offers. These barriers could include restrictive specifications, unreasonably large bonding requirements, or unrealistic delivery schedules.

In addition to these duties involving specific procurements, TPCRs are active ombudsmen for small businesses having problems with an agency. They participate in procurement conferences, seminars and business fairs, explain SBA's procurement assistance programs, and introduce small businesses to buying activities. Should you have a specific problem or general questions about contracting at an agency, the nearest SBA field office or regional office can put you in touch with the TPCR.

Breakout Procurement Center Representatives (BPCRs) are located at major procurement centers of the Government. The BPCRs and their technical advisors are advocates for the breakout of items for procurement through full and open competition. All BPCRs are technically trained accredited engineers familiar with the supplies and services procured at their center. The BPCRs review the method by which the activity intends to procure goods and services to ensure that competition is not unnecessarily restricted.

BPCRs recommend appropriate acquisition methods when competition can be expanded. The breakout program creates many opportunities to bid on new items and services and small businesses generally win a majority of the items and services procured through full and open competition.

Prime contracting also conducts surveillance reviews of Federal contracting offices. These reviews assess the effectiveness of an agency's small business utilization program in providing the small business community the maximum opportunity to participate either as a prime contractor or subcontractor in performance of contracts awarded by that office. Recommendations for any noted program weaknesses or omissions are submitted to the department level authority.

SUBCONTRACTING ASSISTANCE

The Government's role in subcontracting assistance to small business has been changed significantly by P.L. 95-507, which amended Section 8(d) of the Small Business

Act: Prior to the enactment of the law, the emphasis was on voluntary best efforts by cooperating prime contractors. Once contractors had made their make-or-buy decisions, they attempted to subcontract many of the buy items to small business. Over the years the percentage of small business subcontracts grew, but as Federal prime contracting became more complex and specialized, it was realized that more could and should be done for small business in subcontracting in the high-dollar, complex procurements.

P.L. 95-507 changed the emphasis from voluntary to mandatory and from best efforts to maximum practicable opportunity. The Act directs that Federal Government contracts greater than the simplified acquisition threshold shall contain a clause entitled, Utilization of Small Business Concerns and Small Business Concerns Owned and Controlled by Socially and Economically Disadvantaged Individuals.

For larger contracts, i.e., those over $500,000 ($1,000,000 for construction), the law also requires a subcontracting plan setting forth percentage goals for utilizing small business concerns, including separately identified goals for disadvantaged small business and women-owned small business. In addition, the prime contractor must describe the efforts it will take to assure that such firms have an equitable opportunity to compete for subcontracts.

For large negotiated contracts, the contracting officer may approve, cause to be modified, or reject the submitted subcontracting plan. Although the agency's contracting officer has the final decision, SBA may perform a preaward review and evaluation of the subcontracting plan. In most cases, if SBA has serious objections to a proposed plan, the contracting officer will require the large business submitting the plan to make changes to overcome SBA's objections. If the contracting officer determines that the plan provides "the maximum practicable opportunity" for small, small disadvantaged, and women-owned business concerns to participate as subcontractors in the performance of the contract, the approved plan is incorporated as part of the contract. Failure by the large prime contractor to carry it out can constitute a material breach of the contract and, unless remedied, could result in termination.

For large sealed bid (as opposed to negotiated) contracts, the plan submitted by the successful bidder is incorporated into the contract and, if not carried out, can constitute a material breach. The plan is not negotiated ahead of time between the large business and the buying agency. If the agency's contracting officer believes that the subcontracting plan submitted does not reflect the best effort by the bidder to award subcontracts to small, small disadvantaged, and women-owned concerns to the fullest extent, the agency will request a review by SBA. Although this request does not delay award of the contract, prior compliance of the bidder with such subcontracting plans will be considered by the Federal agency in determining the responsibility of the bidder for the award of the contract.

Requirements for subcontracting plans do not apply to: small business prime contractors; contracts under the prescribed amounts; prime contracts not offering subcontracting possibilities; or contracts that are to be performed entirely outside the United States.

SBA has Commercial Market Representatives (CMRs) located throughout the country. Their basic responsibilities are to:

- Assist small businesses in discovering and expanding subcontracting opportunities;

- Work with large prime contractors to identify competent small business contractors, and assist them in interpreting Section 8(d) and its implementing regulations, including the formulation of subcontracting plans;

- Conduct preaward evaluation of sub-contracting plans upon request;

- Conduct postaward review and evaluation of contractually required subcontracting plans; and

- Conduct subcontract program reviews and compliance evaluations to make sure that prime contractors are implementing their subcontracting program requirements under Section 8(d).

The Six Elements of a Subcontracting Plan

Section 8(d) outlines six specific elements for an acceptable subcontracting plan. These six elements are also cited in FAR 19.704. They are: (1) separate percentage goals for small, small disadvantaged, and women-owned small businesses; (2) the name of the subcontracting administrator and a description of his or her duties; (3) a description of the efforts that the company will make to ensure that all small businesses will have an equitable opportunity to compete for subcontracts; (4) assurances that the company will "flow down" the subcontracting requirements to its subcontractors; (5) assurances that the company will cooperate in any studies or surveys and submit periodic reports to the Government, including the Standard Forms (SF) 249 and 295; and (6) a recitation of the types of records the company will maintain to demonstrate its compliance with the plan. The clause at FAR 52-219-9 provides a detailed outline for preparing a subcontracting plan that fulfills these six requirements.

The Flow-Down Process

The requirement for subcontracting plans flows down to all other-than-small business subcontractors with subcontracts over $5000,000 (over $1 million for construction of a public facility). According to the statute, an other-than-small prime contractor with a subcontracting plan must require all other-than-small subcontractors to adopt a plan similar to its own. The prime contractor is responsible for obtaining, approving, and monitoring the subcontracting plans of its other-than-small subcontractors.

A prime contractor's subcontractor is referred to as the first-tier subcontractor. If the first-tier subcontractor is an other-than-small business and it subcontracts to another other-than-small business, it must require that firm (the second tier subcontractor) to adopt a subcontracting plan similar to its own. If the second-tier subcontractor subcontracts to yet another other-than-small business (the third-tier subcontractor), it would have to require that company to adopt a subcontracting plan as well. This process continues indefinitely, as long as the subcontractors are not small businesses and their subcontracts are over $500,000 (over $1 million for construction of a public facility).

Under the flow-down provision, other-than-small business subcontractors with subcontracting plans must submit SF 294 and SF 295 just as the prime contractors do. However, the other-than-small subcontractor must submit the SF 294 to its prime contractor or immediate higher-tier subcontractor rather than to the Government. This is done for monitoring purposes, and continues in this manner for all tiers. The other-than-small subcontractor still submits the SF 295 to the Government in accordance with the instructions on the back of the form. This enables the Government to collect subcontracting statistics from all of the subcontracting tiers.

The flow-down process is intended to ensure that all small businesses receive "maximum practical opportunity" to perform on Government contracts and subcontracts in accordance with Section 8(d), regardless of the subcontracting tier.

Commercial Products Plans

If an other-than-small business is selling a product or service to the Government that differs just slightly from what it is selling to the general public, it may be eligible for a Commercial Products Plan. Such a plan is company-wide or division-wide and relates to the company's production generally, for both commercial and noncommercial products or services, rather than solely to the Government contract. It must be approved by the first Federal agency awarding the company a contract requiring a subcontracting plan during the fiscal year. Once approved, the plan remains in effect during the company's fiscal year and covers all of its commercial products or services.

A commercial products plan has several advantages over individual subcontracting plans. Paperwork and record keeping are vastly reduced, since there is only one plan for the entire company or division. Perhaps even more attractive is the fact that the company is required to submit on annual SF 295 to the Government; no SF 294s for individual contracts are required. However, if the company's fiscal year is different from that of the Government, it must file two SF 295s -- one for the company's fiscal year and one for the Government's fiscal year.

Master Subcontracting Plans

A Master Subcontracting Plan is a subcontracting plan that contains all of the elements required by the Federal Acquisition Regulations (see "The Six Elements of a Subcontracting Plan" above) except goals for small, small disadvantaged, and women-owned small business. Thereafter, as the company receives Government contracts requiring subcontracting plans, it simply develops specific goals for each plan. This process avoids redundant effort on the five other elements of a subcontracting plan, allowing more time and effort for the substantive task of developing goals.

As in the case of a Commercial Products Plan, a Master Plan must be approved by the first Federal agency awarding the company a contract requiring a subcontracting plan during the fiscal year. A Master Plan is effective for three years; however, when incorporated into an individual plan, a master plan applies to that contract throughout the life of the contract.

Specific Goal Requirements

Section 15(g) of the Small Business Act (15 USC 644(g)) requires the President to establish annual subcontract goals of not less than 5% of the total value of all subcontract awards each fiscal year for both small disadvantaged businesses and women-owned small businesses. There is no established percentage subcontract goal for small businesses; however, the achievements have ranged from 35% to 42%.

Reporting Requirements for Other-Than-Small Businesses

STANDARD FORM 294 (SF 294): Other-than-small business prime contractors must file an SF 294, "Subcontract Report for Individual Contract," with their procuring agencies semi-annually during the performance of the contract and also upon each contract's completion. Other-than-small business subcontractors must file the SF 294 with the prime contractor or immediate higher-tier subcontractor rather than with the Government. The SF 294 is not required if the company is operating under a Commercial Products Plan or participating in the Department of Defense Test Program for Negotiation of Comprehensive Subcontracting Plans.

STANDARD FORM 295 (SF 295): Other-than-small business prime contractors and subcontractors must periodically file an SF 295, "Summary Subcontract Report," with their procuring agencies. If the procuring agency is a civilian agency, the SF 295 is required annually (by October 30th for the previous fiscal year ended September 30th); if the procuring agency is the Department of Defense, the SF 295 is required semi-annually (by April 30th for the first six months of the fiscal year and by October 30th for the entire fiscal year).

In the case of a Commercial Products Plan, the SF 295 is required only once a year (by October 30th for the previous fiscal year ended September 30th). Other-than-small prime contracts and subcontractors must submit a copy of the SF 295 to the cognizant SBA Commercial Market Representative.

The SF 294 and SF 295 are intended to document the dollars awarded to small, small disadvantaged, and women-owned small businesses. It is important to note that prime contractors may take credit for only their own subcontracting dollars, not for the dollars awarded by subcontractors at lower tiers. This is explained in more detail on the instructions on the back of the forms.

CERTIFICATE OF COMPETENCY

SBA's procurement assistance effort is greatly strengthened by the Certificate of Competency (COC) program. SBA is authorized by the Congress to certify as to a small company's "capability, competency, credit, integrity, perseverance and tenacity" to perform a specific Government contract. If a contracting officer proposes to reject the offer of a small business firm that is a low offeror because he or she questions the firm's ability to perform the contract on any of the above grounds, the case is referred to SBA. SBA personnel then contact the company concerned to inform it of the impending decision, and to offer the firm an opportunity to apply to SBA for a COC, which, if granted, would require award of the contract to the firm in accordance with the Small Business Act. SBA may also, at its discretion, issue a COC in connection with the sale of Federal property if the responsibility (capacity, credit, integrity, tenacity and perseverance) of the purchaser is questioned, and for firms found ineligible by a contracting officer due to a provision of the Walsh-Healey Public Contracts Act which requires that a Government contractor be either a manufacturer or a regular dealer.

The COC program is carried out by a specialized SBA field staff of individuals with technical, engineering, and Government procurement backgrounds in cooperation with financial specialists, also of the field organization. Upon receipt of a COC application, the SBA notifies the contracting officer of the purchasing agency that the prospective contractor has applied, and a team of financial and technical personnel is sent to the firm to survey its potential. Although SBA has access to the purchasing agency's preaward survey, that served as the basis of the contracting officer's decision, SBA conducts a completely new review, that evaluates the characteristics of the applicant in terms of the needs of the specific acquisition in question. Credit ratings, past performance, management capabilities, management schedules, and the prospects for obtaining needed financial help or equipment are considered.

The team's findings are presented to a COC Review Committee composed of legal, technical and financial representatives, that makes a detailed review of the case and recommends approval or disapproval. If the decision is negative, the firm and the purchasing agency are so informed; if affirmative, a letter certifying the responsibility of the firm to perform the contract (the Certificate of Competency) is sent to the purchasing agency. By terms of the Small Business Act, the COC is conclusive on questions of responsibility, and the contract is awarded.

A COC is valid only for the specific contract for which it is issued. A business concern that is capable of handling one contract may not be qualified to handle another. Each case is considered separately, and each case is considered only if and after the contracting officer has made a negative determination of responsibility or eligibility. Firms may not apply for a COC until a contracting officer makes a non-responsibility determination and refers the matter to the SBA.

SBA's Natural Resources Sales Assistance Program

Natural Resources Sales Assistance Program Manager:

Richard J. Sadowski Internet: rjs@pa.sba.gov

The Federal Government sells large quantities of many kinds of real and personal property -- property surplus to Federal needs -- and resources authorized for sale in accordance with public law. SBA cooperates with other Federal agencies to channel a fair share of this property and resources to small businesses. However, SBA does not sell real or personal property, except property held as collateral for SBA loans foreclosed because of default.

SBA's Natural Resources Sales Assistance Program is intended to (a) ensure small business concerns obtain a fair share of Government property sales/leases to include, where necessary, small business set-asides, and (b) provide counseling, and other assistance to small business concerns on all matters pertaining to Government sales/leases.

The program is directed by SBA's Central Office staff and carried out by the Industrial Specialists listed below. Industrial Specialists:

Robert L. Davis
Mail Code 0405
SBA - Timber Sales Programs
1720 Peachtree Road, N.W., Room 503
Atlanta, GA 30309
Voice: (404) 347- 4270
Fax: (404) 347 –5215

Mary Ellen Casco (Clerk)
SBA - Timber Sales Program
633 17th Street, Suite 700
Denver, CO 80202-3607
Voice: (303) 294-7605
Fax: (303) 294-7153

Gerald J. Gruber
Mail Code: 1086
SBA - Timber Sales Program
222 S. W. Columbia St. , Suite 500

Portland, OR 97201-6605

Voice: (503) 326-5217
Fax: [503] 326-5103

Sally Larson (Clerk)
Mail Code: 1000
SBA - Timber Sales Program
1200 Sixth Avenue, Suite 1805
Seattle, WA 98101-1128
Voice: (206) 553-8541
Fax: (206) 553-4155

Robert C. Rand
Mail Code: 1086
SBA - Timber Sales Program
222 S. W. Columbia St., Suite 500
Portland, OR 97201-6605
Voice: (503) 326-7245
Fax: [503] 326-5103

The five categories of Federal resources covered by the program are:

1.   Timber and related forest products

Timber is regularly sold from the Federal forests managed by the U.S. Department of Agriculture's, Forest Service, http://www.fs.fed.us/, and the U.S. Department of the Interior's, Bureau of Land Management, http://www.blm.gov. On occasion, timber is sold from Federal forests that are under the supervision of the Department of Defense, Department of Energy, Fish and Wildlife Service and the Tennessee Valley Authority.

SBA and these agencies work together to ensure opportunities for small business concerns to bid on Federal timber sales. In addition, SBA and the sales agencies jointly set aside timber sales for bidding by small concerns when it appears that under open sales, small business would not obtain its fair share.

2.   Strategic materials from the National Stockpile

The General Services Administration, http://www.gsa.gov, regulates the procurement and disposal of strategic materials in accordance with statutory requirements. Whenever a stockpile requirement is lowered, excess material may be sold.

In those instances where small business may find it difficult to purchase its fair share because of large quantities, the agencies may agree to divide materials into small parcels, and/or set aside a reasonable amount for exclusive bidding by small business.

3.   Royalty Oil

Royalties due the Government under leases of Federal oil rights for the exploration of oil may be accepted by the Secretary of the Interior in the form of oil or money. If the Secretary elects to accept oil in lieu of money, the oil is identified as "royalty oil."

When the Secretary of the Interior determines that sufficient supplies of crude oil are not available in the open market to small business refineries, preference will be granted to these refineries for processing royalty oil.

SBA refers qualified small business refineries to the U.S. Department of the Interior's, Minerals Management Service, http://www.mms.gov, to assist small concerns in obtaining royalty oil.

4.   Leases involving rights to minerals, coal, oil and gas.

The Federal Government is an extensive owner of mineral, oil, coal and gas rights. Leases to recover these natural resources are normally competitively sold by the Government.

SBA and the sales agency may jointly set aside a reasonable amount of leases for bidding by small concerns when it appears that under open bidding small business would not obtain its fair share.

5.   Surplus real and personal property

The Federal Government disposes of property for which it has no foreseeable need. Such property is first made available for donation to recipients authorized by law, such as educational and public health facilities, state and local governments, etc. The remainder is sold.

The two agencies of the Government principally concerned with surplus personal property sales are the Department of Defense and the General Services Administration. Scheduled sales are widely publicized and are normally competitive bid sales.

SIZE STANDARDS

SBA is responsible for making determinations as to whether a particular business qualifies as a small business under the existing size standards set forth in the Code of Federal Regulations (13 CFR Part 121). In general, these standards vary across industries, with industries dominated by large firms (such as steel mills) having higher size standards than those dominated by small firms (such as barbershops). Currently, the same set of standards applies for both the procurement and financial assistance programs. A few SBA programs, such as Small Business Investment Companies and Surety Bonds, have unique size standards designed to accommodate their own specialized needs.

With regard to procurement or sales of Government property, offerors self-certify that they are small. Another firm will occasionally question the size status of the low offeror; the contracting officer, an SBA official or some other interested party may also protest.

The contracting officer refers the protest to the SBA Government Contracting Area Office in whose territory the principal office of the protested concern is located.

The SBA Government Contracting Area Office makes initial size determinations within very tight time constraints (usually within 10 days of receiving a protest). A procuring (or selling) agency must accept, as conclusive, SBA's determination as to which firms are "small business concerns." Determinations of the Area Office may be appealed to the Office of Hearings and Appeals at SBA headquarters in Washington, D.C., by any of the interested parties.

Minority and Disadvantaged Business Owners

Note

Recent actions of the Supreme Court and the Federal Government have indicated that there may be action to remove "Affirmative Action Programs" in the near future. At the writing of this book, these programs were still active, but you should contact your local SBA office to confirm the continued existence of these programs.

R ecent U.S. Census Bureau statistics indicate that women own 32 percent of all small businesses in the United States and that by the year 2000 the percentages will increase to 40 percent. Despite impressive advancement, women still face unique challenges to starting and growing their businesses.

Selling to the Federal Government can be a large market niche for woman-owned businesses. In fiscal year 1994, only 2.1 percent of all federal prime and subcontracts were awarded to women-owned firms. Women's share of federal contracts has steadily increased, but is still a small percentage of what it will be in the future.

The good news for women-owned firms, is the passage of Public Law 103-355, the Federal Acquisition Streamlining Act, signed by President Clinton on October 13, 1994. This Act is the first major rewrite of Federal procurement laws in a decade. It establishes a Government-wide goal of having not less than 5 percent of the total value of all prime and subcontract awards, for each fiscal year, awarded to women-owned businesses. Government agencies are encouraged to expand procurement opportunities for women.

The most significant provisions of the new law include:

- Establishing a new 5 percent Government-wide procurement goal for women-owned businesses;

- Encouraging agencies to rely on off-the-shelf commercial products instead of those specifically designed to comply with Government-unique requirements;

- Streamlining acquisition procedures through an increased small purchase dollar threshold;

- Amending several current procurement laws to provide uniform treatment of both Department of Defense and civilian agency procurements;

- Authorizing the Office of Federal Procurement Policy to test alternative procurement techniques in 13 pilot acquisition programs; and

- Improving contract protest and oversight procedures.

In order to accomplish the objectives of this law, the following actions will have to be taken by the Government:

- Women-owned firms are specifically incorporated into the procurement preference goal process established for all Government agencies;

- Women-owned firms are added as a class for subcontract goals;

A woman-owned business is presently defined as a small business that is at least 51 percent owned by one or more women, or in the case of any publicly owned business, at least 51 percent of the stock is owned by one or more women and the management and daily business operations are controlled by one or more women.

Although the new legislation makes it clear that Government agencies are expected to expand contract opportunities for women, this does not mean that contracts will be set-aside solely for women-owned firms. Rather, agencies will have a strong incentive to look for qualified women-owned businesses when trying to fill contractual needs. It is still up to women business owners themselves to market their products and services to the government.

Because of these mandates, woman-owned businesses should aggressively market to the Government. Take advantage of your strength in this area while it is at its peak. You can keep up-to-date on the status of woman in Government contracting with the SBA's Office of Advocacy bulletin board. This board electronically publishes a variety of information of interest to small firms. Included in this bulletin board is a sub-board that focuses exclusively on procurement (regulatory and legislative) issues. It can be reached with a computer and modem (9600 baud) by dialing SBA Online, at (800) 697-4636 [in Washington, D.C. call (202) 401-9600]. Once you have logged on to the Main Menu, choose (2) Services Available and then select (7) Advocacy-Small Business Services.

SBA 8(A) PROGRAM

The 8(a) Contracting and Business Opportunity Program is named for the section of the Small Business Act from which it derives its authority. Through the 8(a) Program, small companies owned by socially and economically disadvantaged persons can obtain Federal Government contracts. Under the program, SBA acts as a prime contractor and enters into all types of Government contracts (including but not limited to supply, services, construction, research and development) with other Government departments and agencies and negotiates subcontracts for performance thereof with small companies in the 8(a) Program.

Purpose

The purpose of the 8(a) Program is to:

- Foster business ownership by individuals who are socially and economically disadvantaged;

- Promote the competitive viability of such firms by providing viable contract, financial, technical and management assistance as may be necessary; and

- Clarify and expand the program for the procurement by the United States of articles, equipment, supplies, service materials, and construction work from small business concerns owned by socially and economically disadvantaged individuals.

Eligibility

Applicants for 8(a) Program participation must meet certain program participation requirements that include, but are not limited to the following criteria:

Ownership:

In order to be eligible to participate in the 8(a) Program, an applicant concern must be one that is at least 51 percent owned by an individual(s) who is a citizen of the United States (specifically excluding resident aliens), and who is determined to be socially and economically disadvantaged.

Social Disadvantage:

Socially disadvantaged individuals are those who have been subject to racial or ethnic prejudice or cultural bias because of their identity as a member of a group without regard to their individual qualities.

(a)   Members of Designated Groups: Absent evidence to the contrary, the following individuals are considered socially disadvantaged - Black American, Hispanic American, Native American (American Indian, Eskimo, Aleut or Native Hawaiian), Asian Pacific American (an individual with origins from Burma, Thailand, Malaysia, Indonesia, Singapore, Brunei, Japan, China, Taiwan, Laos, Cambodia, Kampuc, Vietnam, Korea, the Philippines, U.S. Trust Territory of the Pacific Islands, Republic of Palau, Republic of the Marshall Islands, Federated States of Micronesia, the Commonwealth of the Northern Madana Islands, Guam, Samoa, Macao, Hong Kong, Fiji, Tonga, Kiriba, Tuvalu, Naura); Subcontinent Asian American (an individual with origins from India, Pakistan, Bangladesh, Sri Lanka, Bhutan, the Maldives Islands or Nepal), or members of other groups designated from time to time by the SBA.

(b)   Individuals who are not members of the above-named groups must establish their social disadvantage on the basis of clear and convincing case. A clear and convincing case of social disadvantage must include the following elements:

(I)   The individual's social disadvantage must stem from his or her color, national origin, gender, physical handicap, long-term residence in an environment isolated from the mainstream of American society, or other similar cause beyond the individual's control

(ii)   The individual must demonstrate that he or she has personally suffered social disadvantage, not merely claiming membership in a non-designated group that could be considered socially disadvantaged

(iii)   The individual's, social disadvantage must be chronic, long standing, and substantial, not fleeting or insignificant

(iv)   The individual's social disadvantage must be rooted in treatment that he or she has experienced in American society, not in other countries

(v)   The individual's social disadvantage must have negatively impacted his or her entry into, and/or advancement in, the business world

Economic Disadvantage:

Economically disadvantaged individuals are socially disadvantaged individuals whose ability to compete in the free enterprise system has been impaired due to diminished capital and credit opportunities, as compared to others in the same or similar line of business and competitive market area who are not socially disadvantaged.   In determining the degree of economic disadvantage, consideration will be given to the following:

- Personal financial condition of the disadvantaged individual;

- Business financial condition;

- Access to credit and capital; and

- A comparison will be made of the applicant concern's business and financial profile with profiles of businesses in the same or similar type of business and competitive market area.

Control and Management:

An applicant concern's management and daily business operations must be controlled by an individual(s) determined to be socially and economically disadvantaged and such individual(s) must be engaged in the daily management and operation of the business concern.

Size Standard:

In order to be eligible to participate in the 8(a) Program, an applicant concern must qualify as a small business concern as defined in section 121.3-8 of the SBA Rules and Regulations. The particular size standard to be applied will be based on the primary industry classification of the applicant concern.

Potential for Success:

To be eligible to participate in the Section 8(a) Program, an otherwise eligible applicant concern must also be determined to be one that with contract, financial, technical or management support will be able to successfully perform subcontracts awarded under the 8(a) Program, and further, with such support will have a reasonable prospect for success in competition in the private sector. The applicant concern must demonstrate that it has been in business in the primary industry classification in which it seeks 8(a) certification for two full years PRIOR to the date of its 8(a) application by submitting income tax returns showing revenues for each of the two previous years.

Ineligible Businesses:

Brokers, packagers, franchise operators, debarred or suspended firms, non-profit organizations, and firms owned by disadvantaged concerns, are ineligible for participation.

Program Term:

Every 8(a) Program participant is admitted to the program for a nine-year term. The term will consist of a developmental stage of four years and a transitional stage of five years.

Program Termination:

Participation of a Section 8(a) business concern in the Section 8(a) Program may be terminated by SBA for good cause.

OTHER ASSISTANCE AVAILABLE

Financial assistance in the form of loans and advanced payments are available to 8(a) Program participants. Contractors in the program can receive a wide range of assistance in managing their firms, including: pamphlets, individual counseling, seminars, and professional guidance. Bonding to perform on Government contracts may be provided to eligible companies.

HOW TO APPLY

It is SBA's policy that any individual or business has the right to apply for Section 8(a) assistance, whether or not there is an appearance of eligibility. Applications for admission are to be filed in the SBA field office serving the territory in which the principal place of the applicant concern is located. Principal place of business means the location of your books and records, and where the individual who manages the concern's day-to-day operations spends the majority of their working hours.

WAIVER OF MINIMUM PERIOD OF OPERATION

The Administration will provide that any requirement it establishes regarding the period of time a prospective Program Participant must be in operation may be waived and, a prospective Program Participant who otherwise meets the requirements of Section 8(a)(7)(A) of the Small Business Act, will be considered to have demonstrated reasonable prospects for success, if:

- The individual or individuals upon whom eligibility is to be based have substantial and demonstrated business management experience;

- The prospective Program Participant has demonstrated technical expertise to carry out its business plan with a substantial likelihood for success;

- The prospective Program Participant has adequate capital to carry out its business plan;

- The prospective program participant has a record of successful performance on contracts from governmental and non-governmental sources in the primary industry category in which the prospective Program Participant is seeking certification; and

- The prospective Program Participant has, or can demonstrate its ability to timely obtain the personnel, facilities, equipment, and any other requirements needed to perform such contracts.

Note

In order to qualify for the two-year waiver, you MUST meet ALL FIVE criteria as listed above.

FEDERAL OFFICES OF SMALL AND DISADVANTAGED BUSINESS UTILIZATION (OSDBU)

Offices designated as Offices of Small and Disadvantaged Business Utilization (OSDBUs) provide procurement assistance to small, minority, 8(a) and women-owned businesses. Their primary function is to ensure that small and disadvantaged businesses receive their fair share of U.S. Government contracts. "OSDBUs" are the contacts for their respective agencies and are excellent sources of information.

Department of Agriculture
14th and Independence Ave., S.W.,
Room 1323, South Bldg.
Washington, DC 20250
Telephone: (202) 720-7117
FAX (202) 720-3001

Department of Commerce
14th and Constitution Ave., N.W.,
Room H-6411
Washington, DC 20230
Telephone: (202) 482-1472
FAX (202) 482-0501

Department of Defense
Office of the Director for
Small Business Programs
3061 Defense Pentagon, Room 2A340
Washington, DC 20301-3061
Telephone: (703) 614-1151,
697-1688, 697-9383
FAX (703) 693-7014

Department of the Air Force
Office of the Secretary of the Air Force
The Pentagon - Room 5E271
Washington, DC 20330-1060
Telephone: (703) 697-1950
FAX (703) 614-9266

Department of the Army
Office of the Secretary of the Army
106 Army Pentagon
Washington, DC 20310-0106
Telephone: (703) 697-7753
FAX (703) 693-3898

Department of the Navy
Office of the Secretary of the Navy
2211 Jefferson Davis Highway
Arlington, VA 22244-5102
Telephone: (703) 602-2700
FAX (703) 602-2477

Defense Logistics Agency HQ
8725 John J. Kingman Rd., Suite 2533
Ft. Belvoir, VA 22060-6221
Telephone: (703) 767-1650
FAX (703) 767-1670

Department of Education
600 Independence Avenue, S.W.,
Room 3120-ROB-3
Washington, DC 20202-0521
Telephone: (202) 708-9820
FAX (202) 401-6477

Department of Energy
1707 H Street, N.W., Room 904
Washington, DC 20585
Telephone: (202) 254-5583
FAX (202) 254-3989

Department of Health and Human Services
200 Independence Ave., S.W., Room 517D, Humphrey Building
Washington, DC 20201
Telephone: (202) 690-7300
FAX (202) 690-8772

Department of Housing and Urban
Development
451 7th Street, S.W., Room 3130
Washington, DC 20410
Telephone: (202) 708-1428
FAX (202) 708-7642

Department of the Interior
1849 C Street, N.W., Room 2725
Washington, DC 20240
Telephone: (202) 208-3493
FAX (202) 208-5048

Bureau of Indian Affairs
Division of Contracting and Grants
Administration
1951 Constitution Avenue, N.W.,
Mail Stop 334-SIB
Washington, DC 20245
Telephone: (202) 208-2825

Department of Justice
12th and Pennsylvania Avenue, N.W.,
Room 3235, Ariel Rios Bldg.
Washington, DC 20530
Telephone: (202) 616-0521
FAX (202) 616-1717

Department of Labor
200 Constitution Avenue, N.W., Room
C-2318
Washington, DC 20210
Telephone: (202) 219-9148
FAX (202) 219-9167

Department of State
1701 Ft. Myer Drive, Room 633
(SA-6)
Rosslyn, VA 22209

Telephone: (703) 875-6824
FAX (703) 875-6825
Mailing Address Only
SDBU, Room 633, SA 6
Washington, DC 20522-0602

Department of Transportation
400 7th Street, S.W., Room 9414
Washington, DC 20590
Telephone: (202) 366-1930
FAX (202) 366-7228

Department of the Treasury
1500 Pennsylvania Avenue, N.W.,
Room 6100 - Annex
Washington, DC 20220
Telephone: (202) 622-0530
Office of the Comptroller of the
Currency
Acquisitions and Procurement Branch
250 E Street, S.W., Mail Stop 4-13
Washington, DC 20219
Telephone: (202) 874-5040
FAX (202) 874-5625

Office of Thrift Supervision
Department of the Treasury
1700 G Street, N.W., 3rd Floor
Washington, DC 20552
Telephone: (202) 906-6346 or
906-7864
FAX (202) 906-5748

Department of Veterans Affairs
810 Vermont Avenue, N.W. (00SSB)
Washington, DC 20420
Telephone: (202) 565-8127
FAX (202) 565-8156

The majority of independent agencies do not have designated Offices of Small and
Disadvantaged Business Utilization. However, they do have specific personnel
available to assume such responsibilities.

UNITED STATES DEPARTMENT OF COMMERCE MINORITY BUSINESS DEVELOPMENT AGENCY (MBDA)

MINORITY BUSINESS DEVELOPMENT CENTERS MBDA's nationwide network of Minority Development Centers (MBDCs) counsel minority individuals on accounting, administration, business planning, inventory control, negotiations, referrals, networking, construction contracting and subcontracting, marketing, and on SBA's 8(a) certification to participate in minority set-aside contracting opportunities with the federal government. They provide managerial and technical assistance for bonding, bidding, estimating, financing, procurement, international trade, franchising, acquisitions, mergers, joint ventures, and leveraged buyouts. MBDCs facilitate the formation and expansion of minority- owned firms.

ATLANTA REGION

Alabama, Florida, Georgia, Kentucky,
Mississippi, North Carolina,
South Carolina, Tennessee

MBDA Regional Director
401 W. Peachtree Street, N.W., Suite 1930
Atlanta, GA 30308-3516
Telephone: (404) 730-3300

MBDA MIAMI District Office
51 S.W. 1st Avenue, Room 928
Miami, FL 33130
Telephone: (305) 536-5054

ATLANTA MBDC
75 Piedmont Avenue, N.E., Suite 256
Atlanta, GA 30303
Telephone: (404) 586-0953

AUGUSTA MBDC
1394 Laney Walker Blvd.
Augusta, GA 30101-2796
Telephone: (706) 722-0994

BIRMINGHAM MBDC
1732 5th Avenue, N.
Birmingham, AL 35203
Telephone: (205) 324-5231

CHARLESTON MBDC
4 Carriage Lane
Charleston, SC 29407
Telephone: (803) 556-3040

CHEROKEE IBDC
Alquoni Road, Box 1200
Cherokee, NC 28701
Telephone: (704) 497-9335

CHEROKOO IBDC
70 Woodfin Place, Suite 305
Asheville, NC 28801
Telephone: (704) 252-2516

COLUMBIA MBDC
1313 Elmwood Avenue
Columbia, SC 29201
Telephone: (803) 779-5905

COLUMBUS MBDC
233 12th Street, Suite 621
Columbus, GA 31902-1696
FAYETTEVILLE MBDC
PO Box 1387
Fayetteville, NC 28302
Telephone: (910) 483-7513

GREENVILLE/SPARTANBURG MBDC
211 Century Plaza Drive, Suite 100-D
Greenville, SC 29607
Telephone: (803) 271-8753
JACKSON MBDC

5285 Galaxie Drive, Suite A
Jackson, MS 39206
Telephone: (601) 362-2260

JACKSONVILLE MBDC
218 W. Adams Street, Suite 300
Jacksonville, FL 32202-3508
Telephone: (904) 353-3826

LOUISVILLE MBDC
611 W. Main Street
4th Floor
Louisville, KY 40402
Telephone: (502) 589-6232

MEMPHIS MBDC
5 N. 3rd Street, Suite 2020
Memphis, TN 38103
Telephone: (901) 527-2298

MIAMI/FT. LAUDERDALE MBDC
1200 N.W. 78th Avenue, Suite 301
Miami, FL 33126
Telephone: (305) 591-7355

MOBILE MBDC
801 Executive Park Drive, Suite 102
Mobile, AL 36606
Telephone: (205) 471-5165

MONTGOMERY MBDC
770 S. McDonough Street, Suite 209
Montgomery, AL 36104
Telephone: (205) 834-7598

NASHVILLE MBDC
14 Academy Place, Suite 2
Nashville, TN 37210-2026
Telephone: (615) 255-0432

ORLANDO MBDC
132 E. Colonial Drive, Suite 211
Orlando, FL 32801
Telephone: (407) 422-6234

RALEIGH/DURHAM MBDC
817 New Bern Avenue, Suite 8

Raleigh, NC 27601
Telephone: (919) 833-6122

TAMPA/ST. PETERSBURG MBDC
4601 W. Kennedy Blvd., Suite 200
Tampa, FL 33609
Telephone: (813) 289-8824

WEST PALM BEACH MBDC
2001 Broadway, Suite 301C
Riviera Beach, FL 33404
Telephone: (407) 863-0895

CHICAGO REGION

Illinois, Indiana, Iowa, Kansas,
Michigan, Minnesota, Missouri,
Nebraska, Ohio, Wisconsin

MBDA Regional Director
55 E. Monroe Street, Suite 1440
Chicago, IL 60603
Telephone: (312) 353-0182

CHICAGO MEGA CENTER
105 W. Adams Street, 7th Floor
Chicago, IL 60603
Telephone: (312) 977-9190

CINCINNATI MBDC
1821 Summit Road, Suite 111
Cincinnati, OH 45237-2810
(513) 679-6000

CLEVELAND MBDC
601 Lakeside Avenue, E., Suite 335
Cleveland, OH 44114
Telephone: (216) 664-4155

DAYTON MBDC
32 N. Main Street, Suite 1001
Dayton, OH 45402
Telephone: (513) 228-0290

DETROIT MBDC
645 Griswold Street, Suite 2156

Detroit, MI 48226
Telephone: (313) 963-6232

GARY MBDC
567 Broadway
Gary, IN 46402
Telephone: (219) 883-5802

INDIANAPOLIS MBDC
4755 Kingsway Drive, Suite 102
Indianapolis, IN 46205
Telephone: (317) 226-3996

KANSAS CITY MBDC
1101 Walnut Street, Suite 1900
Kansas City, MO 64106-2143
Telephone: (816) 471-1520

MILWAUKEE MBDC
1442 N. Farwell Avenue, Suite 500
Milwaukee, WI 53202
MINNEAPOLIS IBDC
2021 E. Hennepin Avenue, Suite 370
Minneapolis, MN 55413
Telephone: (612) 331-5576

MINNESOTA MBDC
Leech Lake Reservation
PO Box 217
Cass Lake, MN 56633-0217
Telephone: (218) 335-8583

ST. LOUIS MBDC
231 S. Bemiston Street, Suite 750
St. Louis, MO 63101
Telephone: (314) 721-7766

DALLAS REGION

Arkansas, Colorado, Louisiana,
Montana, New Mexico, North Dakota,
Oklahoma, South Dakota, Texas,
Utah, Wyoming

MBDA Regional Director
1100 Commerce Street, Room 7B23

Dallas, TX 75242
Telephone: (214) 767-8001

ALBUQUERQUE MBDC
718 Central Avenue, S.W.
Albuquerque, NM 87102
Telephone: (505) 843-7114

AUSTIN MBDC
1524 S. International Hwy. 35, Suite
218
Austin, TX 78704
Telephone: (512) 447-0800

BATON ROUGE MBDC
2036 Wooddale Blvd., Suite D
Baton Rouge, LA 70814
Telephone: (504) 924-0186

BROWNSVILLE MBDC
2100 Boca Chica Blvd., Suite 301
Brownsville, TX 78521-2265
Telephone: (210) 546-3400

CORPUS CHRISTI MBDC
3649 Leopard Street, Suite 514
Corpus Christi, TX 78408
Telephone: (512) 887-7961

DALLAS/FT. WORTH MBDC
501 Winwood Village Shopping
Center, Suite 202
Dallas, TX 75224-1899
Telephone: (214) 943-4095

DENVER MBDC
930 W. 7th Avenue
Denver, CO 80204
Telephone: (303) 623-5660

EL PASO MBDC
6068 Gateway East, Suite 200
El Paso, TX 79905
Telephone: (915) 774-0626

HOUSTON MBDC

1200 Smith Street, Suite 2870
Houston, TX 77002
Telephone: (713) 650-3831

LAREDO MBDC
1303 Calle del Norte, Suite 400
Laredo, TX 78041
Telephone: (210) 726-8815

LITTLE ROCK MBDC
One Riverfront Plaza, Suite 740
N. Little Rock, AR 72114

MC ALLEN MBDC
1701 W. Bus. Hwy. 83, Suite 306
McAllen, TX 78501
Telephone: (210) 664-0073

NEW MEXICO IBDC
3939 San Pedro Drive, N.E., Suite D
Albuquerque, NM 87190-3256
Telephone: (505) 889-9092

NORTH DAKOTA IBDC
3315 University Drive
Bismarck, ND 58504
Telephone: (701) 255-6849

OKLAHOMA IBDC
5727 S. Garnett Street, Suite C
Tulsa, OK 74146-6823
Telephone: (918) 250-5950

SALT LAKE CITY MBDC
350 East 500 South, Suite 101
Salt Lake City, UT 84111
Telephone: (801) 328-8181

SAN ANTONIO MBDC
UTSA, 6900 North Loop 1604 West
San Antonio, TX 78249-0660
Telephone: (210) 225-6233

TULSA MBDC
240 E. Apache Street
Tulsa, OK 74106
Telephone: (918) 592-1995

NEW YORK REGION

Connecticut, Maine, Massachusetts,
New Hampshire, New Jersey, New
York, Puerto Rico, Rhode Island,
Vermont, Virgin Islands
MBDA Regional Director
26 Federal Plaza, Room 37-20
New York, NY 10278
Telephone: (212) 264-3262

MBDA BOSTON
District Office
10 Causeway Street, Room 418
Boston, MA 02222-1041
Telephone: (617) 565-6850

BOSTON MBDC
10 Causeway Street, Room 418
Boston, MA 02222
Telephone: (617) 565-6850

BROOKLYN MBDC
16 Court Street, Room 1903
Brooklyn, NY 11201
Telephone: (718) 522-5880

BUFFALO MBDC
570 E. Delavan Avenue
Buffalo, NY 14211
Telephone: (716) 895-2218

MANHATTAN MBDC
51 Madison Avenue, Suite 2212
New York, NY 10010
Telephone: (212) 779-4360

MAYAGUEZ MBDC
70 W. Mendez Vigo
PO Box 3146 Marina Station
Mayaguez, PR 00681
Telephone: (809) 833-7783

NASSAU/SUFFOLK MBDC
150 Broad Hollow Road, Suite 304
Melville, NY 11747

NEW BRUNSWICK MBDC
390 George Street, Suite 410
New Brunswick, NJ 08901
Telephone: (908) 249-5511

NEWARK MBDC
60 Park Place, Suite 1601
Newark, NJ 07102
Telephone: (201) 623-7712

PONCE MBDC
19 Salud Street
Ponce, PR 00731
Telephone: (809) 840-8100

QUEENS MBDC
125-10 Queens Blvd.
Kew Gardens, NY 11415
Telephone: (718) 793-3900

ROCHESTER MBDC
350 North Street
Rochester, NY 14605
Telephone: (716) 232-6120
SAN JUAN MBDC
122 Eleanor Roosevelt Avenue
Halo Rey, PR 00918
Telephone: (809) 753-8484

VIRGIN ISLANDS MBDC
81-AB Kronprindsen Gade, 3rd Floor
PO Box 838
St. Thomas, VI 00804
Telephone: (809) 774-7215

VIRGIN ISLANDS MBDC
35 King Street
Christensted
St. Croix, VI 00820
Telephone: (809) 773-6334

WILLIAMSBURG/BROOKLYN MBDC
12 Heyward Street
Brooklyn, NY 11211
Telephone: (718) 522-5620

SAN FRANCISCO REGION
Alaska, American Samoa, Arizona,
California, Hawaii, Idaho,
Nevada, Oregon, Washington

MBDA Regional Director
221 Main Street, Room 1280
San Francisco, CA 94105
Telephone: (415) 744-3001

MBDA LOS ANGELES
District Office
9660 Flair Drive, Suite 455
El Monte, CA 91713
Telephone: (818) 453-8636

ALASKA MBDC
1577 C Street Plaza, Suite 304
Anchorage, AK 99501
Telephone: (907) 274-5400

FRESNO MBDC
4944 E. Clinton Way, Suite 103
Fresno, CA 93727
Telephone: (209) 266-2766

HONOLULU MBDC
1132 Bishop Street, Suite 1000
Honolulu, HI 96813-3652
Telephone: (808) 531-6232

LOS ANGELES MBDC
355 S. Grand Avenue, Suite 1150
Los Angeles, CA 90071
Telephone: (213) 627-1717

PHOENIX MBDC
432 N. 44th Street, Suite 354
Phoenix, AZ 85008
Telephone: (602) 225-0740

PORTLAND MBDC
8959 S.W. Barbur Blvd., Suite 102
Portland, OR 97219
Telephone: (503) 245-9253

SACRAMENTO MBDC
1779 Tribute Road, Suite I
Sacramento, CA 95815
Telephone: (916) 649-2551

SALINAS MBDC
14 Maple Street, Suite D
Salinas, CA 93901
Telephone: (408) 422-8825

SAN DIEGO MBDC
7777 Alvarado Road, Suite 310
La Mesa, CA 91941
Telephone: (619) 668-6232

SAN FRANCISCO/OAKLAND MBDC
221 Main Street, Suite 1570
San Francisco, CA 94105
Telephone: (415) 243-8430
SAN FRANCISCO/OAKLAND MBDC
1212 Broadway, Suite 900
Oakland, CA 94612
Telephone: (510) 271-0180

SANTA BARBARA MBDC
22 N. Milpas Street, Suite H
Santa Barbara, CA 93103
Telephone: (805) 965-2611

SEATTLE MBDC
155 N.E. 100th Avenue, Suite 401
Seattle, WA 98125
Telephone: (206) 525-5617

STOCKTON MBDC
305 N. El Dorado Street, Suite 305
Stockton, CA 95202
Telephone: (209) 467-4774

TUCSON MBDC
1200 N. El Dorado Square, Suite
D-440
Tucson, AZ 85715
Telephone: (520) 721-1187

WASHINGTON REGION
Delaware, Maryland, Pennsylvania,
Virginia, Washington DC, West
Virginia

MBDA Regional Director
1255 22nd Street, N.W., Suite 701
Washington, DC 20036
Telephone: (202) 377-1356

MBDC PHILADELPHIA
District Office
600 Arch Street, Room 10128
Philadelphia, PA 19106
Telephone: (215) 597-9236

BALTIMORE MBDC
301 N. Charles Street, Suite 902
Baltimore, MD 21201
Telephone: (410) 752-7400

NEWPORT NEWS MBDC
6060 Jefferson Avenue, Suite 6016
Newport News, VA 23605
NORFOLK MBDC
355 Crawford Pkwy., Suite 608
Portsmouth, VA 23701
Telephone: (804) 399-0888

PHILADELPHIA MBDC
125 N. 8th Street, 4th Floor
Philadelphia, PA 19106
Telephone: (215) 629-9841

PITTSBURGH MBDC
Nine Parkway Center, Suite 250
Pittsburgh, PA 15220
Telephone: (412) 921-1155

WASHINGTON MBDC
1133 15th Street, N.W., Suite 1120
Washington, DC 20005
Telephone: (202) 785-2886

Chapter

9

Electronic Commerce

H istorically, the Government separated purchases at the $25,000 level. Smaller purchases were made with purchase orders or simple bids. Contracts over that level were made through sealed bidding or negotiated procurements.

Modernization is now taking hold of this unwieldy procurement process, most significantly in the guise of **Electronic Commerce/Electronic Data Interchange (EC/EDI).** The Federal Acquisition Streamlining Act of 1994 was specifically designed to simplify the Federal procurement process. This Act has raised the simplified procurement process level to $100,000 and brought computer technology into play, significantly changing how the Government does business. The Act repeals or modifies more than 225 provisions of law to reduce paperwork burdens, enhance the use of simplified procedures for small purchases, transform the simplified acquisition process to Electronic Commerce, and improve the efficiency of the laws governing the procurement of goods and services.

WHAT IS ELECTRONIC COMMERCE

Electronic Commerce is conducting business transactions within a paperless environment: Electronic Data Interchange (EDI), Electronic Mail (E-Mail), computer bulletin boards, FAX, Electronic Funds Transfer (EFT), and other similar technologies.

WHAT IS ELECTRONIC DATA INTERCHANGE

Electronic Data Interchange is the computer-to-computer exchange of business information using a public standard. EDI is a central part of Electronic Commerce, because it enables businesses to electronically exchange information faster, cheaper and more accurately than by using paperbased systems.

WHAT IS A VALUE ADDED NETWORK

A certified VAN (sometimes called a "third party network") is a company certified by the Government to provide EC/EDI services to the private sector (Trading Partners). The VAN serves as an electronic conduit between Trading Partners and the Government. Trading Partners, however, are responsible for their own internal equipment requirements such as PC, modem, or fax.

WHAT IS A TRADING PARTNER

A Trading Partner is "a business that has agreed to exchange business information electronically with the Government." This term describes any business that has been registered to conduct business electronically with the Government through a VAN.

EDI AND ONLINE SYSTEMS

EDI is not currently conducted using the Internet. While VANs possess the technical capability of sending and receiving EDI documents through the Internet, the Government does not have sufficient confidence in the Internet to allow its use for EDI purposes. The Internet does not offer sufficient security of the transmission, since Internet traffic flows over circuits owned and operated by many different organizations. This may change in the future as technology continues to advance.

WHAT IS THE FEDERAL ACQUISITION NETWORK (FACNET)

The Federal Acquisition Streamlining Act (FASA) essentially sets up four distinct buying systems: simplified acquisition threshold; micro-purchases; commercial items; and the "old" system for major procurements. It requires the government to change the acquisition process from one driven by paperwork to one based on electronic data interchange through the Federal Acquisition Network (FACNET) a computer based source of information that will be readily available to government and private sector users, including small businesses.

Agencies have a big incentive to implement the new system quickly because they may not use the new simplified acquisition procedures for contracts greater than $50,000 until they have developed "interim FACNET capability". This means that they can, at a minimum, provide widespread public notice of solicitations and receive responses to those solicitations and related requests for information.

Agencies may not use the simplified acquisition procedures after December 31, 1999, for contracts greater than $50,000 until they have implemented a "full FACNET capability". Full capability is 75 percent of acquisitions above $2,500 and below $100,000 conducted through EDI. Once there is full government-wide use of electronic commerce, the requirement to publish contract notices in the COMMERCE BUSINESS DAILY (CBD) is waived for all contracts below $250,000 if they are executed using electronic commerce.

The following is a partial list of Value Added Networks (you can find a complete up-to-date list at http://www.acq.osd.mil/ec or call the DoD Electronic Commerce Information Center at 1-800-EDI-3414):

Advanced Communications Systems
Government Program Support
25054 Lorain Road
North Olmstead, OH 44070
Phone: 800-223-5424
Fax: 216-779-9462
Internet: sales@acsmail.com

Advanced Logic Resources, Inc.
Pamela Aksomitas
230 Columbia Avenue
Chapin, SC 29036
Phone: 803-345-6005
Fax: 803-345-0101
Internet: edi@air.net
WWW: http://www.air.net

Advantis
Dave Bolan
3405 E. Dr. M. L. King Jr. Blvd
P.O. Box 30021
Tampa, FL 33630
Phone: 813-878-5462
Fax: 813-878-3398
Internet: dbolan@vnet.ibm.com

ALI Corporation
Sam Saffari
23441 Golden Springs, Suite 334
Diamond Bar, CA 91765
Phone: 909-396-8255
Fax: 909-396-8258

Internet: alicorp@ix.netcom.com
ANGLE Inc.
EDI Sales
7406 Alban Station Court
Springfield, VA 22150
Phone: 800-866-6402
Internet: angle@in.netcom.com

AT&T
Tony Avitollo
P.O. Box 2457
Philadelphia, PA 19147
Phone: 201-331-4393
Fax: 201-331-4598
Internet: avitollo@attmail.com
WWW: http://www.att.com/easylink

Complexity Simplified, Inc.
Thomas A. Godwin
P.O. Box 100280
Denver, CO 80250
Phone: 303-777-1121
Fax: 303-777-5214
Internet: csi@henge.com

Computer Network Corporation
Wesley Holder
335 Hartford Road
South Orange, NJ 07079
Phone: 201-275-0095
Fax: 201-275-0118
Internet: wholder@compnet.com

DATAMATIX
Judith Payne
630 West Germantown Pike,
Suite 300
Plymouth Meeting, PA 19462
Phone: 800-859-3426
Fax: 610-397-0909
Internet: sales@dmx.com
WWW: http://www.dmx.com

EDS
Sue Hodapp
Mail Stop A2N-D51
13600 EDS Drive
Herndon, VA 22071
Phone: 800-483-2954 x363
Fax: 703-742-2576
Internet: msecedi@gsg.eds.com
WWW: http://www.eds.com

ELOCO, Inc.
Lou Klotz
90 Main Mast Circle
New Castle, NH 03854
Phone: 603-430-4041
Fax: 603-430-4041
Internet: eloco@gap.net
WWW: http://www.eloco.com

GAP Instrument Corporation
Federal VAN/EDI Service Cntr.
100 Horse Block Road
Long Island, NY 11980
Phone: 516-924-1700
Fax: 516-924-1799
Internet: edi@gap.net
WWW: http://www.gap.net

GE Information Services, Inc.
Robert L. Schuler
401 North Washington Street
Rockville, MD 20850
Phone: 800-742-4852 opt.1
Fax: 301-517-3967
Internet: schu@geis.com
WWW: http://www.geis.com

Harbinger EDI Services
Government Sales Department
1055 Lenox park Blvd.
Atlanta, GA 30319
Phone: 800-367-4272
Fax: 404-841-4364
Internet: gvtmsg@harbinger.com
WWW: http://www.harbinger.com

Maple Information Services
Hany Hamza
93 Water Street
St. John's NF A1C 1A5
Canada
Phone: 709-739-6778
Fax: 709-739-6773
Internet: hany@maple-
com.cs.mun.ca

MCI Electronic Commerce Sales
201 Centennial Avenue
Piscataway, NJ 08854
Phone: 800-999-2096
Fax: 800-866-9329
Internet: 6482262@mcimail.com

Network Information Services
Charlotte Lakeotes
359 San Miguel Drive, Ste 204
Newport Beach, CA 92660
Phone: 800-989-5800
Fax: 800-958-5850
Internet:
71750.2555@compuserve.com

Premenos Corporation
Kevin Thornton
1000 Burnett Avenue
Concord, CA 94520
Phone: 510-602-2000
Fax: 510-602-2133
Internet: kevin@templar.net
WWW: http://www.premenos.com

Sidereal Corporation
EDI Sales Department
7426 Alban Station Blvd.
Suite A104
Springfield, VA 22150
Phone: 703-912-6200
Fax: 703-912-6204
Internet: mhall@sidnet.com

Simplix
Audrey Helou
3780 Rochester Road

Suite 100
Troy, MI 48083
Phone: 800-Simplix
Fax: 810-740-8180
Internet: sales@edi.com

Softshare, EDI Sales Department
2241 Stanwood Drive
Santa Barbara, CA 93103
Phone: 800-346-6703
Fax: 805-882-2599
Internet: sales@sshare.com

Electronic Commerce Acquisition Instructions

The Government is creating a single, master registration database of all contractors that want to do business with any Federal Government agency. The primary purpose is to avoid repetitive registrations with each procurement office, and also to create an accurate business profile for each business. Registration involves preparing and sending a complete Trading Partner Profile. The secondary purpose is to streamline the acquisition and payment process by collecting standard procurement information. You will register one time and have your Trading Partner Profile shared with all Federal Government agencies.

All contractors are encouraged to complete a Trading Partner Profile. There are two categories of contractors who will register with the Federal Government: (1) Electronic Commerce Trading Partners: those trading with the Federal Government using Electronic Data Interchange (EDI); and (2) Non-Electronic Commerce contractors: those trading with the Federal Government using telephone orders, paper orders, or other non-Electronic Commerce methods. If you are a Non-Electronic Commerce contractor, you may become an Electronic Commerce trading partner at any time by changing your existing registration. In like manner, if you are an Electronic Commerce trading partner you may change your registration to Non-Electronic Commerce contractor. You can also cancel your registration at any time. When you cancel your registration the Government will no longer furnish your organization's name to Federal Government agencies.

Your Trading Partner Profile will be validated before it is accepted. An incomplete or inaccurate Trading Partner Profile will be rejected, and you will be notified. Therefore, it is important that you provide accurate and complete information. If you submit fraudulent registration information, you may be subject to administrative, civil, and/or criminal penalties.

Electronic Commerce transactions are the equivalent of paper documents for purposes of conducting business with the Federal Government. It has been determined that contracts entered into electronically with the Federal Government by using EDI are valid, enforceable contracts in the same manner as documents signed on paper. For Electronic Commerce Trading Partners, EDI transactions will be the ordinary course of business with the Federal Government and, therefore, records of those transactions will be admissible as evidence in the same manner as paper documents. Transactions transmitted via EDI are subject to all applicable statutes, the Federal Acquisition Regulations (FAR), and agency supplements to the FAR.

STANDARDS

Electronic Commerce/Electronic Data Interchange (EC/EDI) is conducted using national or international standards as prescribed by the Federal Information Processing Standards (FIPS). The versions of the standards and the implementation conventions being used will vary over time as updates are made and new transaction sets are adopted by the Government. (A transaction set is, in the standard syntax, information of business or strategic significance consisting of one or more data segments in a specified order.) The details of how these standards are being implemented can be found in the Federal Implementation Convention Guidelines. As a matter of common practice, standards are seldom used in their entirety. For this reason, the Government (in a manner similar to many private-sector industry groups) has written a series of Implementation Conventions that are subsets of the standards. The National Institute of Standards and Technology (NIST) maintains these guidelines on a federal registry. These guidelines identify which data elements are required or are optional (with conditions for use) and include tables and examples.

> **Note**
>
> The guidelines are available on the Internet via File Transfer Protocol (FTP), Telnet or Electronic Mail. The Federal Implementation Conventions are based on the American National Standards Institute (ANSI) Accredited Standards Committee (ASC) X12. You may call 1-800-334-3414 for information on how to obtain the Federal Implementation Convention Guidelines.

If the Government requires an upgrade to a new version or release of standards to achieve certain functionality, the Government and the trading partner will use the current version of a standard within the following time frame: the Government will give the trading partner at least 90 calendar days notice of intent to upgrade to a new standard. The Government will discontinue support of the oldest supported release 90 calendar days after providing notice of intent to support an updated release. It is the Government's intent to support the current version and two previous versions as new versions are introduced.

Throughout this document you will see numeric references in parentheses. These numeric references are the numeric references to transactions that correspond to different business documents. The following transactions are currently in use:

- 810 - Invoice

- 820 - Payment Order/Remittance Advice

- 824 - Application Advice (to accept or reject translated data)

- 836 - Award Notice

- 838 - Trading Partner Profile

- 840 - Request for Quotations (RFQ)

- 843 - Response to Request for Quotations

- 850 - Purchase Order or Delivery Order

- 855 - Purchase Order Acknowledgment

- 864 - Text Message

- 997 - Functional Acknowledgment

VALUE ADDED NETWORK SERVICE PROVIDERS

As described in the previous chapter, Value-Added Network (VAN) service provider means an enterprise that provides network connectivity and value-added service, such as X12 translation services, EDI to facsimile services, and database services. Any enterprise certified by the Government as providing connectivity to the network may declare itself a VAN. The Government will only send transactions to certified network service providers. Accordingly, the Government advises you to investigate the range of services and prices approved VANs offer, and to work closely with a network service provider of your choice. If your current network service provider is not certified, an interconnection with an approved network service provider must be established. You may change your network service provider by giving advance notice (preferably 30 days) and changing your registration profile to show your new electronic address (mail box).

It is your responsibility to acquire, test, maintain, and operate your Electronic Commerce system at your expense, including the cost of receiving and sending transactions through a VAN service provider.

When the trading partner chooses a VAN to transmit, translate, or carry data between the parties, the trading partner:

- Is responsible for the cost of VAN services;

- Is responsible for ensuring that the VAN is capable of providing acceptable (to the trading partner) services such as system/data security, data integrity, error-free protocols, identification codes and password protection, encryption, etc. ; and

- May terminate use of a VAN at any time. The Government may require 30 days after written notification to implement necessary system changes.

The Government will not incur any liability for costs associated with such a termination.

There is no contractual relationship between the Government and the trading partner's chosen VAN. The Government will not incur any liability for any incidental, exemplary, or consequential damages resulting from any delay, omission, or error in electronic transmissions resulting from the trading partner's use of or choice of or agreement with a VAN to transmit or carry data between the trading partner and the Government.

Note

The trading partner may elect to perform as its own VAN by qualifying for and obtaining a Government VAN certification. Information on VAN testing and certification is available from the Defense Information Systems Agency (DISA). The telephone number is (614) 692-5541.

ELECTRONIC PAYMENTS AND FINANCIAL INSTITUTIONS

As part of your registration, the Government will ask you to provide:

- Your Taxpayer Identification Number (TIN);

- Your financial institution's routing and transit number (RTN) for electronic payments;

- Your account number at your financial institution where payments will be credited; and

- Your account type (checking, savings, or lockbox).

The Federal Government's standard and preferred method of paying you is by Electronic Funds Transfer (EFT) through the Automated Clearing House (ACH). Payments will be electronically sent to your financial institution for credit to your account, as designated above. Carefully check your banking information, and double check the information with a representative from your financial institution before you send your Trading Partner Profile. Most Government agencies are capable of originating EFT payments and will do so. The remaining agencies are developing and implementing EFT payment capability.

Under the new Electronic Commerce architecture, the Government will send payments and remittance information describing the reason for the payment (e.g., invoice number) in one of two ways:

- TOGETHER. This means both the transfer of dollars and remittance information are received and processed together through your financial institution. This is accomplished by either of two EFT/ACH formats: ACH/CTX (Corporate Trade Exchange) or ACH/CCD+ (Cash Concentration or Disbursement plus addendum). CTX and CCD+ are NACHA (National Automated Clearinghouse Association) formats for moving funds and payment information between businesses via the ACH network. Under CTX, a full Remittance Advice (820) accompanies the transfer of dollars. Under CCD+, segments comprising a shorter version of the Remittance Advice (820) accompany the transfer of dollars.

- SEPARATE. This means the transfer of dollars is processed through your financial institution, but the remittance information travels separately through your VAN. Generally, the transfer of dollars will be completed using the ACH/CCD+ or CTX format. Information in the Remittance Advice

(820) will be transmitted to you through your VAN. The CCD+ transfer will include a reassociation number that will allow you to reconcile it with the Remittance Advice (820) you separately receive.

In order to successfully implement EFT, the trading partners -- both vendor and Government agency -- must agree on which model (together or separate including format) will be utilized. It is important that any financial institution or VAN you choose be capable of receiving and transmitting remittance advice in the agreed upon manner.

> **Note**
>
> If you need information on EDI capable banks (i.e., Value Added Banks) in your area, that are able to process remittance information that accompanies ACH/CTX or ACH/CCD+ transactions, you may call the National Automated Clearing House Association (NACHA) at (703) 742-9190 or Department of the Treasury at (202) 874-6810. It is your responsibility to check out any financial institution.

COMMODITY AND SERVICE IDENTIFIERS

Standard Industrial Classification (SIC) numbers identify industries by major economic industrial classifications. The Dun & Bradstreet (D&B) SIC 2+2 numbers include greater detail about specific business lines. Federal Supply Class (FSC) numbers and the Product Service Code (PSC) numbers are used by most Federal agencies to identify commonly purchased commodities and services. It is to your benefit to use the SIC/SIC 2+2 and the FSC/PSC in combination to identify the commodities or services you sell. These classification systems are used extensively by Government and industry. Carefully identify those SIC/SIC 2+2 and FSC/PSC that apply to you. Be sure to inform the Government when you add or drop an identifier by sending an updated Trading Partner Profile (838).

BUSINESS CLASSIFICATION

Your business status is important in determining future business opportunities with the Government. Be sure to provide accurate information about the number of employees and 3-year average annual receipts for you and all your affiliates, as these values can affect your business size in certain commodities.

CONFIDENTIAL TRADING PARTNER IDENTIFICATION NUMBER

The Government will validate your Trading Partner Profile information within approximately one week of receipt. When you have successfully completed registration, they will send you a Trading Partner Profile Confirmation (838) with a confidential Trading Partner Identification Number (TPIN). The TPIN is your Electronic Commerce identification. Your confidential TPIN must be used to change, renew or cancel existing registration information. You must also use the TPIN when submitting a Response to Request for Quotations (843). If you suspect your TPIN has been compromised, you should immediately notify the Government. A new TPIN will be issued.

ACCESS TO REGISTRATION INFORMATION

Appropriate information collected during registration will be provided to Government agencies for purposes of doing business with your firm. Consistent with the Freedom of Information Act (FOIA), some of your information might be furnished on request to State and Local governments to assist their procurement programs by identifying potential contractors, and to other businesses looking for suppliers or subcontractors. No information specific to your business income, financial institution, financial accounts, key business information, or similar confidential information will be released to Non- Federal government sources. When other businesses are looking for suppliers or subcontractors, they may request your name and addresses. Their request must reference a SIC/SIC 2+2 or a FSC/PSC.

UPDATING REGISTRATION

You are responsible for updating your registration information as it changes. Any change in the status of your registration information must be immediately provided to the Government in a revised Trading Partner Profile (838). Information that will change at a future date should be provided with the effective date as soon as possible in advance of the change. When preparing to change your name, business affiliation, financial institution, financial account number, VAN, or mail box, you should provide this information in advance of the change (preferably 30 days). Your renewal registration (see below) can also include proposed changes and the effective date of the changes.

Annually, starting one year from the date the Government accepts your registration by issuing a Trading Partner Profile Confirmation (838) and your TPIN, and every year thereafter, you must renew your registration. If you do not renew your registration, the Government will cancel your registration and notify you and all Government agencies of your canceled registration.

ACKNOWLEDGING TRANSACTIONS

All transactions, except Request for Quotations (840), must be acknowledged at the time they are received by sending a Functional Acknowledgment (997). Some Government agencies may require you to accept a purchase order or a delivery order by sending them a Purchase Order Acknowledgment (855). Your Purchase Order Acknowledgment (855) must be promptly sent to the requesting office when it is required by the Purchase Order (850).

TERMINATION OF EDI OPERATIONS

Either party may terminate EDI operations at any time without notice to the other party. Emergency temporary termination of computer connections may be made to protect data from illegal access or other incidental damage.

DATA INTEGRITY AND VERIFICATION

The parties will verify that the ASC X12 and United Nations Electronic Data Interchange for Administration, Commerce, and Transport (International Standard) (UN/EDIFACT) transactions received are intact. Either party may reject (i.e., return as unprocessable) any transaction that is missing information, contains altered data, or does not comply with the appropriate syntax or conventions. The parties may also reject a transaction if it is found to contain invalid data after translation by transmitting an ASC X12.824, Application Advice transaction set. Translation is the conversion of computer system specific formats to ASC X12 or UN/EDIFACT syntax and vice versa. It is a function of the automated process that an ASC X12.997, Functional Acknowledgment transaction set will be transmitted by the end of the business day following the arrival of the transmission in the recipient's mailbox to notify the sender that an ASC X12 transaction has been accepted or rejected.

> **Note**
>
> You may call 1-800-334-3414 for more information about doing Electronic Commerce with the Federal Government. They can provide you with the most up-to-date information available. Other information is available from the EDI User Groups listed on the following pages.

EDI User Groups

Alabama

Birmingham EDI User Group
Birmingham, AL 35244
Debra Taylor
205-988-1248

Alaska

Alaska EDI Users Group
Anchorage, AK
907-265-6126

Arizona

Arizona EDI Roundtable
Tempe, AZ 85284
Dave Darnell
602-838-5316

Arkansas

Little Rock EDI Users Group
Little Rock, AR 72201
501-373-5686

California

So. California EDI Roundtable
Rosemead, CA 91770
818-302-5347
San Diego EDI Users Group
San Diego, CA 92121
Pam Templeton
619-535-3436

No. California EDI Users Group
San Rafael, CA 94901
Sigrid Marmann
415-258-0256

TRI EDI Group (North Valley)
Los Angeles, CA 91320
Robert Grant
818-586-3983

Colorado

Colorado EDI Users Group
Denver, CO 80202
Drew Burnett
303-896-7090

Connecticut

Connecticut EDI Users Group
Monroe, CT 06468
Ken Midzenski
203-771-7845

Florida

Florida EDI
Jacksonville, FL 32250
Ms. Margo Noel
904-247-9286

Georgia

EDI Business Forum
Atlanta, GA 30301
Kevin Hayes
404-239-5783

Columbus, GA
Raymond Swain
706-660-9223

Illinois

Greater Chicago EDI Forum
Chicago, IL 60606
Jim Locascio
312-207-6152

Indiana

Fort Wayne, IN
Trent Thompson
219-455-6030

Indianapolis EDI Users Group
Indianapolis, IN 46250
Linda Perdue
317-576-3344

Kansas

Midwest EDI Association
Wichita, KS
Marshall Owens
316-689-3676

Kentucky

Louisville EDI User Group
Buckner, KY 40010
Ron Reesor
502-222-1424

Maine

EC Forum of Maine
Portland, ME 04122
Scott Charette
207-865-4100 x6045

Maryland

Baltimore EDI User Group
Renee Cookerly
410-771-2572

Massachusetts

New England EDI Users Group
Boston, MA 02149
Wayne Marshall
617-386-3169

Michigan

Michigan EDI Users Goup
Detroit, MI 48335
Lydia Maes
810-442-8540

Minnesota

Twin Cities EDI Forum
Minneapolis, MN 55435
John Moriarty
612-933-1629

Missouri

Great St. Louis EDI Forum
Stl Louis, MO 63169
314-331-1478

Kansas City EDI User Group
Kansas City, MO 54141
Kathy Morris
816-556-2665

Missouri State EDI Interest Group
Jefferson City, MO 65102
Faye Zumwart
314-751-9110

Nebraska

Midlands EDI Association
Omaha, NE 68154
Steve Brownfield
402-422-4232

New Jersey

EDI Forum of New Jersey
Morganville, NJ 07751
Paul Daisy
908-972-2970

New Mexico

Albuquerque EDI User Group
Albuquerque, NM 87125
Becky Berwinkle
505-282-4091

New York

EDI Forum of New York City
New York, NY 10121
Lloyd Solomon
212-556-9664

Long Island EDI Users Group
Rochester, NY 14692
Liz Filipiak
716-424-9227

North Carolina

Piedmont EDI Business Forum
Cary, NC 27511
Jeff LeRose
910-370-8914

Ohio

Central Ohio EDI Users Group
Columbus, OH
Marcia Scanlon
614-225-3606

Northeast Ohio EDI Users Group
Cleveland, OH
Michael Martz
800-851-6636 x4111

Southwest Ohio EDI Users Group
Dayton, OH 45408
Christine Karas
513-443-1003

Oklahoma

Green Coiuntry EDI User Forum
Tulsa, OK
Karen Raper
918-832-3027

Oklahoma City EDI Users Group
Oklahoma City, OK 73103
Judy Robbins
405-733-7348

Oregon

Portland Infoshare
Portland, OR 97208
Mark Federspiel
503-231-5000

Pennsylvania

Laurel Highlands EC User Group
Johnstown, PA
Gary Bell
814-269-2446

Philadelphia EDI Users Group
Broomall, PA 19008
Robert J. Richter, Jr.
610-325-9755
Northeast Penn. EDI Users Group
Scranton, PA 18510
Harry Mumford
800-575-3272

Central Penn. EDI Users Group
Harrisburg, PA 17105
Mark Caruso
717-986-5102

Tennessee

Memphis EDI User Group
Memphis, TN 38197
James Myers
901-224-9166

Nashville EDI Users Group
Nashville, TN 37228
Michael Keef
615-734-4660

Texas

Central Texas EDI Users Group
San Antonio, TX
Julie Tereschchuk
512-345-5376

Dallas-Ft. Worth EDI Business Forum
Fort Worth, TX 75301
Ann Weaver
214-383-4566

Texas Gulf Coast EDI User Group
Houston, TX 77208
Susan Colles
713-275-8514
Amarillo, TX
Ray Schell
806-376-4223
Utah

Utah Strategic EDI Resource User
Group
Salt Lake City, UT 84103
Nia Sherar
801-220-2825

Virginia

Washington, DC EDI Users Group
Mclean, VA 22102

Ms. Theresa Yee
703-917-7409

Richmond EDI Users Group
Richmond, VA 32361
Sharon Smith
804-527-4147

Washington

Northwest EDI Roundtable
Seattle, WA 98124
Abigail Cooke
360-405-5404

Wisconsin

Bar Code/EDI Council
Cedarburg, WI 53012
Mark Thibadeau
414-375-1150
Madison, WI
Barry Widera
608-267-2950

Freedom of Information Act

The Freedom of Information Act (FOIA) can be a very effective tool in submitting winning proposals, if used properly. Most Government contracting sites have a FOIA officer attached to them. When bidding on a contract that is already in place (i.e., has an incumbent contractor), you should always make a FOIA request for information on the existing contract and contractor.

SAMPLE FOIA REQUEST

> **Note**
>
> The following is an example of how you can incorporate your request for a solicitation with your request for information on the incumbent contractor.

To: Department of Justice, Procurement Services
Attn: Patricia A. Waters, Contracting Officer
Solicitation: DOJ-SAS-X-XXX

Please forward the above described solicitation to our company. In addition, we request that you include with the copy of the solicitation, the following information:

The Bidders/Plan Holders List
The name of the Incumbent Contractor
Releasable abstract of Bids or Existing Contract
Releasable Schedule "B" Pricing of Existing Contract

The above referenced information is requested in accordance with the Freedom of Information Act (FOIA). If there is a cost for production of this material, please forward a bill (not to exceed $15) with the materials shipped to our company.

Note

You should always tell the FOIA Officer that you will pay for the materials and give them a cut-off amount, such as the $15 I have used above. It is unusual to receive a bill for these services, but you need to include a statement of this type in your request.

THE ACT

(Ch. 116, par. 201 et seq.)

AN ACT in relation to access to public records and documents P.A. 83-1013, certified Dec. 27, 1983, eff. July 1, 1984.

Section 201. Public Policy--Legislative intent

Pursuant to the fundamental philosophy of the American constitutional form of government, it is declared to be the public policy of the State of Illinois that all persons are entitled to full and complete information regarding the affairs of government and the official acts and policies of those who represent them as public officials and public employees consistent with the terms of the Act. Such access is necessary to enable the people to fulfill their duties of discussing public issues fully and freely, making informed political judgments and monitoring government to ensure that it is being conducted in the public interest.

This Act is not intended to be used to violate individual privacy, nor for the purpose of furthering a commercial enterprise, or to disrupt the duly-undertaken work of any public body independent of the fulfillment of any of the fore-mentioned rights of the people to access to information.

This Act is not intended to create an obligation on the part of any public body to maintain or prepare any public record which was not maintained or prepared by such public body at the time when this Act becomes effective, except as otherwise required by applicable local, State or federal law.

The restraints on information access should be seen as limited exceptions to the general rule that the people have a right to know the decisions, policies, procedures, rules, standards, and other aspects of government activity that affect the conduct of government and the lives of any or all the people. The provisions of this Act shall be construed to this end.

This Act shall be the exclusive State statute on freedom of information, except to the extent that other State statutes might create additional restrictions on disclosure of information or other laws in Illinois might create additional obligations for disclosure of information to the public.

Section 201.1. Short title

This Act shall be known and may be cited as "The Freedom of Information Act".

Section 202. Definitions

Definitions. As used in this Act:

(a) "Public body" means any legislative, executive, administrative, or advisory bodies of the State, state universities and colleges, counties, townships, cities, villages incorporated towns, school districts and all other municipal corporations, boards, bureaus, committees, or commissions of this State, and any subsidiary bodies of any of the foregoing including but not limited to committees and subcommittees which are supported in whole or in part by tax revenue, or which expend tax revenue.

(b) "Person" means any individual, corporation, partnership, firm, organization or association, acting individually or as a group.

(c) "Public records" means all records, reports, forms, writings, letters, memoranda, books, papers, maps, photographs, microfilms, cards, tapes, recordings, electronic data processing records, recorded information and all other documentary materials, regardless of physical form or characteristics, having been prepared, or having been or being used, received, possessed or under the control of any public body.

"Public records" includes, but is expressly not limited to: (I) administrative manuals, procedural rules, and instructions to staff, unless exempted by Section 7(p) of this Act; (ii) final opinions and orders made in the adjudication of cases, except an educational institution's adjudication of student or employee grievance or disciplinary cases; (iii) substantive rules; (iv) statements and interpretations of policy which have been adopted by a public body; (v) final planning policies, recommendations, and decisions; (vi) factual reports, inspection reports, and studies whether prepared by or for the public body; (vii) all information in any account, voucher, or contract dealing with the receipt or expenditure of public or other funds of public bodies; (viii) the names, salaries, titles, and dates of employment of all employees and officers of public bodies; (ix) materials containing opinions concerning the rights of the state, the public, a subdivision of state or a local government, or of any private persons; (x) the name of every official and the final records of voting in all proceedings of public bodies; (xi) applications for any contract, permit, grant, or agreement except as exempted from disclosure by subsection (g) of Section 7 of this Act; (xii) each report, document, study or publication prepared by independent consultants or other independent contractors for the public body; (xiii) all other information required by law to be made available for public inspection or copying and (xiv) information relating to any grant or contract made by or between a public body and another public body or private organization.

(d)   "Copying" means the reproduction of any public record by means of any photographic, electronic, mechanical or other process, device or means.

(e)   "Head of the public body" means the president, mayor, chairman, presiding officer, director, superintendent, manager, supervisor or individual otherwise holding primary executive and administrative authority for the public body, or such person's duly authorized designee.

Section 203. Inspection or copying of public records--Request procedures

(a)   Each public body shall make available to any person for inspection or copying all public records, except as otherwise provided in Section 7 of the Act.

(b)   Subject to the fee provisions of Section 6 of this Act, each public body shall promptly provide, to any person who submits a written request, a copy of any public record required to be disclosed by subsection (a) of this Section and shall certify such copy if so requested.

(c)   Each public body shall, promptly, either comply with or deny a written request for public records within 7 working days after its receipt. Denial shall be by letter as provided in Section 9 of this Act. Failure to respond to a written request within 7 working days after its receipt shall be considered a denial of the request.

(d)   The time limits prescribed in paragraph (c) of this Section may be extended in each case for not more than 7 additional working days for any of the following reasons:

(i)   the requested records are stored in whole or in part at other locations than the office having charge of the requested records;

(ii)   the request requires the collection of a substantial number of specified records;

(iii)   the request is couched in categorical terms and requires an extensive search for the records responsive to it;

(iv)   the requested records have not been located in the course of routine search and additional efforts are being made to locate them;

(v)   the requested records require examination and evaluation by personnel having the necessary competence and discretion to determine if they are exempt from disclosure under Section 7 of this Act or should be revealed only with appropriate deletions;

(vi)   the request for records cannot be complied with by the public body within the time limits prescribed by paragraph (c) of this Section without unduly burdening or interfering with the operations of the public body;

(vii)   there is a need for consultation, which shall be conducted with all practicable speed, with another public body or among two or more components of a public body having a substantial interest in the determination or in the subject matter of the request.

(e)   When additional time is required for any of the above reasons, the public body shall notify by letter the person making the written request within the time limits specified by paragraph (c) of this Section of the reasons for the delay and the date by which the records will be made available or denial will be forthcoming. In no instance, may the delay in processing last longer than 7 working days. A failure to render a decision within 7 working days shall be considered a denial of the request.

(f)   Requests calling for all records falling within a category shall be complied with unless compliance with the request would be unduly burdensome for the complying public body and there is no way to narrow the request and the burden on the public body outweighs the public interest in the information. Before invoking this exemption, the public body shall extend to the person making the request an opportunity to confer with it in an attempt to reduce the request to manageable proportions. If any body responds to a categorical request by stating that compliance would unduly burden its operation and the conditions described above are met, it shall do so in writing, specifying the reasons why it would be unduly burdensome and the extent to which compliance will so burden the operations of the public body. Such a response shall be treated as a denial of the request for information. Repeated requests for the same public records by the same person shall be deemed unduly burdensome under this provision.

(g)   Each public body may promulgate rules and regulations in conformity with the provisions of this Section pertaining to the availability of records and procedures to be followed, including:

(i)   the times and places where such records will be made available, and

(ii)   the persons from whom such records may be obtained.

Section 204. Dissemination of information about public body

Each public body shall prominently display at each of its administrative or regional offices, make available for inspection and copying, and send through the mail if requested, each of the following:

(a)   A brief description of itself, which will include, but not be limited to, a short summary of its purpose, a block diagram giving its functional subdivisions, the total amount of its operating budget, the number and location of all of its separate offices, the approximate number of full and part-time employees, and the identification and membership of any board, commission, committee, or council which operates in an advisory capacity relative to the operation of the public body, or which exercises control over its policies or procedures, or to which the public is required to report and be answerable for its operations; and

(b)   A brief description of the methods whereby the public may request information and public records, a directory designating by titles and addresses those employees to whom requests for public records should be directed, and any fees allowable under Section 6 of this Act.

Section 205. List of records available from public body

As to public records prepared or received after the effective date of this Act, each public body shall maintain and make available for inspection and copying a reasonably current list of all types or categories of records under its control. The list shall be reasonably detailed in order to aid persons in obtaining access to public records pursuant to this Act. Each public body shall furnish upon request a description of the manner in which public records stored by means of electronic data processing may be obtained in a form comprehensible to persons lacking knowledge of computer language or printout format.

Section 206. Fees

(a)   Each public body may charge fees reasonably calculated to reimburse its actual cost for reproducing and certifying public records and for the use, by any person, of the equipment of the public body to copy records. Such fees shall exclude the costs of any search for and review of the record, and shall not exceed the actual cost of reproduction and certification, unless otherwise provided by State statute. Such fees shall be imposed according to a standard scale of fees, established and made public by the body imposing them.

(b)   Documents shall be furnished without charge or at a reduced charge, as determined by the public body, if the person requesting the documents states the specific purpose for the request and indicates that a waiver or reduction of the fee is in the public interest. Waiver or reduction of the fee is in the public interest if the principal purpose of the request is to access and disseminate information regarding the health, safety and welfare of the legal rights of the general public and is not for the principal purpose of personal or commercial benefit. In setting the amount of the waiver or reduction, the public body may take into consideration the amount of materials requested and the cost of copying them.

(c)   The purposeful imposition of a fee not consistent with subsections (6)(a) and (b) of this Act shall be considered a denial of access to public records for the purposes of judicial review.

(d)   The fee for an abstract of a driver's records shall be as provided in Section 6-118 of "The Illinois Vehicle Code", approved September 29, 1969, as amended.

Section 207. Exemptions

(1) The following shall be exempt from inspection and copying:

(a)   Information specifically prohibited from disclosure by Federal or State law or rules and regulations adopted pursuant to federal or State law.

(b)   Information that, if disclosed, would constitute a clearly unwarranted invasion of personal privacy, unless such disclosure is consented to in writing by the individual subjects of the information. The disclosure of information that bears on the public duties of public employees and officials shall not be considered an invasion of personal privacy. Information exempted under this subsection (b) shall include but is not limited to:

(i)   files and personal information maintained with respect to clients, patients, residents, students or other individuals receiving social, medical, educational, vocational, financial, supervisory or custodial care or services directly or indirectly from federal agencies or public bodies;

(ii)   personnel files and personal information maintained with respect to employees, appointees or elected officials of any public body or applicants for those positions;

(iii)   files and personal information maintained with respect to any applicant, registrant or licensee by any public body cooperating with or engaged in professional or occupational registration, licensure or discipline;

(iv)   information required of any taxpayer in connection with the assessment or collection of any tax unless disclosure is otherwise required by State statute; and

(v)   information revealing the identity of persons who file complaints with or provide information to administrative, investigative, law enforcement or penal agencies.

(c) Records compiled by any public body for administrative enforcement proceedings and any law enforcement or correctional agency for law enforcement purposes or for internal matters of a public body, but only to the extent that disclosure would:

(i)   interfere with pending or actually and reasonably contemplated law enforcement proceedings conducted by any law enforcement or correctional agency;

(ii)   interfere with pending administrative enforcement proceedings conducted by any public body;

(iii)   deprive a person of a fair trial or an impartial hearing;

(iv)   unavoidably disclose the identity of a confidential source or confidential information furnished only by the confidential source;

(v)   disclose unique or specialized investigative techniques other than those generally used and known or disclose internal documents of correctional agencies related to detection, observation or investigation of incidents of crime or misconduct;

(vi) constitute an invasion of personal privacy under subsection (b) of this Section;

(vii) endanger the life or physical safety of law enforcement personnel or any other person; or

(viii) obstruct an ongoing criminal investigation.

(d) Criminal history record information maintained by State or local criminal justice agencies, except the following which shall be open for public inspection and copying:

(i) chronologically maintained arrest information, such as traditional arrest logs or blotters;

(ii) the name of a person in the custody of a law enforcement agency and the charges for which that person is being held;

(iii) court records that are public;

(iv) records that are otherwise available under State or local law; or

(v) records in which the requesting party is the individual identified, except as provided under paragraph (vii) of subsection (c) of this Section.

"Criminal history record information" means data identifiable to an individual and consisting of descriptions or notations of arrests, detentions, indictments, informations, pre-trial proceedings, trials, or other formal events in the criminal justice system or descriptions or notations of criminal charges (including criminal violations of local municipal ordinances) and the nature of any disposition arising therefrom, including sentencing, court or correctional supervision, rehabilitation and release. The term does not apply to statistical records and reports in which individuals are not identified and from which their identities are not ascertainable, or to information that is for criminal investigative or intelligence purposes.

(e) Records that relate to or affect the security of correctional institutions and detention facilities.

(f) Preliminary drafts, notes, recommendations, memoranda and other records in which opinions are expressed, or policies or actions are formulated, except that a specific record or relevant portion of a record shall not be exempt when the record is publicly cited and identified by the head of the public body. The exemption provided in this subsection (f) extends to all those records of officers and agencies of the General Assembly which pertain to the preparation of legislative documents.

(g) Trade secrets and commercial or financial information obtained from a person or business where the trade secrets or information are proprietary, privileged or confidential, or where disclosure of such trade secrets or information may cause competitive harm. Nothing contained in this subsection shall be construed to prevent a person or business from consenting to disclosure.

(h) Proposals and bids for any contract, grant, or agreement, including information which if it were disclosed would frustrate procurement or give an advantage to any person proposing to enter into a contractor agreement with the body, until an award or final selection is made. Information prepared by or for the body in preparation of a bid solicitation shall be exempt until an award or final selection is made.

(i) Valuable formulae, designs, drawings and research data obtained or produced by any public body when disclosure could reasonably be expected to produce private gain or public loss.

(j) Test questions, scoring keys and other examination data used to administer an academic examination or determined the qualifications of an applicant for a license or employment.

(k) Architects' plans and engineers' technical submissions for projects not constructed or developed in whole or in part with public funds and for projects constructed or developed with public funds, to the extent that disclosure would compromise security.

(l) Library circulation and order records identifying library users with specific materials.

(m) Minutes of meetings of public bodies whose meetings are closed to the public as provided in the Open Meetings Act until the time as the public body makes the minutes available to the public under Section 2.06 of the Open Meetings Act.

(n)   Communications between a public body and an attorney or auditor representing the public body that would not be subject to discovery in litigation, and materials prepared or compiled by or for a public body in anticipation of a criminal, civil or administrative proceeding upon the request of an attorney advising the public body, and materials prepared or compiled with respect to internal audits of public bodies.

(o)   Information received by a primary or secondary school, college or university under its procedures for the evaluation or faculty members by their academic peers.

(p)   Administrative or technical information associated with automated data processing operations, including but not limited to software, operating protocols, computer program abstracts, file layouts, source listings, object modules, load modules, user guides, documentation pertaining to all logical and physical design of computerized systems, employee manuals, and any other information that, if disclosed, would jeopardize the security of the system or its data or the security of materials exempt under this Section.

(q)   Documents or materials relating to collective negotiating matters between public bodies and their employees or representatives, except that any final contract or agreement shall be subject to inspection and copying.

(r)   Drafts, notes, recommendations and memoranda pertaining to the financing and marketing transactions of the public body. The records of ownership, registration, transfer, and exchange of municipal debt obligations, and of persons to whom payment with respect to these obligations is made.

(s)   The records, documents and information relating to real estate purchase negotiations until those negotiations have been completed or otherwise terminated. With regard to a parcel involved in a pending or actually and reasonably contemplated eminent domain proceeding under Article VII of the Code of Civil Procedure, records, documents and information relating to that parcel shall be exempt except as may be allowed under discovery rules adopted by the Illinois Supreme Court. The records, documents and information relating to a real estate sale shall be exempt until a sale is consummated.

(t) Any and all proprietary information and records related to the operation of an intergovernmental risk management association or self- insurance pool or jointly self-administered health and accident cooperative or pool.

(u) Information concerning a university's adjudication of student or employee grievance or disciplinary cases, to the extent that such disclosure would reveal the identity of the student or employee and information concerning any public body's adjudication of student or employee grievances or disciplinary cases, except for the final outcome of the cases.

(v) Course materials or research materials used by faculty members.

(w) Information related solely to the internal personnel rules and practices of a public body.

(x) Information contained in or related to examination, operating, or condition reports prepared by, on behalf of, or for the use of a public body responsible for the regulation or supervision of financial institutions or insurance companies, unless disclosure is otherwise required by State law.

(y) Information the disclosure of which is restricted under Section 5-108 of The Public Utilities Act.

(z) Manuals or instruction to staff that relate to establishment or collection of liability for any State tax or that relate to investigations by a public body to determine violation of any criminal law.

(aa) Applications, related documents, and medical records received by the Experimental Organ Transplantation Procedures Board and any and all documents or other records prepared by the Experimental Organ Transplantation Procedures Board or its staff relating to applications it has received.

(bb)   Insurance or self insurance (including any intergovernmental risk management association or self insurance pool) claims, loss or risk management information records, data, advice or communications.

(cc)   Information and records held by the Department of Public Health and its authorized representatives relating to known or suspected cases of sexually transmissible disease or any information the disclosure of which is restricted under the Illinois Sexually Transmissible Disease Control Act.

(dd)   Information the disclosure of which is exempted under Section 7 of the "Radon Mitigation Act", enacted by the Eighty-Sixth General Assembly.

(2)   This Section does not authorize withholding of information or limit the availability of records to the public, except as stated in this Section or otherwise provided in this Act.

Section 207.1 Receipt of benefits or payments suspended or terminated--Publication of names and address

Nothing in this Act shall be construed to prohibit publication of and dissemination by the Department of Public Aid of the names and addresses of entities which have had receipt of benefits or payments under the Illinois Public Aid Code suspended or terminated or future receipt barred, pursuant to Section 11-26 of that Code.

Section 208. Nonexempt materials contained in exempt records

If any public record that is exempt from disclosure under Section 7 of this Act contains any material which is not exempt, the public body shall delete the information which is exempt and make the remaining information available for inspection and copying.

Section 209. Denial of request for public records--Notice

(a)   Each public body or head of a public body denying a request for public records shall notify by letter the person making the request of the decision to deny such, the reasons for the denial, and the names and titles or positions of each person responsible for the denial. Each notice of denial by a public body shall also inform such person of his right to appeal to the head of the public body. Each notice of denial of an appeal by the head of a public body shall inform such person of his right to judicial review under Section 11 of this Act.

(b)   When a request for public records is denied on the grounds that the records are exempt under Section 7 of this Act, the notice of denial shall specify the exemption claimed to authorize the denial. Copies of all notices of denial shall be retained by each public body in a single central office file that is open to the public and indexed according to the type of exemption asserted and, to the extent feasible, according to the types of records request.

Section 210. Denial of request for public records--Appeal

(a)   Any person denied access to inspect or copy any public record may appeal the denial by sending a written notice of appeal to the head of the public body. Upon receipt of such notice the head of the public body shall promptly review the public record, determine whether under the provisions of this Act such record is open to inspection and copying, and notify the person making the appeal of such determination within 7 working days after the notice of appeal.

(b)   Any person making a request for public records shall be deemed to have exhausted his administrative remedies with respect to such request if the head of the public body affirms the denial or fails to act within the time limit provided in subsection (a) of this Section.

Section 211. Denial of request for public records--Injunctive or declaratory relief

(a)   Any person denied access to inspect or copy any public record by the head of a public body may file suit for injunctive or declaratory relief.

(b)   Where the denial is from the head of a public body of the State, suit may be filed in the circuit court for the county where the public body has its principal office or where the person denied access resides.

(c)   Where the denial is from the head of a municipality or other public body, except as provided in subsection (b) of this Section, suit may be filed in the circuit court for the county where the public body is located.

(d)   The circuit court shall have the jurisdiction to enjoin the public body from withholding public records and to order the production of any public records improperly withheld from the person seeking access. If the public body can show that exceptional circumstances exist, and that the body is exercising due diligence in responding to the request, the court may retain jurisdiction and allow the agency additional time to complete its review of the records.

(e)   On motion of the plaintiff, prior to or after in camera inspection, the court shall order the public body to provide an index of the records to which access has been denied. The index shall include the following:

(i)   A description of the nature or contents of each document withheld, or each deletion from a released document, provided, however, that the public body shall not be required to disclose the information which it asserts is exempt; and

(ii)   A statement of the exemption or exemptions claimed for each such deletion or withheld document.

(f)   In any action considered by the court, the court shall consider the matter de novo, and shall conduct such in camera examination of the of this Act.

Chapter

12

Federal Stock Groups (FSGs) and Federal Service Codes (FSCs)

Service Code	Description
A	Research and Development
B	Special Studies and Analyses -- Not R&D
C	Architect and Engineering Services -- Construction
D	Automatic Data Processing and Telecommunication Services
E	Purchase of Structures and Facilities
F	Natural Resources and Conservation Services
G	Social Services
H	Quality Control, Testing, and inspection Services
I	Maintenance, Repair and Rebuilding of Equipment
K	Modification of Equipment
L	Technical Representative Services
M	Operation of Government Owned Facility
N	Installation of Equipment
P	Salvage Services
Q	Medical Services
R	Professional, Administrative and Management Support Services
S	Utilities and Housekeeping Services
T	Photographic, Mapping, Printing, and Publications Services
U	Education and Training Services
V	Transportation, Travel and Relocation Services
W	Lease or Rental of Equipment
X	Lease or Rental of Facilities
Y	Construction of Structures and Facilities
Z	Maintenance, Repair or Alteration of Real Property

The FSG codes for Supplies are as follows:

Supply Code Description

10	Weapons
11	Nuclear Ordinance
12	Fire Control Equipment
13	Ammunition and Explosives
14	Guided Missiles
15	Aircraft and Airframe Structural Components
16	Aircraft Components and Accessories
17	Aircraft Launching, Landing, and Ground Handling Equip.
18	Space Vehicles
19	Ships, Small Craft, Pontoons, and Floating Docks
20	Ship and Marine Equipment
22	Railway Equipment
23	Ground Effect Vehicles, Motor Vehicles, Trailers, and Cycles
24	Tractors
25	Vehicular Equipment Components
26	Tires and Tubes
28	Engines, Turbines, and Components
29	Engine Accessories
30	Mechanical Power Transmission Equipment
31	Bearings
32	Woodworking Machinery and Equipment
34	Metalworking Machinery
35	Service and Trade Equipment
36	Special Industry Machinery
37	Agricultural Machinery and Equipment
38	Construction, Mining, Excavating, and Highway Maint. Equip.
39	Materials Handling Equipment
40	Rope, Cable, Chain, and Fittings
41	Refrigeration, Air Conditioning and Air Circulating Equip.
42	Fire Fighting, Rescue, and Safety Equipment
43	Pumps and Compressors
44	Furnace, Steam Plant, and Drying Equip, Nuclear Reactors
45	Plumbing, Heating and Sanitation Equipment
46	Water Purification and Sewage Treatment Equipment
47	Pipe, Tubing, Hose, and Fittings
48	Valves
49	Maintenance and Repair Shop Equipment
51	Hand Tools
52	Measuring Tools
53	Hardware and Abrasives
54	Prefabricated Structures and Scaffolding
55	Lumber, Millwork, Plywood, and Veneer

56	Construction and Building Materials
58	Communications, Detection and Coherent Radiation Equipment
59	Electrical and Electronic Equipment Components
60	Fiber Optics Materials and Components, Assemblies and Access.
61	Electric Wire, and Power and Distribution Equipment
62	Lighting Fixtures and Lamps
63	Alarm, Signal and Security Detection Systems
65	Medical, Dental, and Veterinary Equipment and Supplies
66	Instruments and Laboratory Equipment
67	Photographic Equipment
68	Chemicals and Chemical Products
69	Training Aids and Devices
70	ADP Equipment Software, Supplies and Support Equip
71	Furniture
72	Household and Commercial Furnishings and Appliances
73	Food Preparation and Serving Equipment
74	Office Machines
75	Office Supplies and Devices
76	Books, Maps, and Other Publications
77	Musical Instruments, Phonographs, and Home-Type Radios
78	Recreational and Athletic Equipment
79	Cleaning Equipment and Supplies
80	Brushes, Paints, Sealers, and Adhesives
81	Containers, Packaging, and Packing Supplies
83	Textiles, Leather, Furs, Apparel and Shoes, Tents, Flags
84	Clothing, Individual Equipment, and Insignia
85	Toiletries
87	Agricultural Supplies
88	Live Animals
89	Subsistence (Food)
91	Fuels, Lubricants, Oils, and Waxes
93	Nonmetallic Fabricated Materials
94	Nonmetallic Crude Materials
95	Metal Bars, Sheets, and Shapes
96	Ores, Minerals, and Their Primary Products
99	Miscellaneous

13.1 Service Codes
PSC A - Research and Development
All research and development is broken down into the following sub-classifications:

1	Basic Research
2	Exploratory Development
3	Advanced Development
4	Engineering Development
5	Operational System Development

6	Management and Support of R&D
7	Commercialization
0	Unclassified.

Note

O(Unclassified) is heavily used by agencies reporting to the Federal Procurement Data System.

PSC	Description
AAI	Insect and Disease Control
AA2	Agricultural Marketing
AA3	Agricultural Production
AA9	Other Agricultural
AB1	Crime Prevention and Control
AB2	Fire Prevention and Control
AB3	Rural Services and Development
AB4	Urban Services and Development
AB9	Other Services and Development
AC1	Defense - Aircraft
AC2	Defense - Missile and Space Systems
AC3	Defense - Ships
AC4	Defense - Tank and Automotive
AC5	defense - Weapons
AC6	Defense - Electronics and Communications Equipment
AC9	Defense - Miscellaneous Hard Goods
AD1	Defense - ammunition
AD2	Defense - Services
AD3	Defense - Subsistence
AD4	Defense - Textiles, Clothing, Etc
AD5	defense - Fuels and Lubricants
AD6	Defense - Construction
AD9	Other Defense
AE1	Employment Growth-Productivity
AE2	Product or Service Improvement
AE3	Manufacturing Tech
AE9	Economic Growth-Productivity
AF1	Educational
AG1	Energy - Coal
AG2	Energy - Gas
AG3	Energy - Geothermal
AG4	Energy - Wind
AG5	Energy - Nuclear
AG6	Energy - Petroleum
AG7	Energy - Solar/Photovoltaic

AG8	Conservation of Energy
AG9	Other Energy
AH1	Pollution Control/Abatement
AH2	Air Pollution
AH3	Water Pollution
AH4	Noise Pollution
AH5	Other Pollution
AH9	Other environment
AJ1	Physical Science
AK1	Housing
AL1	Employment
AL2	Income Maintenance
AL9	Other Income Security
AM1	International Affairs
AN1	Biomedical
AN2	Drug Dependency
AN3	Alcohol Dependency
AN4	Health Services
AN5	Mental Health
AN6	Medical Rehabilitative Engineering
AN7	Spec Medical Services
AN9	Other Medical
AP1	Natural Resources - Aquaculture
AP2	Natural Resources - Land
AP3	Natural Resources - Mineral
AP4	Natural Resources - Recreation
AP5	Natural Resources - Marine and Ocean
AP9	Other Natural Resource
AQ1	Social Services-Geriatric
AQ9	Other Social Services
AR1	Aeronautics and Space Tech
AR2	Space Science
AR3	Space Transportation Systems
AR4	Space Tracking Data Acquisition
AR5	Space and Terrestrial
AR9	Other Space
AS1	Transportation - Air
AS2	Transportation - Motor Vehicle
AS3	Transportation - Rail
AS4	Transportation - Marine
AS9	Transportation - Other Modal
AT1	Transportation - Roads and bridges
AT2	Transportation - Human Factors
AT3	Transportation - Navigation Aids
AT4	Transportation - Passenger Safety
AT5	Transportation - Pipeline Safety

AT6	Transportation - Traffic Management
AT7	Transportation - Tunnels
AT9	Other General Transportation
AU1	Transportation of Hazard Materials
AU9	Other Commodity Transportation
AV1	Subsurface Mining Equipment
AV2	Surface Mining Equipment
AV3	Subsurface Mining Methods
AV4	Surface Mining Methods
AV5	Mining Reclamation Methods
AV6	Mining Safety
AV7	Mining Metallurgical
AV9	Other Mining Activities
AZ1	Other Research and Development

PSC B - Special Studies

Note

B5 was formerly R5.

PSC	Description
B502	Air Quality
B503	Archeological-Paleontological
B504	Chemical-Biological
B505	Cost Benefit
B506	Data - Other Than Scientific
B507	Economic
B509	Endangered Species-Plant/Animal
B510	Environmental Assessments
B513	Feasibility - Non-Construct
B516	Fisheries and Animal
B517	Geological
B518	Geophysical
B519	Geotechnical
B520	Grazing-Range Use
B521	Historical
B522	Legal
B524	Mathematical-Statistical
B525	Natural Resource
B526	Oceanological
B527	Recreation
B528	Regulatory
B529	Scientific Data
B530	Seismological

B532 Soils
B533 Water Quality
B534 Wildlife
B537 Medical and Health
B538 Intelligence
B539 Aeronautic/Space
B540 Building Technology
B541 Defense
B542 Educational
B543 Energy
B544 Technology
B545 Housing and Community Develop
B546 Security (Physical and Personal)
B547 Accounting/Financial Mgt
B548 Trade Issues
B549 Foreign and National Security Policy
B550 Organization/Admin/Personnel
B551 Mobilization/Preparedness
B552 Manpower
B553 Communications
B554 Acquisition Policy/Procedures
B555 Elderly-Handicapped
B599 Other Special Studies and Analyses

PSC C - Architect and Engineer Services

Note

C 1 was formerly R1.

PSC   Description
C111 Buildings and Facilities Administrative and Services Bldgs
CI12 Buildings and Facilities / Airfield, missile and Communications
CI13 Buildings and Facilities / Educational Bldgs
C114 Buildings and Facilities / Hospital Buildings
CI15 Buildings and Facilities / Industrial Bldgs
CI16 Buildings and Facilities / Residential Bldgs
CI17 Buildings and Facilities / Warehouse Bldgs
C118 Buildings and Facilities / R&D Facilities
C119 Buildings and Facilities / Other Buildings
C121 Non-Building / Conservation and Development
C122 Non-Building / Highways, Roads and Bridges
C123 Non-Building / Electric Power Generation
C124 Non-Building / Utilities
C129 Non-Building / Other

C130 Restoration
C211 A/E - Non Construction - General
C212 A/E - Drafting Engineering
C213 A/E - Inspection - Non Construct
C214 A/E - Management Engineering
C215 A/E - Production Engineering
C216 A/E - Marine Engineering
C217 A/E - Mapping
C218 A/E - Surveying
C219 Other Architect and Engineering Services

PSC D - Automatic Data Processing Services

Note

D3 was formerly R3.

PSC   Description
D301 ADP Facility Management
D302 ADP Systems Develop
D303 ADP Services/Data Entry
D304 ADP Services/Telecomm and Transmission
D305 ADP Teleprocessing and Timeshare
D306 ADP System Analysis
D307 Automated Information System Services
D308 ADP Programming Services
D309 ADP Inf, Broadcast and Dist Services
D310 ADP Backup and Security Services
D311 ADP Data Conversion Services
D312 ADP Optical Scanning Services
D313 Computer Aided Design/Mfg Services
D314 ADP Acquisition Sup Services
D315 Digitizing Services
D316 Telecommunication Network Management Services
D317 Auto News, Data and Other Services
D399 Other ADP Services

PSC F - Natural Resources Management

PSC   Description
F00I Aerial Fertilization - Spraying
F002 Aerial Seeding
F003 Forest-Range Fire Suppression
F004 Forest-Range Fire Rehabilitation
F005 Forest Tree Planting

F006 Land Treatment Practices
F007 Range Seeding - Ground Equipment
F008 Recreation Site Maint/Non-Constr
F009 Seed Collection-Production
F010 Seedling Production-Transplanting
F011 Surface Mining Reclam/Non-Constr
F012 Survey line Clearing
F013 Tree Breeding
F014 Tree Thinning
F015 Well Drilling - Exploratory
F016 Wildhorse-Burro Control
F018 Other Range-Forest Improvement/Non-Construction
F019 Other Wildlife Management
F020 Fisheries Res Management
F021 Site Preparation
F099 Other Natural Resource Management and Conservation
F101 Air Quality Supplies
F102 Ind Invest Surv/Tch Supplies
F103 Water Quality Supplies
F104 Ind Invest Surv/Tch Supplies
F105 Pesticides Supplies
F106 Toxic Subst Supplies
F107 Harz Subst Analysis
F108 Harz Remv/clean-Up/Disp/Op
F109 Leak Underground Store Tank Supplies
F110 Dev Environmental Impact Stmt/Assess
F111 Mult Pol Ind Invst Surv/Tech Supplies
FI12 Oil Spill Response
F999 Other Environmental Services/Studies/Supplies

PSC G - Social Services

PSC Description
G001 Care of Remains and/Or Funeral Services
G002 Chaplain Services
G003 Recreational Services
G004 Rehabilitation - Social
G005 Geriatrics Services
G006 Govt Life Ins Programs
G007 Govt Health Ins Programs
G008 Other Govt Ins Programs
G009 Non-Govt Insurance Programs
G010 Dir Aid Tribal Govt-Di (PL93-638)
G099 Other Social Services

PSC H - Quality Control, Testing and Inspection Services

Note

For the PSCs for category H replace ___ with the appropriate Federal Supply Group. For example, Quality Control Services (HI) for Ammunition (FSG 13) would be H110.

PSC	Description
H1__	Quality Control Services
H2__	Equipment and Materials Testing
H3__	Inspection Services
H999	Miscellaneous Testing and Inspection Services

PSC J   Maintenance, Repair and Rebuilding of Equipment

PSC	Description
J0	Use the appropriate Federal Supply Group

PSC K - Modification of Equipment

PSC	Description
K0	Use the appropriate Federal Supply Group

PSC L - Technical Representative Services

PSC	Description
L0	Use the appropriate Federal Supply Group

PSC P - Salvage Services

PSC	Description
P100	Disposal of Surplus Property
P200	Salvage of Aircraft
P300	Salvage of Marine Vessels
P400	Demolition of Buildings
P500	Demolition of Structures/Facilities
P999	Other Salvage Services

PSC Q - Specialized Medical Service

PSC	Description
Q101	Dependent Medicare
Q201	General Health Care
Q301	Laboratory Test - Medical

Q401 Nursing Services
Q402 Nursing Home Care
Q403 Evaluation and Screening
Q501 Anesthesiology
Q502 Cardio-Vascular
Q503 Dentistry
Q504 Dermatology
Q505 Gastroentorology
Q506 Geriatric
Q507 Gynecology
Q508 Hematology
Q509 Internal Medicine
Q510 Neurology
Q511 Ophthalmology
Q512 Optometry
Q513 Orthopedics
Q514 Otolaryngology
Q515 Pathology
Q516 Pediatrics
Q517 Pharmacology
Q518 Physical Medicine and Rehabilitation
Q519 Psychiatry
Q520 Podiatry
Q521 Pulmonary
Q522 Radiology
Q523 Surgery
Q524 Thoracic
Q525 Urology
Q526 Psychological Consultation Services
Q527 Nuclear Medicine
Q999 Other Medical Services

PSC R4 - Professional Services

PSC   Description
R404 Land Surveys - Cadastral
R405 Operations Research
R406 Policy Review - Develop
R407 Program Evaluation
R408 Program Management-Support
R409 Program Review-Development
R411 Real Property Appraisals
R412 Simulations
R413 Specifications Develop
R414 Systems Engineering
R415 Tech Sharing-Util

R416 Veterinary/Animal Care
R418 Legal Services
R419 Educational Services
R420 Certifications and Accredit
R421 Technical Assistance
R422 Phone and Field Interview
R423 Intelligence Services
R424 Expert Witnesses
R425 Engineering Technical
R426 Communications Services
R427 Weather Report-Observation
R428 Industrial Hygienic
R497 Personal Services
R498 Other Professional Services
R499 Other Professional Services

PSC R6 - Administrative Support Services

PSC   Description
R601 Material Management
R602 Courier and Messenger
R603 Transcription
R604 Mailing and Distribution
R605 Library Services
R606 Court Reporting
R607 Word Processing/Typing
R608 Translation-Sign Language
R609 Stenographic Services
R610 Personal Property Management Service
R611 Credit Reporting
R612 Information Retrieval
R699 Other Administrative Support Services

PSC R7 - Management Support Services

PSC   Description
R701 Advertising
R702 Data Collection
R703 Acct and Financial Services
R704 Auditing Services
R705 Debt Collection
R706 Logistics Support
R707 Contract and Procurement Supplies
R708 Public Relations
R709 Ongoing Audit Operations Support
R710 Relocation Services

R799 Other Management Support Services

PSC SI - Utilities

PSC   Description
S111 Gas Services
S112 Electricity Services
S113 Telephone and/or Communications Services
S114 Water Services
S119 Other Utilities

PSC S2 - Housekeeping Services

PSC   Description
S201 Custodial - Janitorial
S202 Fire Protection
S203 Food Service
S204 Fueling Service
S205 Trash/Garbage Collection
S206 Guard Services
S207 Insect and Rodent Control
S208 Landscaping - Groundskeeping
S209 Laundry and Dry Cleaning
S211 Surveillance Services
S212 Solid Fuel Handling Services
S213 Messenger Services
S214 Carpet Laying and Cleaning
S215 Warehousing and Storage Services
S216 Facilities Operations Support Services
S217 Interior Plantscaping
S218 Snow Removal/Salt Service
S219 Asbestos Removal
S220 Travel Agent Services
S221 Hazardous Waste Removal
S222 Waste Treatment and.Storage
S299 Other Housekeeping Services

PSC T Photographic, Mapping, Printing and Publication Services

PSC   Description
T001 Arts-Graphics
T002 Cartography
T003 Cataloging
T004 Charting
T005 Film Processing
T006 Film-Video Tape Production

T007   Microform
T008   Photogrommetry
T009   Photographic - Aerial
T010   Photographic - General - Still
T011   Printing - Binding
T012   Reproduction
T013   Technical Writing
T014   Topography
T015   Photographic - General - Motion
T016   audiovisual Services
T099   Other Photo Mapping Printing Services

PSC U - Training Services

PSC   Description
U001   Lectures for Training
U002   Personnel Testing
U003   Reserve Training - Military
U004   Scientific and Management Education
U005   Tuition, Registration and Membership Fees
U006   Vocational-Technical Training
U007   Faculty Salaries Dependent Schools
U008   Training/Curriculum Dvlp
U009   Education
U010   Cert and Accrediations
U011   AIDS Training
U099   Other Educational and Training Services

PSC V1 - Transportation and Travel

PSC   Description
V001   GBL and GTR Procurements
V002   Motor Pool Operations
V003   Packing/Crating Services

PSC V1 - Transportation of Things

PSC   Description
V111   Air Freight
V112   Motor Freight
V113   Rail Freight
V114   Stevedoring
V115   Vessel Freight
V119   Other Cargo Freight Services
V121   Air Charter for Things
V122   Motor Charter for Things

V123 Rail Charter for Things
V124 Marine Charter for Things
V125 Vessel Towing
V126 Space Transportation and Launch
V 129 Other Vehicle Charter for Transportation of Things
V211 Air Passenger Service
V212 Motor Passenger Service
V213 Rail Passenger Service
V214 Marine Passenger Service
V221 Air Charter for Persons
V222 Motor Charter for Persons
V223 Rail Charter for Persons
V224 Marine Charter for Persons
V225 Ambulance Service
V226 Taxicab Services
V231 Lodging - Hotel/Motel
V241 Military Personnel Recruiting Services
V251 Civilian Personnel Recruitment
V301 Relocation Services
V302 Travel Agent Services
V999 Other Travel Services

PSC Multiple Use Codes

> **Note**
>
> For the following major categories use the letter followed by a three digit multiple use code to form the 4 character PSC. For example, the construction (Y) of a new dam would be PSC Y211.

E   Purchase of Structures and Facilities
M   Operation of Government Owned Facilities
X   Lease or Rental of Facilities
Y   Construction of Facilities
Z   Maintenance. Repair or Alteration of Real Property

Code Description

111   Office Buildings
112   Conference Space and Facilities
119   Other Administrative and Services Buildings
121   Air Traffic Control Towers
122   Air Traffic Training Facilities
123   Radar and Navigational Facilities
124   Airport Runways

125	Airport Terminals
126	Missile System Facilities
127	Elct and Communications System Facilities
129	Other Airfield Structures
131	Schools
139	Other Educational Buildings
141	Hospitals and Infirmaries
142	Laboratories and Clinics
149	Other Hospital Buildings
151	Ammunition Facilities
152	Maint Buildings
153	Production Buildings
154	Ship Constr and Rep Fac
155	Tank Automotive Fac
159	Other Industrial Buildings
161	Family Housing
162	Recreational Buildings
163	Troop Housing
164	Dining Facilities
165	Religious Facilities
166	Penal Facilities
169	Other Residential Buildings
171	Ammunition Storage Building
172	Food/Grain Storage Buildings
173	Fuel Storage Buildings
174	Open Storage Facilities
179	Other Warehouse Buildings
181	R&D - GOCO Facilities
182	R&D - GOGO Facilities
183	R&D - GOCO Environmental Labs
184	R&D - GOGO Environmental Labs
191	Museums and Exhibition Building
192	Test and Measurement Buildings
199	Misc Buildings
211	Dams
212	Canals
213	Mine Fire Control Facilities
214	Mine Subsidence Control Facilities
215	Surface Mine Reclamation Facilities
216	Dredging Facilities
219	Other Conservation Facilities
221	Airport Service Roads
222	Highways, Roads, Streets and Bridges
223	Tunnel and Subsurface Struct
224	Parking Facilities
231	Electric Power Generation Facilities - Coal

232   Electric Power Generation Facilities - Gas
233   Electric Power Generation Facilities - Geothermal
234   Electric Power Generation Facilities - Hydro
235   Electric Power Generation Facilities - Nuclear
236   Electric Power Generation Facilities - Petroleum
237   Electric Power Generation Facilities - Solar
239   Electric Power Generation Facilities - Other Incl Transm
241   Fuel Supply Facilities
242   Heating and Cooling Plants
243   Pollute Abatement and Control Facilities
244   Sewage and Waste Facilities
245   Water Supply Facilities
249   Other Utilities
291   Recreational Facilities (Non-Building)
292   Exhibit Design (Non-Building)
293   Unimproved Real Property (Land)
294   Waste Treatment-Storage Facilities
299   All Other Non-building Facilities
300   Restoration

Section 14.0 Supply Codes

PSC10-Weapons

PSC   Description
1005 Guns through 30 mm
1010 Guns over 30 mm Up to 75 mm
1015 Guns 75 mm through 125 mm
1020 Guns over 125 mm through 150 mm
1025 Guns over 150 mm through 200 mm
1030 Guns over 200 mm through 300 mm
1035 Guns over 300 mm
1040 Chemical Weapons and Equipment
1045 Launchers, Torpedo and Depth Charge
1055 Launchers, Grenade, Rocket and Pyrote
1070 Nets and Booms Ordnance
1075 Degaussing and Mine Sweeping Equipment
1080 Camouflage and Deception Equipment
1090 Assemblies Interchangeable between Two or More Classes
1095 Misc Weapons

PSC 11 - Nuclear Ordnance

PSC   Description
1105 Nuclear Bombs
1110 Nuclear Projectiles

1115 Nuclear Warheads and Warhead Sections
1120 Nuclear Depth Charges
1125 Nuclear Demolition Charges
1127 Nuclear Rockets
1130 Conversion Kits, Nuclear Ordnance
1135 Fusing and Firing Devices, Nuclear Ordnance
1140 Nuclear Components
1145 Explosive and Pyrotechnic Comps, Nuclear
1190 Special Test and Handling Equipment, Nuclear Equipment
1195 Misc Nuclear Ordnance

PSC 12 - Fire Control Equipment

PSC Description
1210 Fire Control Directors
1220 Fire Control Computing Sights and Device
1230 Fire Control Systems, Complete
1240 Optical Sighting and Ranging Equipment
1250 Fire Control Stabilizing Mechanisms
1260 Fire Control Designating-Indicating Equipment
1265 Fire Control Equipment Except Airborne
1270 Aircraft Gunnery Fire Control Comps
1280 Aircraft Bombing Fire Control Comps
1285 Fire Control Radar Equipment Except Airborne
1287 Fire Control Sonar Equipment
1290 Misc Fire Control Equipment

PSC 13 - Ammunition and Explosives

PSC   Description
1305 Ammunition through 30mm
1310 Ammunition over 30 mm Up to 75 mm
1315 Ammunition 75 mm through 125 mm
1320 Ammunition over 125 mm
1325 Bombs
1330 Grenades
1336 Guided Missile Warheads-Explosive Components
1337 Missile and Space Vehicle Explosive Propulsion Units, Solid Fuel
1338 Missile and Space Vehicle Inert Propulsion Units, Solid Fuel
1340 Rockets and Rocket Ammunition
1345 Land Mines
1350 Underwater Mine Inert Components
1351 Underwater Mine Explosive Components
1355 Torpedo Inert Components
1356 Torpedo Explosive Components
1360 Depth Charge Inert Components

1361 Depth Charge Explosive Components
1365 Military Chemical Agents
1370 Pyrotechnics
1375 Demolition Materials
1376 Bulk Explosives
1377 Cartridge and Propellant Devices
1380 Military Biological Agents
1385 Surface Explosive Ord Disposal Tool
1386 Underwater Explosive Ord Disposal
1390 Fuse and Primers
1395 Miscellaneous Ammunition
1398 Ammunition Handling and Servicing Equipment

PSC 14 - Guided Missiles

PSC Description
1410 Guided Missiles
1420 Guided Missile Components
1425 Guided Missile Systems, Complete
1427 Guided Missile Subsystems
1430 Guided Missile Remote Control Systems
1440 Launchers, Guided Missile
1450 Guided Missile Handling Service Equipment

PSC 15   Aircraft and Airframe Structural Components

PSC Description
1510 Aircraft, Fixed Wing
1520 Aircraft, Rotary Wing
1540 Gliders
1550 Drones
1560 Airframe Structural Components

PSC 16 - Aircraft Components and Accessories

PSC Description
1610 Aircraft Propellers
1615 Helicopter Rotor Blades-Drive Mech
1620 Aircraft Landing Gear Components
1630 Aircraft Wheel and Brake systems
1650 Aircraft Hydraulic Vacuum De-Icing
1660 Aircraft Air Condition Heating Equipment
1670 Parachutes, Aerial Pick-Up, Delivery and Recovery Systems and Tie Down Equipment
1680 Miscellaneous Aircraft Accessories Components

PSC 17 — Aircraft Launching, Landing, and Ground Handling Equip

PSC Description
1710 Aircraft Arresting Barrier and Equipment
1720 Aircraft Launching Equipment
1730 Aircraft Ground Servicing Equipment
1740 Airfield Special Trucks and Trailers

PSC 18 - Space Vehicles

PSC Description
1810 Space Vehicles
1820 Space Vehicle Components
1830 Space Vehicle Remote Control Systems
1840 Space Vehicle Launchers
1850 Space Vehicle Handling and Service Equipment
1860 Space Survival Equipment

PSC 19 — Ships, Small Craft, Pontoons, and Floating Docks

PSC Description
1900 Frigates and Corvettes
1901 Aircraft Carriers
1902 Cruisers
1903 Destroyers
1904 Submarines
1905 Subchasers
1906 Minelayers and Minesweepers
1907 Landing Craft
1908 Torpedo Boats and Gun Boats
1909 Hydrofoils
1910 Transport Vessels-Passenger and Troop
1911 Amphibious Assault Ships
1915 Cargo and Tanker Vessels
1920 Fishing Vessels
1921 Tugs and Towboats
1922 Fire Boats
1923 Ice Breakers
1924 Repair Ships
1925 Tender Vessels
1926 Lightships
1927 Cable Ships
1928 Salvage Vessels
1929 Rescue Vessels
1930 Barges and lighters Cargo
1935 Barges and lighters Special Purpose

1940   Small Craft
1945   Pontoons and Floating Docks
1950   Floating Dry-docks
1955   Dredges
1990   Miscellaneous Vessels

PSC 20 - Ship and Marine Equipment

PSC   Description
2010   Ship and Boat Propulsion Components
2020   Rigging and Rigging Gear
2030   Deck Machine
2040   Marine Hardware and Hull Items
2050   Buoys
2060   Commercial Fishing Equipment
2090   Miscellaneous ship and Marine equipment

PSC 22 - Railway Equipment

PSC   Description
2210   Locomotives
2220   Rail Cars
2230   Railroad Right of Way Constr Equipment
2240   Locomotive and Rail Car Accessories
2250   Track Materials Railroad

PSC 23 - Motor Vehicles, Trailers, and Cycles

PSC   Description
2305   Ground Effect Vehicles
2310   Passenger Motor Vehicles
2320   Trucks and Truck Tractors Wheeled
2330   Trailers
2340   Motorcycle,Motor Scooters and Bikes
2350   Combat Assault and Tactical Veh

PSC 24 - Tractors

PSC   Description
2410   Tractors Full Track Low Speed
2420   Tractors Wheeled
2430   Tractors Track Laying High Speed

PSC 25 - Vehicular Equipment Components

PSC   Description
2510 Vehicle Cab Body Frame Structural Components
2520 Vehicle Power Transmission Components
2530 Vehicle Brake Steering Axle Wheel Components
2540 Vehicle Furniture and Accessories
2590 Miscellaneous Vehicular Components

PSC 26 - Tires and Tubes

PSC   Description
2610 Tires and Tubes Pneumatic Except Aircraft
2620 Tires and Tubes Pneumatic Aircraft
2630 Tires Solid and Cushion
2640 Tires and Tubes Rebuilding-Repair Material

PSC 28 - Engines, Turbines, and Components

PSC   Description
2805 Gas Reciprocating Engine - Except Aircraft
2810 Gas Reciprocating Engine - Aircraft
2815 Diesel Engines and Components
2820 Steam Engines Reciprocating and Components
2825 Steam Turbines and Components
2830 Water Turbines,Water Wheels and Components
2835 Gas Turbines and Jet Engines Except Aircraft
2840 Gas Turbines and Jet Engines Aircraft
2845 Rocket Engines and Components
2850 Gasoline Rotary Engines and Components
2895 Miscellaneous Engines and Components

PSC 29 - Engine Accessories

PSC   Description
2910 Engine Fuel Sys Components Nonaircraft
2915 Engine Fuel System Components Aircraft
2920 Engine Electrical Sys Comps Nonaircraft
2925 Engine Electrical Sys Comps - Aircraft
2930 Engine Cooling Sys Comps - Nonaircraft
2935 Engine Cooling Sys Components - Aircraft
2940 Engine Air and Oil Filters - Nonaircraft
2945 Engine Air and Oil Filters - Aircraft
2950 Turbosuperchargers
2990 Miscellaneous Engine Accessories - Nonaircraft
2995 Miscellaneous Engine Accessories - Aircraft

PSC 30   Mechanical Power Transmission Equipment

PSC   Description
3010   Torque Converters and Speed Changers
3020   Gear Pulley Sprocket and Transmission Chain
3030   Belting Drive Belts Fan Belts and Accessories
3040   Miscellaneous Power Transmission Equipment

PSC 31 - Bearings

PSC   Description
3110   Bearings Antifriction Unmounted
3120   Bearings Plain Unmounted
3130   Bearings Mounted

PSC 32 - Woodworking

PSC   Description
3210   Sawmill and Planing Mill Machine
3220   Woodworking Machines
3230   Tools - Attachments for Woodwork Machinery

PSC 34 - Metalworking Machinery

PSC   Description
3405   Saws and Filing Machines
3408   Maching Centers and Way-Type Machines
3410   Electrical and Ultrasonic Erosion Machines
3411   Boring Machines
3412   Broaching Machines
3413   Drilling and Tapping Machines
3414   Gear Cutting and Finishing Machines
3415   Grinding Machines
3416   Lathes
3417   Milling Machines
3418   Planers and Shapers
3419   Miscellaneous Machine Tools
3422   Rolling Mills and Drawing Machines
3424   Metal Heat Treating Equipment
3426   Metal Finishing Equipment
3431   Electric Arc Welding Equipment
3432   Electric Resistance Welding Equipment
3433   Gas Weld Heat Cut - Metalizing Equipment
3436   Welding Positioners and Manipulators

3438 Miscellaneous Welding Equipment
3439 Miscellaneous Weld Solder and Brazing Supply
3441 Bending and Forming Machines
3442 Hydraulic/Pneumatic Power Press Dr
3443 Mechanical Presses Power Driven
3444 Manual Presses
3445 Punching and Shearing Machines
3446 Forging Machine and Hammers
3447 Wire and Metal Ribbon Forming Machs
3448 Riveting Machines
3449 Miscellaneous Secondary Metal Form-Cut Mach
3450 Machine Tools Portable
3455 Cutting Tools for Machine Tools
3456 Secondary Metal Mach-Cutting Tools
3460 Machine Tool Accessories
3461 Secondary Metalworking Mach-Access
3465 Production Jigs Fixtures and Template
3470 Machine Shop Sets Kits and Outfits

PSC 35 - Service and Trade Equipment

PSC   Description
3510 Laundry and Dry Cleaning Equipment
3520 Shoe Reparing Equipment
3530 Ind Sew Mach and Mobile Textile Shops
3540 Wrapping and Packaging Machine
3550 Vending and Coin Operated Machines
3590 Miscellaneous Service and Trade Equipment

PSC 36 - Special Industry Machinery

PSC   Description
3605 Food Products Machine and Equipment
3610 Printing,Duplicating and Bookbind Equipment
3611 Industrial Marking Machines
3615 Pulp and Paper Industries Machine
3620 Rubber and Plastic Working Machine
3625 Textile Industries Machine
3630 Clay-Concrete Products Mach
3635 Crystal and Glass Industries Machine
3640 Tobacco Manufacturing Machine
3645 Leather Tanning and Working Machine
3650 Chemical and Pharmaceutical Machine
3655 Gas Generating and Dispensing System
3660 Industrial Size Reduction Machine
3670 Printed Circuit Board Mfg Mach

3680 Foundry Machine - Related Equipment and Supplies
3685 Special Metal Container Mfg Mach
3690 Special Ammunition and Ordnance Mach
3693 Industrial Assembly Machines
3694 Clean Work Stations Environment Equipment
3695 Miscellaneous Special Industry Machine

PSC 37 - Agricultural Machinery and Equipment

PSC Description
3710 Soil Preparation Equipment
3720 Harvesting Equipment
3730 Dairy Poultry and Livestock Equipment
3740 Pest Disease and Frost Control Equipment
3750 Gardening Implements and Tools
3760 Animal Drawn Vehicle and Farm Trailer
3770 Saddlery, Hamess, Whips and Furnishing

PSC 38   Construction, Mining, Excavating, and Highway Maint Equip

PSC Description
3805 Earth Moving and Excavating Equipment
3810 Cranes and Crane-Shovels
3815 Crane and Crane-Shovel Attachments
3820 Mining, Rock Drilling, Earth Bore Equipment
3825 Road Clearing and Cleaning Equipment
3830 Truck and Tractor Attachments
3835 Petroleum Production-Distrib Equipment
3895 Miscellaneous Contruct Equipment

PSC 39 - Materials Handling Equipment

PSC Description
3910 Conveyors
3915 Materials Feeders
3920 Mat Handling Equipment - Nonself-Propelled
3930 Warehouse Trks and Tractors Self-Prop
3940 Blocks Tackle Rigging and Slings
3950 Winches Hoists Cranes and Derricks
3960 Elevators and Escalators
3990 Miscellaneous Materials Handling Equipment

PSC 40 - Rope, Cable, Chain, and Fittings

PSC Description
4010 Chain and Wire Rope

4020 Fiber Rope Cordage and Twine
4030 Fittings for Rope Cable and Chain

PSC 41   Refrigeration and Air Conditioning Equipment

PSC   Description
4110 Refrigeration Equipment
4120 Air Conditioning Equipment
4130 Refrigeration and Air Condition Components
4140 Fans Air Circulators and Blower Equipment

PSC 42   Fire Fighting, Rescue, and Safety Equipment

PSC   Description
4210 Fire Fighting Equipment
4220 Marine Lifesaving and Diving Equipment
4230 Decontaminating and Impregnating Equipment
4240 Safety and Rescue Equipment

PSC 43 - Pumps and Compressors

PSC   Description
4310 Compressors and Vacuum Pumps
4320 Power and Hand Pumps
4330 Centrifugals Separators and Filters

PSC 44   Furnace, Steam Plant, and Drying Equip, Nuclear Reactors

PSC   Description
4410 Industrial Boilers
4420 Heat Exchangers and Steam Condensers
4430 Industrial Furnaces, Kilns and Ovens
4440 Dryers Dehydrators and Anhydrators
4460 Air Purification Equipment
4470 Nuclear Reactors

PSC 45   Plumbing, Heating and Sanitation Equipment

PSC   Description
4510 Plumbing Fixtures and Accessories
4520 Space Heating Equipment and Water Heaters
4530 Fuel Burning Equipment Units
4540 Miscellaneous Plumbing, Heat and Sanitation Equipment

PSC 46   Water Purification and Sewage Treatment Equipment

4610   Water Purification Equipment
4620   Water Distill Equipment-Marine and Indust
4630   Sewage Treatment Equipment

PSC 47 - Pipe, Tubing, Hose, and Fittings

PSC   Description
4710   Pipe and Tube
4720   Hose and Tubing Flexible
4730   Fittings - Hose Pipe and Tube

PSC 48 - Valves

PSC   Description
4810   Valves Powered
4820   Valves Nonpowered

PSC 49   Maintenance and Repair Shop Equipment

PSC   Description
4910   Motor Vehicle Maint Equipment
4920   Aircraft Maint and Rep Shop Equipment
4921   Torpedo Maint Rep and Checkout Equipment
4923   Depth Charges-Mines Maint and Rep Equipment
4925   Ammunition Maint - Checkout Equipment
4927   Rocket Maint and Rep Equipment
4930   Lubrication and Fuel Dispensing Equipment
4931   Fire Control Maint Equipment
4933   Weapons Maint Equipment
4935   Guided Missile Maint Equipment
4940   Miscellaneous Maint Equipment
4960   Space Vehicle Maint Equipment

PSC 51 - Hand Tools

PSC   Description
5110   Hand Tools Edged Nonpowered
5120   Hand Tools Nonedged Nonpowered
5130   Hand Tools Power Driven
5133   Drill Bits, Counterbores and Sinks
5136   Taps,Dies and Collets-Hand and Machine
5140   Tool and Hardware Boxes
5180   Sets Kits and Outfits of Hand Tools

PSC 52 - Measuring Tools

PSC   Description
5210   measuring Tools Craftsmens
5220   Gages and Precision Layout Tool
5280   Sets, Kits and Outfits of Measuring Tools

PSC 53 - Hardware and Abrasives

PSC   Description
5305   Screws
5306   Bolts
5307   Studs
5310   Nuts and Washers
5315   Nails Keys and Pins
5320   Rivets
5325   Fastening Devices
5330   Packing and Gasket Materials
5335   Metal Screening
5340   Miscellaneous Hardware
5345   Disks and Stones Abrasive
5350   Abrasive Materials
5355   Knobs and Pointers
5360   Coil,Flat and Wire Springs
5365   Rings Shims and Spacers

PSC 54   Prefabricated Structures and Scaffolding

PSC   Description
5410   Prefabricated and Portable Buildings
5411   Rigid Wall Shelters
5420   Bridges Fixed and Floating
5430   Storage Tanks
5440   Scaffolding Equipment and Concrete Forms
5445   Prefabricated Tower Structures
5450   Miscellaneous Prefabricated Structures

PSC 55   Lumber, Millwork, Plywood, and Veneer

PSC   Description
5510   Lumber and Related Wood Materials
5520   Millwork
5530   Plywood and Veneer

PSC 56 - Construction and Building Materials

PSC	Description
5610	Mineral Contruct Materials Bulk
5620	Building Glass Tile Brick and Block
5630	Pipe and Conduit Nonmetallic
5640	Wallboard Building and Thermal Insulation
5650	Roofing and Siding Materials
5660	Fencing, Fences and Gates
5670	Building Components Prefabricated
5680	Miscellaneous Construction Materials

PSC 58 - Communications Equipment

PSC	Description
5805	Telephone and Telegraph Equipment
5810	Communications Security Equipment and Components
5811	Other Cryptologic Equipment and Components
5815	Teletype and Facsimile Equipment
5820	Radio and TV Equipment - Except Airborne
5821	Radio and TV Equipment - Airborne
5825	Radio Navigation Equipment - Except Airborne
5826	Radio Navigation Equipment - Airborne
5830	Intercom Public Address Sys - Except Airborne
5831	Intercom Public Address Sys - Airborne
5835	Sound Recording and Reproducing Equipment
5836	Video Recording and Reproducing Equipment
5840	Radar Equipment - Except Airborne
5941	Radar Equipment - Airborne
5845	Underwater Sound Equipment
5850	Visible Invisible Light Communications Equipment
5855	Night Vision Equipment
5860	Stimulated Coherent Radiation Devices
5865	Electronic Countermeasure and Quick Reaction Equipment
5895	Miscellaneous Communications Equipment

PSC 59   Electrical and Electronic Equipment Components

PSC	Description
5905	Resistors
5910	Capacitors
5915	Filters and Networks
5920	Fuses Arresters Absorbers and Protector
5925	Circuit Breakers
5930	Switches
5935	Connectors, Electrical

5936 5940 Lugs Terminals and Terminal Strips
5945 Relays and Solenoids
5950 Coils and Transformers
5955 Oscillators Piezoelectric Crystals
5960 Electron Tubes and Assoc Hardware
5961 Semi Conductor Devices
5962 Microcircuits - Electronic
5963 Electronic Modules
5965 Headset,Handset,Microphone and Speak
5970 Electrical Insulators and Insulating Materials
5975 Electrical Hardware and Supplies
5977 Electrical Contact Brushes and Electrodes
5980 Optoelectrical Devices and Associated Hardware
5985 Antennas Waveguides and Related Equipment
5990 Synchros and Resolvers
5995 Cable Cord Wire Assembly - Communications Equipment
5998 Electrical Assemb-Bds Cards-Assoc Hardware
5999 Miscellaneous Electrical and Electronic Components

PSC 60 - Fiber Optics Materials

PSC   Description
6004 Rotary Joints
6005 Couplers, Splitters, and Mixers
6006 Attenuators
6007 Filters
6008 Optical Multiplexers/Demultiplexers
6010 Fiber Optic Conductors
6015 Fiber Optic Cables
6020 Fiber Optic Cable Assembly and Harness
6021 Fiber Optic Switches
6025 Fiber Optic Transmitters
6026 Fiber Optic Receivers
6029 Fiber Optic Repeaters
6030 Fiber Optic Devices
6031 Integrated Optical Circuits
6032 Fiber Optic light Sources
6033 Fiber Optic Photo Detectors
6034 Fiber Optic Mod/Demodulators
6035 Fiber Optic Light/Image Transfer
6040 Fiber Optic Sensors
6050 Fiber Optic Passive Devices
6060 Fiber Optic Interconnectors
6070 Fiber Optic Accessories and Supplies
6080 Fiber Optic Kits and Sets
6099 Miscellaneous Fiber Optic Components

PSC 61   Electric Wire, and Power and Distribution Equipment

PSC   Description
6105   Motors Electrical
6110   Electrical Control Equipment
6115   Generators and Generator Sets Elect
6116   Fuel Cell Power Units, Comp, Acc
6117   Solar Elec Power Systems
6120   Transformers - Distrib and Power Sta
6125   Converters Electrical Rotating
6130   Converters Electrical Non Rotating
6135   Batteries Nonrechargeable
6140   Batteries Rechargeable
6145   Wire and Cable, Electrical
6150   Miscellaneous Electric Power and Distribution Equipment

PSC 62 - Lighting Fixtures and Lamps

PSC   Description
6210   Indoor and Outdoor Electrical lighting Fixtures
6220   Electric Vehicular lights and Fixtures
6230   Electric Portable and Hand lighting Equipment
6240   Electric Lamps
6250   Ballasts Lampholders and Starters
6260   Nonelect lighting Fixtures

PSC 63 - Alarm and Signal Systems

PSC   Description
6310   Traffic and Transit Signal Systems
6320   Shipboard Alarm and Signal Systems
6330   Railroad Signal and Warning Devices
6340   Aircraft Alarm and Signal Systems
6350   Miscellaneous Alarm, Signal, Sec Systems

PSC 65   Medical, Dental, and Veterinary Equipment and Supplies

PSC   Description
6505   Drugs, Biologicals and Official Reagents
6506   Blood
6507   Blood Derivatives
6508   Medicated Cosmetics and Toiletries
6510   Surgical Dressing Materials
6515   Medical and Surgical Instruments,Equipment and Supplies

6520   Dental Instruments Equipment and Supplies
6525   X-Ray Equipment Supplies - Medical, Dental and Veterinary
6530   Hosp Furniture,Eq,Utensils and Supplies
6532   Hospital and Surgical Clothing
6540   Ophthalmic Instruments Equipment and Supplies
6545   Medical Sets Kits and Outfits
6550   in vitro Diagnostic Substances,Reagents

PSC 66 - Instruments and Laboratory Equipment

PSC   Description
6605   Navigational Instruments
6610   Flight Instruments
6615   Auto Pilot Mechanisms Airborne Gyro
6620   Engine Instruments
6625   Electrical and Electronic Measuring Instruments
6630   Chemical Analysis Instruments
6635   Physical Properties Test Equipment
6636   Environmental Chambers and Related Equipment
6640   Laboratory Equipment and Supplies
6645   Time Measuring Instruments
6650   Optical Instruments
6655   Geophysical Instruments
6660   Meteorological Instruments and Apparatus
6665   Hazard-Detecting Instru and Apparatus
6670   Scales and Balances
6675   Drafting Surveying and Mapping Instruments
6680   Liquid-Gas-Motion Measuring Instruments
6685   Pressure Temp Humidity Instruments
6695   Combination and Miscellaneous Instruments

PSC 67 - Photographic Equipment

PSC   Description
6710   Cameras, Motion Picture
6720   Cameras, Still Picture
6730   Photographic Projection Equipment
6740   Photo Developing and Finishing Equipment
6750   Photographic Supplies
6760   Photographic Equipment and Accessories
6770   Film Processed
6780   Photographic Sets Kits and Outfits

PSC 68 - Chemicals and Chemical Products

PSC   Description
6810 Chemicals
6820 Dyes
6830 Gases Compressed and Liquefied
6840 Pest Control Agents and Disinfectants
6850 Miscellaneous Chemical Specialties

PSC 69 - Training Aids and Devices

PSC   Description
6910 Training Aids
6920 Armament Training Devices
6930 Operational Training Devices
6940 Communication Training Devices

PSC 70   ADP Equipment Software, Supplies and Support Equip

PSC   Description
7010 ADPE System Configuration
7020 ADP Central Processing Unit-Analog
7021 ADP Central Processing Unit-Digital
7022 ADP Central Processing Unit-Hybrid
7025 ADP Input/Output and Storage Devices
7030 ADP Software
7035 ADP Support Equipment
7040 Punched Card Equipment
7042 Mini and Micro Computer Control Devices
7045 ADP Supplies
7050 ADP Components

PSC 71 - Furniture

PSC   Description
7105 Household Furniture
7110 Office Furniture
7125 Cabinets Lockers Bins and Shelving
7195 Miscellaneous Furniture and Fixtures

PSC 72   Household and Commercial Furnishings and Appliances

PSC   Description
7210 Household Furnishings
7220 Floor Coverings
7230 Draperies Awnings and Shades

7240   Household and Common Utility Containers
7290   Msc Household Furnishings Appliance

PSC 73   Food Preparation and Serving Equipment

PSC   Description
7310   Food Cooking Baking Serving Equipment
7320   Kitchen Equipment and Appliances
7330   Kitchen Hand Tools and Utensils
7340   Cutlery and Flatware
7350   Tableware
7360   Set Kit and Outfit Food Preparation and Service

PSC 74 - Office Machines

PSC   Description
7420   Accounting and Calculating Machines
7430   Typewriter and Office Composing Machines
7435   Office Information System Equipment
7450   Office Sound Recording Reproduction Machines
7460   Visible Record Equipment
7490   Miscellaneous Office Machines

PSC 75 - Office Supplies and Devices

PSC   Description
7510   Office Supplies
7520   Office Devices and Accessories
7530   Stationery and Record Forms
7540   Standard Forms

PSC 76 - Books, Maps, and Other Publications

PSC   Description
7610   Books and Pamphlets
7630   Newspapers and Periodicals
7640   Maps Atlases Charts and Globes
7650   Drawings and Specifications
7660   Sheet and Book Music
7670   Microfilm Processed
7690   Miscellaneous Printed Matter

PSC 77   Musical Instruments, Phonographs, and Home-Type Radios

PSC   Description
7710   Musical Instruments

7720   Musical Instrument Parts and Acc
7730   Phonograph,Radio and TV-Home Type
7740   Phonograph Records

PSC 78 - Recreational and Athletic Equipment

PSC   Description
7810   Athletic and Sporting Equipment
7820   Games Toys and Wheeled Goods
7830   Recreational and Gymnastic Equipment

PSC 79 - Cleaning Equipment and Supplies

PSC   Description
7910   Floor Polishers and Vacuum Cleaners
7920   Brooms Brushes Mops and Sponges
7930   Cleaning polishing Compounds and Prep

PSC 80 - Brushes, Paints, Sealers, and Adhesives

PSC   Description
8010   Paint,Dope,Vamish and Related Prod
8020   Paint and Artists Brushes
8030   Preservative and Sealing Compounds
8040   Adhesives

PSC 81   Containers, Packaging, and Packing Supplies

PSC   Description
8105   Bags and Sacks
8110   Drums and Cans
8115   Boxes Cartons and Crates
8120   Gas Cylinders
8125   Bottles and Jars
8130   Reels and Spools
8135   Packaging and Packing Bulk Materials
8140   Ammunition and Nuclear Ordnance Boxes
8145   Special Shipping and Storage Contain

PSC 83   Textiles, Leather, Furs, Apparel and Shoe Findings, Tents and Flags

PSC   Description
8305   Textile Fabrics
8310   Yarn and Thread
8315   Notions and Apparel Findings

8320   Padding and Sewing Materials
8325   Fur Materials
8330   Leather
8335   Shoe Findings and Soling Materials
8340   Tents and Tarpaulins
8345   Flags and Pennants

PSC 84   Clothing, Individual Equipment, and Insignia

PSC   Description
8405   Outerwear Mens
8410   Outerwear Womens
8415   Clothing Special Purpose
8420   Underwear and Nightwear, Mens
8425   Underwear and Nightwear, Womens
8430   Footwear Mens
8435   Footwear Womens
8440   Hosiery Handwear and Clothing Acc-Men
8445   Hosiery Handwear Clothing Acc-Women
8450   Children and Infants Apparel and Acc
8455   Badges and Insignia
8460   Luggage
8465   Individual Equipment
8470   Armor Personal
8475   Spec Flight Clothing and Accessories

PSC 85 - Toiletries

PSC   Description
8510   Perfume,Toilet Preparation and Powder
8520   Toilet Soap,Shave Prep and Dentifrice
8530   Personal Toiletry Articles
8540   Toiletry Paper Products

PSC 87 - Agricultural Supplies

PSC   Description
8710   Forage and Feed
8720   Fertilizers
8730   Seeds and Nursery Stock

PSC 88 - Live Animals

PSC   Description
8810   Live Animals Raised for Food
8820   Live Animals Not Raised for Food

PSC 89 - Subsistence (Food)

PSC	Description
8900	Perishable Subsistence $IOK - 25K
8905	Meat Poultry and Fish
8910	Dairy Foods and Eggs
8915	Fruits and Vegetables
8920	Bakery and Cereal Products
8925	Sugar Confectionery and Nuts
8930	Jams Jellies and Preserves
8935	Soups and Bouillons
8940	Special Dietary Food and Special Prep
8945	Food Oils and Fats
8950	Condiments and Related Products
8955	Coffee Tea and Cocoa
8960	Beverages Nonalcoholic
8965	Beverages Alcoholic
8970	Composite Food Packages
8975	Tobacco Products
8999	Food Items for Resale

PSC 91 - Fuels, Lubricants, Oils, and Waxes

PSC	Description
9110	Fuels Solid
9130	liquid Propellants - Petroleum Base
9135	liquid Propellants - Chemical Base
9140	Fuel Oils
9150	Oil and Grease - Cutting,Lubricants and Hydraulic
9160	Miscellaneous Waxes Oils and Fats

PSC 93 - Nonmetallic Fabricated Materials

PSC	Description
9310	Paper and Paperboard
9320	Rubber Fabricated Materials
9330	Plastics Fabricated Materials
9340	Glass Fabricated Materials
9350	Refractories and Fire Surfacing Materials
9390	Miscellaneous Fabricated Nonmetal Materials

PSC 94 - Nonmetallic Crude Materials

PSC	Description
9410	Crude Grades of Plant Materials

9420   Fibers Vegetable Animal and Synthetic
9430   Miscellaneous Crude Animal Prods - Inedible
9440   Miscellaneous Crude Agricultural and Forestry Prod
9450   Nonmetallic Scrap Except Textile

PSC 95 - Metal Bars, Sheets, and Shapes

PSC   Description
9505   Wire Nonelect Iron and Steel
9510   Bars and Rods Iron and Steel
9515   Plate Sheet and Strip Iron and Steel
9520   Structural Shapes Iron and Steel
9525   Wire Nonelect Nonferrous Base Metal
9530   Bars and Rods Nonferrous Base Metal
9535   Plate Sheet Strip-Nonferrous Metal
9540   Structural Shapes Nonferrous Metal
9545   Plate,Sheet,Strip and Wire-Prec Metal

PSC 96   Ores, Minerals, and Their Primary Products

PSC   Description
9610   Ores
9620   Minerals Natural and Synthetic
9630   Additive Metal Materials and Master Alloys
9640   Iron and Steel Primary and Semifinished
9650   Nonferrous Base Metal Refinery
9660   Precious Metals Primary Forms
9670   Iron and Steel Scrap
9680   Nonferrous Metal Scrap

PSC 99 - Miscellaneous

PSC   Description
9905   Signs, Advertisement Displays and Identification Plates
9910   Jewelry
9915   Collectors/Historical Items
9920   Smokers Articles and Matches
9925   Ecclesiastical Equipment Furnishing and Supplies
9930   Memorials-Cemetery and Mortuary Equipment
9998   Nonfood Items for Resale
9999   Miscellaneous Unclassifiable Items

Standard Industrial Classifications (SIC Codes)

0111   Cash Wheat Farms
0112   Cash Rice Farms
0115   Cash Corn Farms
0116   Cash Soybean Farms
0119   Cash Grain Farms
0131   Cotton Farms
0132   Tobacco Farms
0133   Sugarcane & Sugar Beet Farms
0134   Irish Potato Farms
0139   Field Crop Farms
0161   Vegetable and Melon Farms
0171   Berry Farms
0171a Cranberry Growers
0172   Grape Farms & Vineyards
0172a Vineyards
0173   Tree Nut Groves & Farms
0174   Citrus Fruit Groves & Farms
0174a Citrus Growers
0175   Deciduous Tree Fruit Orchards & Farms
0179   Fruit & Tree Nut Farms Orchards & Groves
0181   Ornamental Floriculture & Nursery Products
0181a Flower Growers & Shippers
0181b Seed & Bulb Growers
0182   Food Crops Grown under Cover
0182a Mushroom Growers
0191   Primarily Crop Farms
0211   Beef Cattle Feedlots & Stockyards
0212   Beef Cattle Farms & Ranches
0213   Hog Feedlots & Farms
0214   Sheep & Goat Farms
0219   General Livestock Farms

0241 Dairy Farms
0251 Poultry Farms & Ranches
0252 Egg Farms
0253 Turkey Farms & Ranches
0254 Poultry Hatcheries
0259 Poultry & Egg Farms
0271 Fur Bearing Animal Farms
0272 Horse & Other Equine Farms
0273 Animal Aquaculture
0273a Fish Farms
0279 Animal Specialties
0279a Bee Farms
0291 Primarily Livestock & Animal Specialty Farms
0711 Soil Preparation Services
0721 Crop Cultivating Planting & Protection Services
0721a Crop Dusting Services
0721b Citrus Grove Crop Services
0722 Mechanical Crop Harvesting
0723 Crop Preparation Services for Market
0724 Cotton Ginning
0741 Livestock Veterinary Services
0742 Veterinary Services for Animal Specialties
0742a Animal Hospitals
0742b Veterinarian Emergency Services
0751 Livestock Services Except Veterinary
0751a Artificial Insemination Services
0752 Animal Specialty Services Except Veterinary
0752a Dog & Cat Boarding Kennels
0752b Dog & Pet Grooming Services
0752c Horse Breeders
0752d Horse Training
0752e Animal Shelters
0761 Farm Labor Contractors & Crew Leaders
0762 Farm Management Services
0762a Citrus Grove Management
0781 Landscape Counseling & Planning
0781a Land Planning Services
0781b Landscape Design
0782 Lawn & Garden Services
0782a Landscape Contractors
0782b Landscaping & Lawn Maintenance
0783 Ornamental Shrub & Tree Services
0811 Timber Tracts
0831 Forest Nurseries & Gathering of Forest Products
0831a Forest Nurseries
0831b Pine Gum Extraction Services

0851 Forestry Services
0851a Forestry Consultants
0912 Finfish Fishing
0913 Shellfish Catching & Taking
0913a Oyster Dredging or Tonging
0919 Marine Products Miscellaneous
0921 Fish Hatcheries & Preserves
0971 Hunting & Trapping & Game Propagation
1011 Iron Ore Mining
1021 Copper Ore Mining
1031 Lead & Zinc Ore Mining
1041 Gold Ore Mining
1044 Silver Ore Mining
1061 Ferroalloy Ore Mining
1081 Metal Mining Services
1094 Uranium Radium & Vanadium Ore Mining & Services
1099 Miscellaneous Metal Ore Mining & Services
1099a Bauxite & Aluminum Ore Mining
1099b Mercury Ore Preparation
1221 Bituminous Coal & Lignite Surface Mining
1222 Bituminous Coal Underground Mining
1231 Anthracite Coal Mining & Preparation
1241 Coal Mining Services
1241a Anthracite Mining Services on a Contract Basis
1241b Bituminous & Lignite Services
1311 Crude Petroleum & Natural Gas Production
1321 Natural Gas Liquids Producers
1381 Oil & Gas Well Drilling Contractors
1381a Gas Well Drilling
1381b Oil Well Directional Drilling
1382 Oil & Gas Field Exploration Services
1382a Seismograph Services
1389 Oil & Gas Field Services
1389b Oil Field Equipment Repairing
1389d Oil Well Surveyors
1389e Oil Field Hauling
1389f Oil Well Cementing
1389g Oil Well Drilling Mud & Additives
1389h Oil Weel Logging & Perforating
1389j Oil Riggers
1389k Pipe Inspection Service
1411 Dimension Stone Quarrying & Mining
1422 Crushed & Broken Limestone Quarrying & Mining
1423 Crushed & Broken Granite Quarrying & Mining
1429 Crushed & Broken Stone Quarrying & Mining
1442 Construction Sand & Gravel Mining

1446 Industrial Sand Mining
1455 Kaolin & Ball Clay Mining
1459 Clay Ceramic & Refractory Material Mining
1459a Bentonite Mining
1459b Fire Clay Mining
1459c Fullers Earth Mining
1474 Potash Soda & Borate Mineral Mining
1475 Phosphate Rock Mining
1479 Chemical & Fertilizer Mineral Mining
1479a Barite Mining
1479b Fluorspar Mining
1479c Rock Salt Mining
1479d Sulfur Mining
1481 Nonmetallic Minerals Services Except Fuels
1499 Nonmetallic Minerals
1499a Gypsum Mining
1499b Talc & Related Minerals Mining
1521 General Contractors Single Family Houses
1521a Remodeling Contractors
1521b Fire Damage Contractors
1521c Patio & Deck Builders
1521d Home & Industrial Building Contractors
1521e Building Construction
1522 General Contractors Residential Buildings Other than Single Family
1531 Operative Builders
1541 General Contractors Industrial Buildings & Warehouses
1541a Prefabricated Metal Building Erection Industrial
1541d Floor Raising
1541e Grain Elevator Builders
1541z Clean Room Construction & Equipment
1542 General Contractors Nonresidential Buildings Not Industrial & Warehse
1542a Store Front Contractors
1542b Garage Builders
1542c Greenhouse & Solarium Builders
1542z Nonresidentional Builders
1611 Highway & Street Construction Except Elevated Highways
1611b Highway Sign Installation
1611c Road Building Contractors
1611d Pavement Marking Contractors
1611g Culvert Construction
1611j Grading Contractors
1611k Parking Lot & Garage Construction
1611l Road Oiling Contractors
1611z Paving Contractors
1622 Bridge Tunnel & Elevated Highway Construction
1623 Water Sewer Pipeline & Communications & Power Line Construction

1623a Sewer Contractors
1623b Pipe Line Contractors
1623f Gas Line Installation & Repair
1629   Heavy Construction
1629a Tennis Court Contractors
1629c Drainage Contractors
1629d Mining Contractors
1629e Marine Contractors
1629g File Contractors
1629h Ditching Contractors
1629j Dredging Contractors
1629k Pile Driving Contractors
1629l Oil Field Contractors
1629n Engineering Contractors
1629o Water Pollution Control Contractors
1629p Golf Course Construction
1711   Plumbing Heating & Air Condintioning Contractors
1711a Plumbing Contractors
1711b Heating & Ventilation Contractors
1711c Air Conditioning Contractors
1711d Boiler Setting Contractors
1711e Boiler Maintenance Services
1711f Solar Energy Contractors
1711g Irrigation Lawn & Garden Sprinkler Systems Installers
1711j Furnance Maintenance Services
1711k Septic System Construction
1711m Automatic Fire Protection Sprinkler System Contractors
1711n Mechanical Contractors
1711p Pipe Fabricator Contractors
1721   Painting & Paper Hanging Contractors
1721a Painting & Decorating Contractors
1721b Wallpaper Contractors
1721c Spray Painting & Finishing Contractors
1731   Electrical Work Contractors
1741   Masonry Stone Setting & Other Stone Work Contractors
1741a Bricklaying Masonry & Stone Setting
1741b Tuck Pointing
1741c Chimney Builders
1741f Marble Contractors
1742   Plastering Drywall Acoustical & Insulation Contractors
1742a Drywall Contractors
1742b Plastering & Lathing Contractors
1742c Acoustical & Ceiling Contractors
1742d Insulation Contractors
1743   Terrazzo Tile Marble & Mosiac Work Contractors
1751   Carpentry Work Contractors

1751a Mechanized Door & Gate Contractors Including Overhead
1751b Woodworking
1751c Carpenters
1751d Wood Finishing Services
1751z Cabinet Makers
1752 Floor Work Contractors
1752a Floor Laying & Resurfacing
1752b Linoleum & Nonceramic Tile Installation
1752c Carpet & Rug Installation Contractors
1761 Roofing Siding & Sheet Metal Work Contractors
1761a Siding Contractors
1761b Roofing Contractors
1761c Sheet Metal Work Contractors
1761d Gutter & Downspout Contractors
1761e Skylight Contractors
1761h Roof Decking Contractors
1761k Roof Maintenance Contractors
1771 Concrete & Related Work Contractors
1771b Stucco Contractors
1771c Driveway Contractors
1771d Sidewalk Contractors
1771e Foundation Contractors
1781 Water Well Drilling Contractors
1791 Structural Steel Erection Contractors
1791d Metal Fabricators
1793 Glass & Glazing Work Contractors
1794 Excavation Work Contractors
1795 Wrecking & Demolition Contractors
1796 Installation or Erection of Building Equipment
1796a Elevator Installation Contractors
1796b Machinery Movers & Erectors
1796e Pneumatic Tube Systems & Equipment Manufacturing
1799 Special Trade Contractors
1799a Fence Contractors
1799b Swimming Pool Contractors
1799c Waterproofing & Weather Stripping Contractors
1799d Fireproofing Contractors
1799e House Moving Contractors
1799f Scaffolding Construction & Steeple Jacks
1799g Drilling & Boring Contractors
1799h Computer Rooms Equipment & Installation Contractors
1799i Paint Removal Contractors
1799j Parking Lot Marking & Maintenance
1799k Wallpaper Removal Contractors
1799l Sign Installation & Maintenance
1799s Service Station Equipment and Services

1799u Glass Board up Service
1799v Asbestos Removal Contractors
1799w Drapery Installation Contractors
2011   Meat Packing Plants
2013   Sausage & Prepared Meat Manufacturing
2015   Poultry Slaughtering & Processing
2015a Poultry Dressing Plants
2015b Poultry & Egg Processors
2021   Creamery Butter Manufacturing
2022   Natural Processed & Imitation Cheese Manufacturing
2023   Dry Condensed & Evaporated Dairy Product Manufacturing
2024   Ice Cream & Frozen Dessert Manufacturing
2026   Fluid Milk Processing Plants
2032   Specialty Products Except Seafood Canners
2033   Fruit Vegetable Preserve Jam & Jelly Canners
2034   Dried & Dehydrated Fruit Vegetable & Soup Mix Producers
2034a Nuts Processing & Wholesale
2034b Dehydrating Services
2035   Pickled Fruits & Vegetables Vegetable Sauces & Seasons & Salad Dress
2035b Pickles & Pickle Products
2037   Frozen Fruits Fruit Juice and Vegetable Producers
2038   Frozen Specialty Manufacturing
2041   Flour & Other Grain Mill Product Milling
2043   Cereal Breakfast Food Manufacturing
2044   Rice Milling
2045   Prepared Flour Mix and Dough Manufacturing
2046   Wet Corn Milling
2047   Dog & Cat Food Manufacturing
2048   Prepared Feed & Feed Ingredients for Animal & Fowl Except Dogs & Cats
2051   Bread & Bakery Products Except Cookies & Cracker Manufacturing
2052   Cookie & Cracker Manufacturing
2053   Frozen Bakery Product Manufacturing Except Bread
2061   Cane Sugar Manufacturing Except Refining
2062   Cane Sugar Refining
2063   Beet Sugar Manufacturing
2064   Candy & Other Confectionery Product Manufacturing
2066   Chocolate and Cocoa Product Manufacturing
2067   Chewing Gum Manufacturing
2068   Salted and Roasted Nut & Seed Manufacturing
2074   Cottonseed Oil Mills
2075   Soybean Oil Mills
2076   Vegetable Oil Mills Except Corn Cottonseed & Soybean
2077   Animal & Marine, Fat & Oil Manufacturing
2079   Shortening Table Oil Margarine & Other Edible Fat & Oil Mfg
2082   Malt Beverage Manufacturing
2083   Malt Manufacturing

2084 Wine Brandy & Brandy Spirit Manufacturing
2084a Wineries
2085 Distilled & Blended Liquor Manufacturing
2086 Bottled & Canned Soft Drink & Carbonated Water Manufacturing
2087 Flavoring Extract & Syrup Manufacturing
2091 Fish & Seafood Curing & Canning
2091a Canned Fish Cakes
2092 Fish & Seafood Fresh & Frozen Preparation
2095 Coffee Roasters
2096 Potato & Corn Chip & Similar Snack Manufacturing
2097 Ice Manufacturing
2098 Macaroni Spaghetti Vermicelli & Noodle Manufacturing
2099 Food Preparations Manufacturing
2111 Cigarette Manufacturing
2121 Cigar Manufacturing
2131 Chewing & Smoking Tobacco & Snuff Manufacturing
2141 Tobacco Stemming & Redrying
2141z Tobacco Products
2211 Cotton Broadwoven Fabric Mills
2211a Cotton Mills
2221 Manmade Fabric & Silk Broadwoven Fabric Mills
2231 Wool Broadwoven Fabric Mills Including Dyeing & Finishing
2241 Narrow & Other Smallware Cotton Wool Silk & Manmade Fiber Fabric Mill
2251 Womens Full & Knee Length Hosiery Except Socks - Knitting Mills
2252 Hosiery Knitting Mills
2253 Knit Outerwear Mills
2254 Knit Underwear & Nightwear Mills
2254a Underwear Manufacturers & Wholesalers
2257 Weft Knit Fabric Mills
2258 Lace & Warp Knit Fabric Mills
2258a Knitted Fabrics
2258b Lace Goods Manufacturing
2259 Knitting Mills
2261 Cotton Broadwoven Fabric Finishing Plants
2262 Manmade Fiber & Silk Broadwoven Fabric Finishing Plants
2269 Textile Finishing Plants
2273 Carpet & Rug Mills
2273a Woven Carpet & Rug Mills
2273b Tufted Carpet & Rug Mills
2281 Yarn Spinning Mills
2282 Yarn Texturizing Throwing Twisting & Winding Yarn Mills
2284 Thread Mills
2295 Coated Fabric Not Rubberized Manufacturing
2296 Tire Cord & Fabric Manufacturing
2297 Nonwoven Fabric Manufacturing
2298 Cordage & Twine Manufacturing

2299 Textile Goods Processing & Manufacturing
2299a Felt Goods Except Woven Hats
2299b Upholstery Fillings & Padding Manufacturing
2299c Processing of Textile Waste
2311 Men & Boys Suit Coat & Overcoat Manufacturing
2311a Men & Boys Tailored Jackets
2321 Men & Boys Shirt Except Work Shirts Manufacturing
2322 Men & Boys Underwear & Nightwear Manufacturing
2322a Men & Boys Purchased Material Nightwear
2323 Men & Boys Neckwear Manufacturing & Wholesale
2325 Men & Boys Separate Trouser & Slack Manufacturing
2326 Men & Boys Work Clothing Manufacturing
2329 Men & Boys Clothing Manufacturing
2331 Womens Misses & Juniors Blouse & Shirt Manufacturing
2335 Womens Misses & Juniors Dress Manufacturing
2337 Womens Misses & Juniors Suit Skirt & Coat Manufacturing
2339 Womens Misses & Juniors Outerwear Manufacturing
2341 Women Misses Childrens & Infants Underwear & Nightwear Manufacturing
2341a Lingerie Manufacturing & Wholesale
2342 Brassiere Girdle & Allied Garment Manufacturing
2353 Hat Cap & Millinery Manufacturing
2353a Millinery Manufacturing
2353b Hat & Cap Manufacturing
2361 Girls Childrens & Infants Dresses Blouses & Shirts
2369 Girls Childrens & Infants Outerwear Manufacturing
2369a Children & Infant Coats & Suit Manufacturing
2371 Fur Goods Manufacturing
2381 Dress & Work Gloves Except Knit & All Leather Manufacturing
2384 Robe & Dressing Gown Manufacturing
2385 Waterproof Outerwear Manufacturing
2386 Leather & Sheep Lined Clothing Manufacturing
2386a Leather Apparel Manufactures
2387 Apparel Belt Manufacturing & Wholesale
2389 Apparel & Accessory Manufacturing
2391 Curtain & Drapery Manufacturing
2392 Housefurnishing Except Curtain & Drapes Manufacturing
2393 Textile Bag Manufacturing
2394 Canvas & Related Products Manufacturing
2394b Sailmakers
2395 Pleating Decorative & Novelty Stitching & Tucking for the Trade
2395b Quilting for the Trade
2396 Automobile Trimmings Apparel Findings & Related Product Manufacturing
2396a Ribbon Manufacturing & Wholesale
2397 Schiffli Machine Embroideries
2399 Fabricated Textile Products Manufacturing
2399b Coat Manufacturing & Wholesale

2399c Automobile Seatcover Manufacturing & Wholesale
2399d Emblem Manufacturing & Wholesale
2411 Logging
2411b Pulpwood Manufacturing
2421 General Sawmills & Planing Mills
2421a Lumber Manufacturing
2426 Hardwood Dimension & Flooring Mills
2429 Special Product Sawmills
2431 Millwork Plants
2434 Wood Kitchen Cabinet Manufacturing
2435 Hardwood Veneer & Plywood Manufacturing
2436 Softwood Veneer & Plywood Manufacturing
2439 Structural Wood Member Manufacturing
2441 Nailed & Lock Corner Wood Box & Shook Manufacturing
2448 Wood Pallet & Skid Manufacturing
2449 Wood Container Manufacturing
2451 Mobile Home Manufacturing
2452 Prefabricated Wood Building & Component Manufacturing
2491 Wood Preserving Plants
2493 Reconstituted Wood Product Manufacturing
2493a Fiberboard Manufacturing
2493b Particleboard Plants
2493c Hardboard Strandboard & Flakeboard Manufacturing
2499 Wood Product Manufacturing
2499b Cork & Cork Product Manufacturing & Wholesale
2499d Wood Mulch Manufacturing
2511 Wood Household Furniture Except Upholstered Manufacturing
2512 Wood Upholstered Household Furniture Manufacturing
2514 Metal Household Furniture Manufacturing
2515 Mattress Foundation & Convertible Bed Manufacturing
2517 Wood Tv Radio Phonograph & Sewing Machine Cabinet Manufacturing
2519 Household Furniture Manufacturing
2521 Wood Office Furniture Manufacturing
2522 Non-wood Office Furniture Manufacturing
2531 Public Building & Related Furniture Manufacturing
2531a Seating Companies
2541 Wood Office & Store Fixture Partition Shelving & Locker Manufacturing
2541a Wood Showcases Except Refrigerated Manufacturing
2542 Non-wood Office & Store Fixtures Partitions Shelving & Locker Mfrs
2542a Refrigerated Showcases Except Wood
2591 Drapery Hardware & Window Blind & Shade Manufacturing
2599 Furniture & Fixture Manufacturing
2599a Display Fixtures & Materials
2611 Pulp Mills
2621 Paper Mills
2631 Paperboard Mills

2652   Set up Paperboard Box Manufacturing
2653   Corrugated & Solid Fiber Box Manufacturing
2655   Fiber Can Tube Drum & Similar Product Manufacturing
2656   Sanitary Food Except Folding Container Manufacturing
2657   Folding Paperboard Box Including Sanitary Manufacturing
2671   Packaging Paper & Plastic Film Coated & Laminated Manufacturing
2672   Coated & Laminated Paper Manufacturing
2672a Paper Labels
2673   Plastic Foil & Coated Paper Bag Manufacturing
2674   Uncoated Paper & Multiwall Bag Manufacturing
2675   Die Cut Paper Paperboard & Cardboard Manufacturing
2676   Sanitary Paper Product Manufacturing
2677   Envelope Manufacturing & Wholesale
2678   Stationary Tablets & Related Products Manufacturing
2679   Converted Paper & Paperboard Product Manufacturing
2679a Pressed & Molded Pulp Goods
2711   Newspaper Publishing or Publishing & Printing
2721   Periodical Publishing or Publishing & Printing
2731   Book Publishing or Publishing & Printing
2732   Book Printing
2741   Miscellaneous Publishing
2741b Shoppers News Publications
2741c Art Publishers
2741e Catalog Compilers
2741f Map Publishers & Printers
2741g Music Publishers
2752   Commercial Lithographic Printing
2754   Commercial Gravure Printing
2759   Commercial Printing
2759a Silkscreen Printing
2759c Stationary Engravers
2759d Decal Manufacturing & Wholesale
2759e Business Card Printing
2759f Glass Metal & Plastic Etc Printing
2759g Embossing Services
2759h Imprinting
2759j Law Brief Printers
2759k Post Card Printers
2759l Poster Printers
2759m Thermographers
2759n Printing Brokers
2759o Wedding Announcements & Invitations Retail
2761   Manifold Business Form Manufacturing
2761b Sales & Order Books Manufacturing
2771   Greeting Card Publishing or Publishing & Printing
2782   Blankbook Looseleaf Binder & Device Manufacturing

2782a Album Manufacturing & Wholesale
2782b Book Catalog Etc Covers
2782c Loose Leaf Equipment & Supplies
2789 Bookbinding & Related Work
2791 Typesetting
2796 Platemaking & Related Services
2796a Platemaking Services
2796b Gravure Printing Plates
2796c Photoengraving
2796d Lithographing & Electrotying
2796e Positive & Negative Lithographic Plate Manufacturing
2812 Alkalies & Chlorine Manufacturing
2812a Chlorine Manufacturing & Wholesale
2813 Industrial Gas Manufacturing
2816 Inorganic Pigment Manufacturing
2819 Industrial Inorganic Chemical Manufacturing
2819a Hydrazine
2821 Plastics Material Synthetic Resin & Non-vulcanizable Elastomer Mfg
2822 Synthetic Rubber Vulcanizable Elastomers Manufacturing
2823 Cellulosic Manmade Fiber Manufacturing
2824 Non-cellulosic Manmade Organic Fiber Manufacturing
2833 Medical Chemical & Botanical Products Manufacturing
2834 Pharmaceutical Preparations Manufacturing
2835 in Vitro & in Vivo Diagnostic Substance Manufacturing
2836 Biological Products Except Diagnostic Substances Manufacturing
2841 Soap & Other Detergent Except Specialty Cleaners Manufacturing
2842 Specialty Cleaning Polishing & Sanitation Preparation Manufacturing
2842a Polish Manufacturing
2842b Sweeping Compound
2843 Surface Active & Finishing Agents Sulfonated Oil & Assistants Mfg
2844 Perfumes Cosmetics & Other Toilet Preparation Manufacturing
2844a Perfume Manufacturing & Wholesale
2851 Paint Varnish Lacquer Enamel & Allied Product Manufacturing
2851a Laquer Manufacturing
2861 Gum & Wood Chemical Manufacturing
2861a Dye & Dyestuff Manufacturing
2865 Cyclic Organic Crudes & Intermediates & Organic Dyes & Pigment Mfg
2869 Industrial Organic Chemical Manufacturing
2873 Nitrogenous Fertilizer Manufacturing
2874 Phosphatic Fertilizer Manufacturing
2875 Fertilizer Plants Mixing Only
2879 Pesticides & Agricultural Chemical Manufacturing
2879a Soil Conditioners
2891 Adhesive & Sealant Manufacturing
2892 Explosives Manufacturing
2893 Printing Ink Manufacturing

2895 Carbon Black Manufacturing
2899 Chemicals & Chemical Preparation Manufacturing
2899a Anti-freeze Compound Manufacturing & Wholesale
2899b Fireproofing Material Manufacturing
2899c Oil Treating Compounds
2911 Petroleum Refining
2951 Asphalt Paving Mixture & Block Manufacturing
2952 Asphalt Felt & Coating Manufacturing
2992 Lubricating Oil & Grease Manufacturing
2999 Petroleum & Coal Product Manufacturing
3011 Tire & Inner Tube Manufacturing
3021 Rubber & Plastic Footwear Manufacturing
3052 Rubber & Plastic Hose & Belting Manufacturing
3053 Gasket Packing & Sealing Device Manufacturing
3061 Molded Extruded & Lathe Cut Mechanical Rubber Good Manufacturing
3069 Fabricated Rubber Product Manufacturing
3069a Reclaimed Rubber Reworked by Manufacturing Processes
3069b Rubberized Printer Rolls & Blankets Manufacturing
3069c Rubber Band Manufacturing
3069d Rubber Clothing & Footwear Manufacturing
3081 Unsupported Plastics Film & Sheet Manufacturing
3082 Unsupported Plastic Profile Shape Manufacturing
3083 Laminated Plastics Plate Sheet & Profile Shape Manufacturing
3084 Plastic Pipe Manufacturing
3085 Plastic Bottle Manufacturing
3086 Plastic Foam Product Manufacturing
3087 Custom Compounding of Purchased Plastics Resins
3088 Plastics Plumbing Fixture Manufacturing
3089 Plastic Product Manufacturing
3111 Leather Tanning & Finishing
3111a Tanners
3131 Boot & Shoe Cut Stock & Findings Manufacturing
3142 House Slipper Manufacturing
3143 Mens Footwear Except Athletic Manufacturing
3144 Womens Footwear Except Athletic Manufacturing
3149 Footwear Except Rubber Manufacturing
3151 Leather Glove & Mitten Manufacturing
3161 Luggage Manufacturing
3171 Womens Handbag & Purse Manufacturing
3172 Personal Leather Goods Except Womens Handbags & Purses Manufacturing
3199 Leather Goods Manufacturing
3211 Flat Glass Manufacturing
3221 Glass Container Manufacturing
3229 Pressed & Blown Glass & Glassware Manufacturing
3229a Glass Blowers

3229b Glass Blocks & Structural Glass Etc
3231 Glass Products Made from Purchased Glass Manufacturing
3241 Hydraulic Cement Manufacturing
3251 Brick & Structural Clay Tile Manufacturing
3253 Wall & Floor Ceramic Tile Manufacturing
3255 Clay Refractories
3255a Brick Refractories
3259 Structural Clay Product Manufacturing
3261 Vitreous China & Earthenware Plumbing Fixtures Fittings & Bath Acc Mf
3262 Vitreous China Table & Kithchen Article Manufacturing
3263 Fine Earthenware Whiteware Table & Kitchen Article Manufacturing
3264 Porcelain Electrical Supplies Manufacturing
3269 Pottery Product Manufacturing
3271 Concrete Block & Brick Manufacturing
3272 Concrete Products Except Block & Brick Manufacturing
3273 Ready Mix Concrete Manufacturing
3274 Lime Manufacturing
3275 Gypsum Product Manufacturing
3281 Stone & Cut Stone Product Manufacturing
3281a Granite Manufacturing & Wholesale
3291 Abrasive Product Manufacturing
3291a Grinding Wheels
3292 Asbestos Product Manufacturing
3295 Minerals & Earths Ground or Otherwise Treated
3296 Mineral Wool Manufacturing
3297 Non-clay Refractories
3297b Industrial Ceramic Products
3299 Non-metallic Mineral Product Manufacturing
3312 Steel Works Blast Furnaces Including Coke Ovens & Rolling Mills
3313 Electrometallurgical Products Except Steel Manufacturing
3313a Spiegeleisen
3315 Steel Wiredrawing & Steel Nail & Spike Manufacturing
3316 Cold Rolled Steel Sheet Strip & Bar Manufacturing
3317 Steel Pipe & Tube Manufacturing
3321 Gray & Ductile Iron Foundries
3322 Malleable Iron Foundries
3324 Steel Investment Foundries
3325 Steel Foundries
3331 Primary Smelting & Refining of Copper
3334 Primary Production of Aluminum
3339 Primary Smelting & Refining of Nonferrous Metals Exc Copper & Aluminu
3339a Lead Primary Mills
3339b Zinc Primary Mills
3341 Secondary Smelting & Refining of Nonferrous Metals
3351 Rolling Drawing & Extruding of Copper
3353 Aluminum Sheet Plate & Foil Manufacturing

3354 Aluminum Extruded Product Manufacturing
3355 Aluminum Rolling & Drawing
3356 Rolling Drawing & Extruding of Non-ferrous Metals Exc Copper & Aluminu
3357 Drawing & Insulating of Non-ferrous Wire
3363 Aluminum Die Casting Manufacturing
3364 Non-ferrous Die Casting Except Aluminum Manufacturing
3364a Copper & Copper Base Alloy Die Casting Manufacturing
3364b Magnesium & Magnesium Base Die Cast
3365 Aluminum Foundries
3366 Copper Foundries
3369 Non-ferrous Foundries Except Aluminum & Copper
3398 Metal Heat Treating
3399 Primary Metal Product Manufacturing
3411 Metal Can Manufacturing
3412 Metal Shipping Barrel Drum Keg & Pail Manufacturing
3412b Cargo & Freight Container Manufacturing
3421 Cutlery Manufacturing & Wholesale
3423 Hand & Edge Tools Except Machine Tools & Handsaws Manufacturing
3423a Printers Mallets Manufacturing
3425 Saw Blade & Handsaw Manufacturing
3429 Hardware Manufacturing
3429a Clamp Manufacturing & Wholesale
3429b Lock Manufacturing & Wholesale
3431 Enameled Iron & Metal Sanitary Ware Manufacturing
3432 Plumbing Fixture Fitting and Trim Manufacturing
3432a Plastic Faucets & Spigots
3433 Heating Equipment Except Electric & Warm Air Furnances Manufacturing
3433b Solar Energy Equipment & Systems Manufacturing & Distribution
3441 Fabricated Structural Metal Manufacturing
3441a Expansion Joint Manufacturing
3441b Tower Manufacturing
3442 Metal Doors Sash Frames Molding & Trim Manufacturing
3443 Fabricated Plate Work Boiler Shops
3443a Septic Tanks & Systems Manufacturing & Wholesale
3443b Gas Cylinders
3443c Boiler Plate Smokestack Manufacturing
3444 Sheet Metal Work Manufacturing
3446 Architectural & Ornamental Metal Work Manufacturing
3446c Architectural & Ornamental Iron Work Manufacturing & Wholesale
3446d Brass Product Manufacturing
3446e Flag Poles Manufacturing & Wholesale
3446f Grating Manufacturing
3448 Prefabricated Metal Buildings & Component Manufacturing
3449 Miscellaneous Structural Metal Work Manufacturing
3449a Metal Curtain Walls
3451 Screw Machine Product Manufacturing

3452 Bolt Nut Screw Rivet & Washer Manufacturing
3462 Iron & Steel Forging Manufacturing
3463 Non-ferrous Metal Forging Manufacturing
3465 Automobile Stamping Plants
3466 Crown & Closure Manufacturing
3469 Metal Stamping Manufacturing
3471 Electroplating, Plating, Polishing, Anodizing, & Coloring
3471a Metal Polishing
3471b Anodizing
3471c Metal Finishers
3471d Plating
3479 Coating,engraving & Allied Services
3479a Enameling, Japanning & Lacquering
3479c Protective Coating Application for the Trade
3479d Mechanical Engravers
3479e Galvanizing
3479f Pipe Lining & Coating
3479g Engraving Jewelry, Silverware & Metal for the Trade
3482 Small Arms Ammunition Manufacturing
3483 Ammunition Except Small Arms Manufacturing
3484 Small Arms Manufacturing
3489 Ordnance & Accessory Manufacturing
3491 Industrial Valve Manufacturing
3492 Fluid Power Valve & Hose Fitting Manufacturing
3492a Fluid Power Valve Manufacturing
3493 Steel Springs Except Wire Manufacturing
3494 Valves & Pipe Fitting Manufacturing
3495 Wire Spring Manufacturing
3496 Miscellaneous Fabricated Wire Product Manufacturing
3496a Wire Basket Manufacturing & Wholesale
3496b Wire Cloth Manufacturing
3497 Metal Foil & Leaf Manufacturing
3497a Gold Leaf Manufacturing
3498 Fabricated Pipe & Pipe Fitting Manufacturing
3499 Fabricated Metal Product Manufacturing
3511 Steam, Gas, & Hydraulic Turbines, & Turbine Generator Set Unit Mfg
3519 Internal Combustion Engine Manufacturing
3523 Farm Machinery & Equipment Manufacturing
3523e Barn Equipment
3524 Lawn & Garden Tractors & Equipment Manufacturing
3531 Construction Machinery & Equipment Manufacturing
3531a Mixing & Agitation Machinery Manufacturing
3531c Concrete Mixer Manufacturing
3531g Crushing & Pulverising Equipment Manufacturing
3532 Mining Machinery & Equipment, Except Oil & Gas Field Manufacturing
3533 Oil & Gas Field Machinery & Equipment Manufacturing

3534   Elevator & Moving Stairway Manufacturing
3534b Wheelchair Lifts & Ramps Manufacturing
3535   Conveyors & Conveying Equipment Manufacturing
3536   Overhead Traveling Cranes, Hoists, & Monorail System Manufacturing
3537   Industrial Truck, Tractor, Trailer, & Stacker Manufacturing
3537a Automatic Stacking Machine Manufacturing
3541   Metal Cutting Machine Tool Manufacturing
3541b Broaching Machinery Manufacturing
3541c Drilling & Boring Equipment & Supply Manufacturing
3541d Lathe Manufacturing & Wholsale
3541f Pipe Cutting & Threading Equipment
3541h Grinding Machines & Equipment
3542   Metal Forming Machine Tool Manufacturing
3543   Industrial Pattern Manufacturing
3544   Special Dies & Tools Die Sets, Jig Fixture & Industrial Mold Mfg
3544b Jigs & Fixtures
3544d Die Makers
3544e Mold Manufacturing
3545   Cutting Tools, Machine Tool Accessory & Precision Measuring Device Mfg
3546   Power Driven Hand Tool Manufacturing
3547   Rolling Mill Machinery & Equipment Manufacturing
3548   Electric & Gas Welding & Soldering Equipment Manufacturing
3548a Welding Apparatus Non-electric Manufacturing
3548b Welding Apparatus Other Manufacturing
3549   Metalworking Machinery Manufacturing
3552   Textile Machinery Manufacturing
3552a Industrial Textile Drying Equipment
3552b Knitting Machines
3553   Woodworking Machinery Manufacturing
3553a Furniture Manufacturing Equipment & Supplies
3553b Cabinet Maker Equipment & Supplies Manufacturing
3553c Sawmill Equipment & Supply Manufacturing
3554   Paper Industry Machinery Manufacturing
3555   Printing Trade Machinery & Equipment Manufacturing
3555b Bookbinders Machinery Manufacturing
3555d Typesetting Machine Manufacturing
3556   Food Product Machinery Manufacturing
3556b Meat Choppers & Grinders
3556f Ice Cream Manufacturing Equipment
3556h Popcorn Machine Manufacturing
3556j Slicing Machines
3559   Special Industry Machinery Manufacturing
3559a Plastics Machinery & Equipment
3559b Paint Manufacturing Equipment
3559c Metal Finishing Equipment & Supplies
3559d Tanners Equipment & Supply Manufacturing

3559e Rubber Working Equipment Manufacturing
3559f Cotton Ginning Equipment & Supplies Manufacturing
3559g Chemical Plant Equipment & Supplies Manufacturing
3559h Pottery Equipment & Supplies
3559j Tire Retreading & Repairing Equipment & Supplies Manufacturing
3559k Foundry Equipment and Supplies
3559l Shoe Manufacturing Equipment Manufacturing
3559m Wheel Alignment Frame & Axle Equipment Manufacturing
3559n Automobile Diagnostic Equipment Manufacturing
3559o Brake Service Equipment Manufacturing
3559p Tire Changing Equipment Manufacturing
3561 Pump & Pumping Equipment Manufacturing
3562 Ball & Roller Bearing Manufacturing
3563 Air & Gas Compressor Manufacturing
3564 Industrial & Commercial Fan Blower & Air Purification Equipment Mfg
3565 Packaging Machinery Manufacturing
3565a Bread Wrapping Machine Manufacturing
3566 Speed Changers, Industrial High Speed Device & Gear Manufacturing
3566a Gears & Gear Cutting
3567 Industrial Process Furnance & Oven Manufacturing
3568 Mechanical Power Transmission Equipment Manufacturing
3569 General Industrial Machinery & Equipment Manufacturing
3569d Liquid Filters
3569e Fire Department Equipment & Supplies
3569g Jacks Manufacturing & Wholesale
3569h Labeling Equipment Manufacturing & Wholesale
3569j Lubricating Devices & Systems
3571 Electronic Computer Manufacturing
3572 Computer Storage Device Manufacturing
3575 Computer Terminal Manufacturing
3577 Computer Peripheral Equipment Manufacturing
3578 Calculating & Accounting Machines, Except Computer Manufacturing
3579 Office Machine Manufacturing
3579a Typewriter Manufacturing
3581 Automatic Vending Machine Manufacturing
3582 Commercial Laundry Drycleaning & Pressing Machine Manufacturing
3585 Air Conditioning Warm Air Heating & Coml Indl Refrigeration Equipt Mf
3586 Measuring & Dispensing Pump Manufacturing
3589 Service Industry Machinery Manufacturing
3589b Industrial Waste Reduction & Disposal Equipment
3592 Carburetors, Pistons, Piston Rings & Valve Manufacturing
3593 Fluid Power Cylinders & Actuator Manufacturing
3594 Fluid Power Pump & Motor Manufacturing
3594a Hydraulic & Pneumatic Motors
3594b Hydrostatic Drives
3594c Fluid Power Equipment Manufacturing

3594d Hydraulic Aircraft Pumps
3596   Scales & Balance, Except Laboratory Manufacturing
3599   Industrial & Commercial Machinery & Equipment Manufacturing
3599a Machine Shops & Grinding Castings for the Trade
3599d Machine Tools Repairing Rebuilding
3599e Machinery Rebuilding & Repairing
3599f Machinery Custom Designed
3599k Electrical Discharge Machining
3612   Power Distribution & Specialty Transformer Manufacturing
3613   Switchgear & Switchboard Apparatus Manufacturing
3613a Electric Switchboards
3621   Motor & Generator Manufacturing
3624   Carbon & Graphite Product Manufacturing
3625   Relays & Industrial Control Manufacturing
3625a Electric Power Switches
3625b Industrial Control Manufacturing
3625c Electronic Relays & Switches
3625d Timing Devices
3629   Electrical Industrial Apparatus Manufacturing
3631   Household Cooking Equipment Manufacturing
3632   Household Refrigerators, Home & Farm Freezer Manufacturing
3633   Household Laundry Equipment Manufacturing
3634   Electric Houseware & Fan Manufacturing
3635   Household Vacuum Cleaner Manufacturing
3639   Household Appliance Manufacturing
3639a Buttonhole & Eyelet Machine Manufacturing
3641   Electric Lamp Bulb & Tube Manufacturing
3641a Electric Lamp Bulb Parts
3643   Current Carrying Wiring Device Manufacturing
3644   Non-current Carrying Wiring Device Manufacturing
3645   Residential Electric Lighting Fixture Manufacturing
3646   Commercial Industrial & Institutional Electric Lighting Fixture Mfg
3647   Vehicular Lighting Equipment Manufacturing
3648   Lighting Equipment Manufacturing
3651   Household Audio & Video Equipment Manufacturing
3651a Speaker Manufacturing & Wholesale
3652   Phonograph Record, Prerecorded Audio Tape & Disk Manufacturing
3661   Telephone & Telegraph Apparatus Manufacturing
3661a Modems & Other Interface Equipment Manufacturing
3661b Facsimile Communication Equipment
3663   Radio & Television Broadcasting & Communication Equipment Mfg
3663a Television Station Equipment
3669   Communications Equipment Manufacturing
3669a Microwave Communication Equipment & Systems
3669b Traffic Signals & Equipment
3671   Electron Tube Manufacturing

3671a Cathode Ray Television Tube Manufacturing
3671b Special Purpose Electron Tubes
3671c Electron Tubes
3672　Printed Circuit Board Manufacturing
3674　Semiconductor & Related Devices Manufacturing
3675　Electronic Capacitor Manufacturing
3676　Electronic Resistor Manufacturing
3677　Electronic Coil Transformer & Other Inducer Manufacturing
3677a Constant Impedance Transformer Manufacturing
3678　Electronic Connector Manufacturing
3679　Electronic Component Manufacturing
3679a Electrical Wire Harness Manufacturing
3679b Electronic Equipment & Supplies
3679c Electronic Power Supplies
3679d Relay Manufacturing
3691　Storage Battery Manufacturing
3692　Dry & Wet Primary Battery Manufacturing
3694　Electrical Equipment for Internal Combustion Engines Manufacturing
3695　Magnetic & Optical Recording Media Manufacturing
3699　Electrical Machinery Equipment & Supplies Manufacturing
3699a Electronic Transmission & Distribution Equipment Manufacturing
3699b Electronic Research & Development Equipment
3699c Laser Manufacturing
3699d Battery Charging Equipment Manufacturing
3711　Motor Vehicles and Passenger Car Body Manufacturing
3711b Automobile Body Manufacturing
3711d Bus Manufacturing & Distribution
3713　Truck & Bus Body Manufacturing
3714　Motor Vehicle Parts and Accessories Manufacturing
3714a Bus Parts & Supplies Manufacturing
3714b Drive Shaft Manufacturing & Wholesale
3714c Automobile Heater Manufacturing
3715　Truck Trailer Manufacturing
3716　Motor Home Manufacturing
3721　Aircraft Manufacturing
3724　Aircraft Engine & Engine Part Manufacturing
3724a Aircraft Engine Manufacturing
3728　Aircraft Parts & Auxiliary Equipment Manufacturing
3731　Ship Building & Repairing
3732　Boat Building & Repairing
3732a Boat Repairing Yards
3732b Boat Building Yards
3743　Railroad Equipment Manufacturing
3751　Motorcycles, Bicycles & Parts Manufacturing
3761　Guided Missile & Space Vehicle Manufacturing
3764　Guided Missile & Space Vehicle Propulsion Units & Parts Manufacturing

3769 Guided Missle & Space Vehicle Parts & Auxiliary Equipment Mfg
3792 Travel Trailer & Camper Manufacturing
3795 Tank & Tank Component Manufacturing
3799 Transportation Equipment Manufacturing
3812 Search Detection Navigation Guidance Aero & Water Systems & Instrumen
3821 Laboratory Apparatus & Furniture Manufacturing
3822 Automatic Controls for Regulating Environments & Appliances Mfg
3823 Industrial Instruments for Measurement Display & Control of Processin
3824 Totalizing Fluid Meters & Counting Device Manufacturing
3825 Instruments for Measuring & Testing of Electricity & Electrical Signal
3825b Electronic Testing Equipment Manufacturing
3826 Laboratory Analytical Intrument Manufacturing
3826a Scientific Instrument Manufacturing
3826b Analytical Instrument Manufacturing
3827 Optical Instruments & Lense Manufacturing
3829 Measuring & Controlling Device Manufacturing
3829a Geophysical & Meteorological Equipment
3829b Drafting & Survey Apparatus
3829c Photo Surveying Instruments
3841 Surgical & Medical Instruments & Apparatus Manufacturing
3842 Orthopedic Prosthetic & Surgical Appliances & Supplies Manufacturing
3842a Medical Adhesive Tape Manufacturing
3843 Dental Equipment & Supplies Manufacturing

3844 X-ray Apparatus, Tubes & Related Irradiation Apparatus Manufacturing
3845 Electromedical & Electrotherapeutic Apparatus Manufacturing
3851 Ophthalmic Goods Manufacturing
3861 Photographic Equipment & Supplies Manufacturing
3873 Watchs Clocks, Clockwork Operated Devices & Parts Manufacturing
3911 Precious Metal Jewelry Manufacturing
3914 Silverware Plated Ware & Stainless Steel Ware Manufacturing
3915 Jewelers Findings Materials & Lapidary Work Manufacturing
3931 Musical Instrument Manufacturing
3942 Dolls & Stuffed Toy Manufacturing
3944 Games, Toys & Childrens Vehicles Except Doll & Bicycle Manufacturing
3949 Sporting & Athletic Goods Manufacturing
3949a Golfing Equipment Manufacturing
3951 Pens, Mechanical Pencils & Parts Manufacturing
3952 Crayons, Pencils & Artists Materials Manufacturing
3953 Marking Device Manufacturing
3955 Carbon Paper & Inked Ribbon Manufacturing
3961 Costume Jewelry & Costume Novelties Except Precious Metals Mfg
3965 Fasteners, Buttons, Needles & Pin Manufacturing
3965a Button Manufacturing
3965b Needles, Pins & Other Notions Manufacturing
3965c Buckle Manufacturing

3991 Broom & Brush Manufacturing
3993 Sign & Advertising Specialty Manufacturing
3993a Display Designers & Producers
3993c Electric & Neon Sign Manufacturing
3993e Name Plate Makers
3995 Burial Casket Manufacturing
3996 Linoleum Asphalted Felt Base & Other Hard Floor Covering Mfg
3999 Manufacturing Industries
3999a Model Makers
3999b Puppets & Marionettes Manufacturing & Wholesale
3999c Lamp Shade Manufacturing & Wholesale
3999d Artificial Flower Manufacturing
3999e Gold Stamping for the Trade
3999f Match Manufacturing
3999k Marine Shells
3999l Die Cutting
4011 Line Haul Operating Railroads
4013 Railroad Switching & Terminal Establishments
4111 Local & Suburban Transit
4111a Airport Transportation Services
4119 Local Passenger Transportation
4119a Ambulance Services
4119b Limousine Services
4121 Taxicab Companies
4131 Intercity & Rural Bus Transportation
4141 Local Bus Charter Services
4142 Bus Charter Services Except Local
4151 School Bus Services
4173 Terminal & Service Facilities for Motor Vehicle Passenger Transportin
4173a Bus Terminal Services
4173b Motor Vehicle Services
4212 Local Trucking Without Storage
4212a Local Delivery Services
4212b Cartage & Express Service Local
4213 Trucking Except Local
4213a Mobile Home Transporting Companies
4213b Contract Haulers Except Local
4213c Heavy Hauling Trucking
4213k Horse Transporting
4213m Refrigerated Trucking
4214 Local Trucking with Storage
4215 Courier Services Except by Air
4215a Messenger Services
4221 Farm Product Warehousing & Storage
4221a Grain Elevators
4221c Tobacco Warehouses

4221f Commodity Warehouses
4222   Refrigerated Warehousing & Storage
4222a Cold Storage Warehouses
4222b Frozen Food Lockers
4225   General Warehouses
4225d Rental & Self Service Warehouses
4226   Special Warehousing & Storage
4226a Private & Public Household Warehouses
4226b Camping & Travel Trailer Storage
4226c Recreational Vehicle Storage
4226e Trailer Storage
4231   Terminal Maintenance Facilities for Motor Freight Transportation
4311   Government Postal Service
4412   Deep Sea Foreign Transportation of Freight
4412b Containerized Freight Service
4424   Deep Sea Domestic Transportation of Freight
4424a Intercoastal Transportation
4424b Coastwise Transportation
4432   Freight Transportation on the Great Lakes & St Lawrence Seaway
4449   Water Transportation of Freight
4481   Deep Sea Transportation of Passengers Except Ferry
4482   Ferries
4489   Water Transportation of Passengers
4491   Marine Cargo Handling
4491a Marine Terminals
4491d Moorages
4492   Towing & Tugboat Services
4493   Marinas
4493h Marine Repairs
4499   Water Transportation Services
4499a Lighterage
4499b Canal Operation
4499d Ship Cleaning
4499e Boat Launching Services
4499f Boat Cleaning
4499j Boat Transporting Services
4499k Marine Salvage
4512   Air Transportation Scheduled
4512a Airlines Certified
4512b Airlines Non-certified
4512c Air Cargo & Express Package Services
4513   Air Courier Services
4522   Air Transportation Nonscheduled
4522a Air Ambulance Services
4522b Helicopter Charter & Rental Services
4581   Airports Flying Fields & Airport Terminal Services

4581a Airports & Aircraft Maintenance
4581b Airports with Terminals
4581c Airports Without Terminals
4581d Flying Fields
4581e Military Fields
4581f Aircraft Services & Maintenance
4581g Airport Terminal Services
4581j Aircraft Storage
4581k Aircraft Upholsterers
4581l Aircraft Ferrying & Transportation Services
4612 Crude Petroleum Pipelines
4613 Refined Petroleum Pipelines
4619 Pipelines
4724 Travel Agencies
4724a Transportation Arrangements
4725 Tour Operators
4725g Wholesale Tours
4729 Arragement of Passenger Transportation
4729a Airline Ticket Offices
4729b Steamship Ticket Offices
4729c Passenger Transportation Services
4731 Arrangement of Transportation of Freight & Cargo
4731a Freight Transportation Services
4731b Freight Forwarders
4731c Freight Consolidators
4731e Transportation Brokerage
4731f Customs & Custom House Brokers
4741 Railroad Cars Rental
4741a Railroad Car Rental with Services
4741b Railroad Car Rental Without Services
4783 Packing & Crating Services for Shipping
4785 Fixed Facilities, Inspection & Weighing Services for Motor Vehicles
4785a Motor Vehicle Inspection & Weighing Services
4785b Tunnels Toll Roads & Bridges
4789 Transportation Services
4812 Radiotelephone Communications
4812d Paging & Signaling Services
4812e Mobile Telephone Services
4813 Telephone Communication Except Radiotelephone
4813a Long Distance Telephone Services
4822 Telegraph & Other Message Communications
4822b Facsimile Transmission Service
4832 Radio Broadcasting Stations
4833 Television Broadcasting Stations
4833c Community Tv Services Antennas
4841 Cable & Other Pay Television Services

4841a Cable Television Services
4899 Communication Services
4899a Data Communications Services
4899c Statellite Communication Services
4911 Electric Services
4922 Natural Gas Transmission
4923 Natural Gas Transmission & Distribution
4924 Natural Gas Distribution
4925 Mixed Manufactured or Lpg Production &/or Distribution
4931 Electric and Other Services Combined
4932 Gas and Other Services Combined
4939 Combination Utilities
4941 Water Supply
4952 Sewerage Systems
4953 Refuse Systems
4959 Sanitary Services
4961 Steam and Air Conditioning Supply
4971 Irrigation Systems
5012 Automobile & Other Motor Vehicles Distribution & Wholesale
5012a Trucks Wholsale
5012b Automobile & Truck Trailers Wholsale
5012c Campers, Recreational Vehicles & Pickup Coachs Distribution & Wholesal
5012e Automobile Brokers
5012h New & Used Buses Distribution & Wholesale
5013 Motor Vehicle Supplies & New Parts Wholesale
5013a Automobile Parts Wholesale
5013b Truck Trailer Equipment Wholsale
5013c Automobile Services Equipment Wholesale
5013d Motorcycle Parts Wholesale
5013t Automobile Radio & Stereo Systems Wholesale
5013u Mufflers & Exhaust Systems Wholesale
5013w Automobile Radiators Wholesale
5013z Truck Bodies Wholesale
5014 Tires & Tubes Wholesale
5015 Used Motor Vehicle Parts Wholesale or Retail
5015a Used & Rebuilt Auto Supplies Wholesale or Retail
5015c Used Automobile Parts Wholesale or Retail
5021 Furniture Wholesale
5021a Office Furniture Wholesale
5021b Lockers Wholesale
5021c Shelving Wholesale
5021h Kitchen Cabinets Wholesale
5021j Water Beds Wholesale
5021k Outdoor Furniture Wholesale
5021l Beds Wholesale
5021m Mattresses Wholesale

5023　Homefurnishings Wholesale
5023a Carpet Rug & Floor Coverings Wholesale
5023b Chinaware & Glassware Wholesale
5023c Draperies Wholesale
5023d Housewares Wholesale
5023e Decorating Supplies Wholesale
5023f Lamps & Lampshades Wholesale
5023g Fireplace Equipment Wholesale
5023h Bedding Wholesale
5023j Venetian Blinds Wholesale
5023n Bedspreads Wholesale
5023p Bathroom Fixtures & Accessories Wholesale
5023s Closets & Closet Accessories Wholesale
5023w Vertical Blinds Wholesale
5023x Linens Wholesale
5023y Towels Wholesale
5023z Shower Curtains Wholesale
5031　Lumber, Plywood, Millwork & Wood Panels Wholesale
5031d Plywood & Veneers Wholesale
5031f Cabinets Wholesale
5031j Door Frames Wholesale
5031k Moldings Wholesale
5031l Doors Wholesale
5032　Brick Stone & Related Construction Materials Wholesale
5032b Ceramic Tile Wholesale
5032c Concrete Blocks, Shapes & Construction Products Wholesale
5032d Crushed & Natural Stone Wholesale
5032f Sand & Gravel Wholesale
5032g Brick Dealers Wholesale
5032h Cement Wholesale
5033　Roofing Siding & Insulation Materials Wholesale
5039　Construction Materials Wholesale
5039a Building Materials Wholesale
5039e Non-ceramic Tile Wholesale
5039n Glass Wholesale
5039p Mosiacs Wholesale
5039q Poles Wholesale
5039s Fence Materials Wholesale
5039u Mobile Home Dealers Wholesale
5039v Energy Conversation Construction Materials Wholesale
5043　Photographic Equipment & Supplies Wholesale
5043b Audio Visual Equipment Wholesale
5043d Motion Picture Film Wholesale
5043e Motion Picture Equipment & Supplies Wholesale
5043f Projection Apparatus Wholesale
5044　Office Equipment Wholesale

5044a Duplicating Machines Wholesale
5044b Blue Print Equipment & Supplies Wholesale
5044c Dictating Machines Wholesale
5044d Cash Registers Wholesale
5044e Accounting Machines Except Machines Readable Wholesale
5044f Safes & Vaults Wholesale
5044g Calculators Wholesale
5044h Photocopy Machines Wholesale
5044i Addressing Machines Wholesale
5044m Bank Equipment & Supplies Wholesale
5044n Word Processing Equipment Wholesale
5044o Paper Shredding Machines Wholesale
5044x Accounting & Bookkeeping Systems Wholesale
5045 Computers & Computer Peripheral Equipment & Software Wholesale
5045a Machine Readable Programed Accounting Machines Wholesale
5046 Commercial Equipment Wholesale
5046a Hotel & Motel Equipment & Supplies Wholesale
5046b Restaurant & Food Service Equipment Wholesale
5046c Store Fixtures Wholesale
5046d Scales Except Laboratory Wholesale
5046e Coin Operated Vending & Amusement Devices Wholesale
5047 Medical Dental & Hospital Equipment & Supplies Wholesale
5047a Dental Equipment & Supplies Wholesale
5047b Oxygen Therapy Equipment Wholesale
5047c Hospital & Lab Equipment & Supplies Wholesale
5047d Veterinarian Supplies Wholesale
5047e Physician Equipment & Supplies Wholesale
5047f Hospital Beds Wholesale
5048 Ophthalmic Goods Wholesale
5048a Opticians Goods Wholesale
5049 Professional Equipment & Supplies Wholesale
5049b Drafting Supplies Wholesale
5049c Scientific Apparatus Wholesale
5049d Surveyors Instruments Wholesale
5049e Religious Equipment & Supplies Wholesale
5049h School Supplies Wholesale
5051 Metal Service Centers & Offices Wholesale
5051a Aluminum Distributors
5051b Brass & Copper Distributors
5051d Steel Service and Warehousing
5051h Concrete Reinforcements Wholesale
5051l Investment Castings Wholesale
5051m Non-electrical Wire & Cable Wholesale
5051n Iron Wholesale
5051r Nails & Tacks Wholesale
5051z Pipe Wholesale

5052   Coal & Other Minerals & Ores Wholesale
5052a Coal & Coke Wholesale
5063   Electrical Apparatus Equipment Wiring Supplies & Construction Material
5063a Burglar Alarm Systems Equipment & Supplies Wholesale
5063c Electric Motors Wholesale
5063d Generators Wholesale
5063e Fire Alarm System Distribution & Wholesale
5063f Electric Lighting Fixtures Equipment & Apparatus Wholesale
5063g Electrical Signs Wholesale
5063h Storage Batteries Wholesale
5063n Electrical Meters Wholesale
5063o Transformers Wholesale
5063q Dry Cell Batteries Wholesale
5063r Electric Motor Supplies Wholesale
5063s Electrical Signal Systems Wholesale
5064   Electrical Appliances Television & Radio Sets Wholesale
5064a Radio & Hi Fi Equipment Wholesale
5064b Refrigerators & Freezers Wholesale
5064d Vacuum Cleaners Wholesale
5064e Major Appliances Wholesale
5064f Small Appliances Wholesale
5064g Video Recorders & Players Wholesale
5064m Electric Shavers Wholesale
5064n Television Sets Wholesale
5065   Electronic Parts & Equipment Wholesale
5065a Paging & Signaling Equipment Wholesale
5065b Closed Circuit Television Equipment Wholesale
5065c Radio Supplies & Parts Wholesale
5065d Recording & Sound Equipment & Supplies Wholesale
5065e Telephone Equipment Intercoms & Related Equipment Wholesale
5065f Television or Television & Radio Parts & Supplies Wholesale
5065g Data Communication Systems Wholesale
5065j Electronic Manufacturer Representatives
5065k Electronic Intruments Wholesale
5065l Electronic Parts Assemblers
5065t Mobile Telephone Equipment & Supplies Wholesale
5065v Stereo Parts Wholesale
5065w Radar Equipment & Supplies Wholesale
5065x Facsimile Equipment & Supplies Wholesale
5072   Hardware Wholesale
5072d Pneumatic Tools Wholesale
5072e Hand & Hand Power Tools Wholesale
5072g Cutlery Wholesale
5072j Builders Hardware Wholesale
5072k Door Checks & Closers Wholesale
5072l Locks & Related Materials Wholesale

5074 Plumbing & Hydronic Heating Equipment & Supplies Wholesale
5074a Oil Burners Wholesale
5074b Plumbing Supplies Wholesale
5074c Water Heaters Wholesale
5074d Boiler Distribution & Wholesale
5074e Solar Heating Panels & Equipment Wholesale
5075 Warm Air Heating & Air Conditioning Equipment & Supplies Wholesale
5075a Furnaces Wholesale
5075b Electrical Heating Equipment & Supplies Wholesale
5075d Air Cleaning & Conditioning (Humidity Control Etc) Equipment Wholesale
5075p Heating Systems & Units Wholesale
5075q Furnance Parts & Supplies Wholesale
5075r Air Conditioning Systems & Equipment Wholesale
5078 Refrigeration Equipment & Supplies Wholesale
5078a Ice Making Equipment Wholesale
5082 Construction & Mining Except Petroleum Machinery & Equipment Wholesale
5082a Contractor Machinery Equipment & Supplies Wholesale
5082d Sewer Cleaning Equipment & Supplies Wholesale
5082e Mason Contractors Equipment & Supplies Wholesale
5082g Rubbish Removal Contractors Equipment & Supplies Wholesale
5082h Water Well Drilling Equipment & Supplies Wholesale
5082j Excavating Equipment Wholesale
5082k Dry Wall Contractor Equipment & Supplies Wholesale
5082n Sandblasting Equipment & Supplies Wholesale
5082x Mining Equipment Wholesale
5083 Farm & Garden Machinery & Equipment Wholesale
5083a Farm Tractors Wholesale
5083g Baling Equipment Equipment & Supplies Wholesale
5083j Sprinklers Garden & Lawn Wholesale
5083m Poultry Equipment & Supplies Wholesale
5083n Farm & Livestock Machinery & Equipment Exc Dairy Wholesale
5083o Dairy Equipment & Supplies Wholesale
5084 Industrial Machinery & Equipment Wholesale
5084a Air & Gas Compressor Dealers Wholesale
5084b Drilling Equipment Wholesale
5084c Industrial Trucks Wholesale
5084d Machinery & Machine Tools Wholesale
5084e Material Handling & Shop Equipment Wholesale
5084f Printing & Lithographing Equipment Wholesale
5084g Pumps Wholesale
5084h Industrial Waste Compactors Wholesale
5084i Welding Equipment & Supplies Wholesale
5084j Safety Equipment Wholesale
5084k Silk Screening Materials Wholesale
5084l Gasoline or Diesel Engines Wholesale
5084m Tool & Die Makers Equipment Wholesale

5084n Industrial Fans Wholesale
5084o Garbage Container Receptacles Wholesale
5084p Robots Wholesale
5084q Audio & Video Recording Studio Equipment Wholesale
5084r Tanks Wholesale
5084s Measuring & Testing Equipment Wholesale
5084v Gauges & Gages Wholesale
5084y Cutting Tools Wholesale
5084z Plating Equipment & Supplies Wholesale
5085   Industrial Supplies Wholesale
5085a Abrasives Wholesale
5085d Packaging Materials Including Rope & Twine Wholesale
5085g Industrial Fasteners Wholesale
5085h Hose & Tubing Wholesale
5085i Buffing & Polishing Supplies Wholesale
5085l Sprockets Wholesale
5085mMechanical Packings Wholesale
5085p Industrial Fittings Wholesale
5085q Elevator Supplies & Parts
5085r Filtering Materials & Supplies Wholesale
5085s Industrial Diamonds Wholesale
5085z Valves & Valve Fittings Wholesale
5087   Service Establishment Equipment & Supplies Wholesale
5087a Barber Shop Equipment & Supplies Wholesale
5087b Beauty Shop Equipment & Supplies Wholesale
5087c Cleaners & Laundry Equipment & Supplies Wholesale
5087d Funeral Director Equipment Wholesale
5087e Janitor Supplies Wholesale
5087f Upholsterer Supplies Wholesale
5087l Shoe Findings & Supplies Wholesale
5087n Bird Barriers, Repellents & Controls Wholesale
5088   Transportation Equipment & Supplies Except Motor Vehicles Wholesale
5088e Ship Chandlers
5091   Sporting & Recreational Goods & Supplies Wholesale
5091a Swimming Pools & Hot Tubs Equipment & Supplies Wholesale
5091f Golf Equipment & Supplies Wholesale
5091h Pleasure Boat Distribution & Wholesale
5091j Pleasure Boat Equipment & Supplies Wholesale
5091k Bicycles Wholesale
5092   Toys & Hobby Goods & Supplies Wholesale
5092a Home Video Games Wholesale
5092c Dolls Wholesale
5093   Scrap & Waste Materials Wholesale
5093a Scrap Iron & Metal Wholesale
5093b Wastepaper Wholesale
5093c Automobile & Truck Wreckers for Scrap

5093i Plastic Scrap Wholesale
5093j Cotton Wool & Synthetic Waste Etc Wholesale
5093l Oil Waste Wholesale
5094   Jewelry Watches Precious Stones & Precious Metals Wholesale
5094c Clocks Wholesale
5094d Precious Metal Buyers & Sellers
5094e Diamonds Wholesale
5094f Watches Wholesale
5094h Jewelers Supplies Wholesale
5094j Jewerly Buyers
5094m Precious Semi Precious & Synthetic Gem Stones Wholesale
5099   Durable Goods Wholesale
5099a Fire Protection Equipment Wholesale
5099b Luggage Wholesale
5099c Manufacturers Agents
5099d Musical Instruments & Parts & Supplies Wholesale
5099e Compact Discs
5099f Import Products & Services Wholesale
5099t Sunglasses & Sun Goggles Wholesale
5099u Brooms Wholesale
5099v Solar Energy Equipment & Supplies Wholesale
5111   Printing & Writing Paper Wholesale
5112   Stationery & Office Supplies Wholesale
5112a Data Processing Supplies Wholesale
5112g Pens & Pencils Wholesale
5112h Commercial Stationary Wholesale
5112l Legal Forms Wholesale
5113   Industrial & Personal Service Paper Wholesale
5113a Packing Materials for Shipping Wholesale
5113d Paper Tubes & Cores Wholesale
5113e Specialty & Fancy Boxes Wholesale
5122   Drugs, Drug Proprietaries & Druggist Sundries Wholesale
5122a Druggists Pharmaceutical Products Wholesale
5122b Cosmetics Wholesale
5122f Abdominal Supports Wholesale
5122g Ostomy Equipment & Supplies Wholesale
5122h Hair Preparations Wholesale
5131   Piece Goods Notions & Other Dry Goods Wholesale
5131a Piece Goods Wholesale
5131c Bridal Supplies Wholesale
5131d Knit Goods Wholesale
5131e Zippers Wholesale
5131f Cotton Goods Wholesale
5131g Drapery Fabric Wholesale
5131h Textile Converters Except Kint Goods Wholesale
5131i Clothing Buttons Wholesale

5131j Textile Brokers
5131k Cotton Goods Converters
5136 Men & Boys Clothing & Furnishings Wholesale
5136a Work & Industrial Gloves Wholesale
5136b Mens Sportswear Wholesale
5136e Shirts Wholesale
5136f Hats Wholesale
5136h Caps Wholesale
5137 Women Children & Infants Clothing & Accessories Wholesale
5137a Womens Rack Merchandise Jobbers
5137b Womens Sportswear Wholesale
5137f Dresses Wholesale
5137g Womens Swimming Suits Wholesale
5137h Womens Uniforms Wholesale
5137j Handbag Wholesale
5137k Womens Hosiery Wholesale
5139 Footwear Wholesale
5141 General Line Groceries Wholesale
5141a Food Brokers
5142 Packaged Frozen Foods Wholesale
5143 Dairy Products Except Dried or Canned Wholesale
5143b Cheese Wholesale
5143c Butter Wholesale
5144 Poultry & Poultry Products Wholesale
5145 Confectionery Wholesale
5145d Syrup Wholesale
5145e Pretzels Wholesale
5146 Fish & Seafood Wholesale & Brokers
5146a Fish & Seafood Wholesale
5146b Fish & Seafood Brokers
5147 Meat & Meat Products Wholesale
5147a Meat Brokers
5148 Fresh Fruits & Vegetables Wholesale
5148c Produce Brokers
5148d Citrus Fruit Wholesale
5148f Fruit & Vegetable Growers & Shippers
5148g Citrus Fruit & Vegetable Brokers
5148h Potatoes Wholesale
5149 Groceries and Related Products Wholesale
5149g Rice Wholesale
5149h Vegetable Oil Wholesale
5149k Coffee Wholesale
5149l Fruit & Vegetable Juice Distribution & Wholesale
5149m Ice Cream Cone Distribution & Wholesale
5149n Tortillas Wholesale
5149p Chocolate Wholesale

5149r Dried Fruits Wholesale
5149s Coffee & Tea Wholesale
5149x Salads Wholesale
5153   Grain & Field Beans Wholesale
5153a Grain Brokers
5154   Livestock Wholesale
5159   Farm Product Raw Materials Wholesale
5159a Peanut Products Wholesale
5159b Cotton Wholesale
5159c Hides Wholesale
5162   Plastics Materials & Basic Forms & Shapes Wholesale
5162h Polyurethane Products Wholesale
5169   Chemicals & Allied Products Wholesale
5169a Compressed Gas Except Lpg Wholesale
5169l Ammonia Wholesale
5171   Petroleum Bulk Stations & Terminals Wholesale
5172   Petroleum & Petroleum Products Except Bulk & Terminals Wholesale
5172a Liquefied Petroleum Gas Wholesale
5172p Grease Wholesale
5181   Beer & Ale Wholesale
5182   Wine & Distilled Alcoholic Beverages Wholesale
5191   Farm Supplies Wholesale
5191a Feed & Fertilizer Dealers Wholesale
5191r Agricultural Chemicals Exc Fertilizers Wholesale
5191t Beekeepers Supplies Wholesale
5192   Books, Periodicals & Newspapers Wholesale
5192a Books Wholesale
5192b Newspaper & Magazine Distributors
5193   Flowers Nursery Stock & Florists Supplies Wholesale
5193a Plants Wholesale
5194   Tobacco & Tobacco Products Wholesale
5194d Tobacco Products Wholesale
5198   Paint Varnish & Supplies Wholesale
5198a Paint & Varnish Wholesale
5198b Wallpaper Wholesale
5198d Colors & Pigments Wholesale
5199   Nondurable Goods Wholesale
5199a Advertising Specialties Wholesale
5199b Burlap Cotton or Canvas Bags Wholesale
5199c Carnival Supplies Wholesale
5199e Foam Rubber Wholesale
5199f General Merchandise Wholesale
5199g Giftware & Novelties Wholesale
5199h Art Gallery Supplies Wholesale
5199j Leather & Leather Goods Wholesale
5199m Variety Store Merchandise Wholesale

5199n Yarn Wholesale
5211 Building Materials Dealers Retail
5211a Lumber Plywood & Building Materials Retail
5211b Roofing & Siding Materials Retail
5211c Window Jalousy & Door Dealers Retail
5211d Home Centers Retail
5211e Brick Dealers Retail
5211f Wallboard & Paneling Dealers Retail
5211g Fencing Materials Dealers Retail
5211h Door & Window Screens Retail
5211i Cement & Concrete Retail
5211j Portable Buildings Retail
5211k Energy Conservation Building Materials Retail
5211l Hardwoods Retail
5211mCeiling Materials Retail
5211n Overhead Doors Retail
5211o Heating & Plumbing Supplies Retail
5231 Paint Glass & Wallpaper Stores
5231a Paint & Glass Dealers Retail
5231b Wallpaper & Wallcovering Dealers Retail
5231c Stained & Leaded Glass Retail
5251 Hardware Stores
5251a Chainsaw Dealers Retail
5261 Nurseries Lawn & Garden Supply Shops Retail
5261a Nurserymen
5261b Lawn & Garden Supply Stores Retail
5261c Lawn Mower Dealers Retail
5261d Fertilizer Dealers Retail
5261f Insecticides Retail
5261t Weed Control Equipment & Supplies Retail
5261v Bark Retail
5271 Mobile Home Dealers Retail
5271a Mobile Home Equipment & Parts Dealers Retail
5311 Department Stores
5311a Discount Department Stores
5331 Variety Stores
5399 Miscellaneous General Merchandise Stores
5399a Army & Navy Goods Stores
5399b Salvage & Surplus Stores Retail
5411 Grocery Stores
5411c Convenience Food Stores
5411f Food Marts
5411g Food Plans Retail
5421 Meat & Fish & Seafood Markets Including Freezer Provisioners Retail
5421a Freezer Meat Provisioners Retail
5421c Meat & Fish Markets Combined Retail

5421d Meat Markets Retail
5421e Fish & Seafood Stores Retail
5431 Fruit & Vegetable Markets Retail
5431b Farm Markets Retail
5441 Candy Nut & Confectionery Stores Retail
5441a Candy & Confectionery Stores Retail
5441b Nut Stores Retail
5451 Dairy Products Stores Retail
5451a Cheese Stores Retail
5451b Milk & Dairy Products Stores Retail
5451d Yogurt Retail
5461 Bakeries Retail
5461a Bakeries Baking & Selling Retail
5461b Bakeries Selling Only Retail
5461c Bagels Stores Retail
5461d Donut Shops
5461e Cake & Pie Bakers Retail
5461f Cookie Shops Retail
5499 Miscellaneous Food Stores
5499a Health Food Herb & Vitamin Stores Retail
5499b Coffee & Tea Dealers Retail
5499c Poultry Stores Retail
5499d Gourmet Shops Retail
5499e Japanese Food Products Retail
5499f Delicatessens
5511 New & Used Motor Vehicle Dealers Retail
5511a New & Used Car Dealers Retail
5511b Truck & Trailer Dealers Retail
5521 Used Only Motor Vehicle Dealers Retail
5521a Antique & Classic Car Dealers Retail
5521b Used Car Dealers Retail
5531 Automobile & Home Supply Stores Retail
5531a Automobile Parts & Accessory Stores Retail
5531b Truck Equipment & Parts Dealers Retail
5531c Tire Dealers Retail
5531e Racing Car Supply Dealers Retail
5541 Gasoline Service Stations
5551 Boat & Marine Supply Dealers Retail
5551a Boat Dealers Retail
5551b Marine Supply Stores Retail
5551c Outboard Motor Dealers Retail
5551f Raft Dealers Retail
5551j Yacht Dealers Retail
5561 Recreational Vehicle Dealers Retail
5561a Camper & Pickup Coach Dealers Retail
5561b Camping & Travel Trailer Dealers Retail

5561c Motorized Home Dealers Retail
5561j Recreational Vehicle Parts & Accessories Retail
5571 Motorcycle Dealers Retail
5571b Moped Dealers Retail
5571c All Terrain Vehicle Dealers Retail
5599 Automobile Dealers Retail
5599a Aircraft Dealers Retail
5599b Snowmobile Dealers Retail
5599c Utility Trailers Retail
5599d Aircraft Brokers
5611 Men & Boys Clothing & Accessory Stores Retail
5611a Work Clothing Stores Retail
5611b Boys Clothing & Furnishings Retail
5611k Mens Stores Retail
5621 Womens Clothing Stores Retail
5621a Boutiques
5621b Bridal Shops Retail
5621c Maternity Shops Retail
5632 Womens Accessory & Specialty Stores Retail
5632a Bra & Corset Shops Retail
5632c Lingerie Shops Retail
5632d Millinery Shops Retail
5632e Handbag Shops Retail
5632f Hosiery Stores Retail
5632h Furriers & Fur Shops Retail
5641 Childrens & Infant Wear Stores Retail
5641c Girls Apparel Retail
5651 Family Clothing Stores Retail
5651a Pants & Jean Stores Retail
5651b Knit Goods Shops Retail
5651c Glove & Mitten Shops Retail
5651d Sweater Shops Retail
5661 Shoe Stores Retail
5661a Custom & Orthopedic Shoe Stores Retail
5661b Athletic Footwear Stores Retail
5699 Miscellanous Apparel & Accessory Stores Retail
5699a Mens Custom Shirtmakers
5699b Mens Custom Tailors
5699c Custom Dressmakers
5699d Riding Apparel & Western Shops Retail
5699e Sports Apparel Stores Retail
5699f Uniform Stores Retail
5699g Wig, Toupee & Wiglet Stores Retail
5699h Caps & Gowns Retail
5699i Fashion Designers
5699j Clothing Designers

5699k Dancing Supplies Retail
5699l Costume Sales & Rental Retail
5699w Garments Printing & Lettering
5699x Sheepskin Specialty Stores Retail
5699z Swimwear & Accessories Retail
5712 Furniture Stores Retail
5712a Youth Furniture Stores Retail
5712b Custom Built Furniture Makers
5712d Kitchen Cabinets & Counter Stores Retail
5712e Mattress Stores Retail
5712f Outdoor & Garden Furniture Stores Retail
5712g Waterbed Dealers Retail
5712h Unfinished Furniture Stores Retail
5713 Floor Covering Stores Retail
5713a Carpet & Rug Dealers Retail
5713b Tile & Linoleum Dealers Retail
5714 Drapery Curtain & Upholstery Stores Retail
5719 Miscellanous Homefurnishing Stores Retail
5719a China & Glassware Stores Retail
5719b Fireplaces & Fireplace Equipment Stores Retail
5719c Kitchenware & Houseware Stores Retail
5719d Lamp & Lampshade Shops Retail
5719e Linen & Bedding Shops Retail
5719f Mirror Stores Retail
5719g Blinds & Shades Stores Retail
5719h Closet & Bathroom Accessories Retail
5719i Lighting Fixtures Stores Retail
5719j Wood & Coal Etc Stoves Retail
5719v Carved & Ornamental Glass Retail
5719x Pillows Retail
5722 Household Appliance Stores Retail
5722a Residential Room Air Conditioner Dealers Retail
5722b Major Appliance Dealers Retail
5722c Sewing Machine & Sewing Supplies & Attachment Dealers Retail
5722d Vacuum Cleaner Dealers Retail
5722e Household Fan Dealers Retail
5722f Small Electric Appliance Dealers Retail
5731 Consumer Electronics Stores Retail
5731a Radio Equipment & Parts Stores Retail
5731b Hi Fi Equipment Stores Retail
5731c Citizens Band Radio Stores Retail
5731d Television Dealers Retail
5731f Video Equipment & Supplies Retail
5731h Automobile Radio & Stereo Stores Retail
5731i Audio Visual Equipment Dealers Retail
5734 Computer & Computer Software Stores Retail

5734a Computers & Computer Equipment & Supplies Retail
5734b Computer Software Supplies & Parts Retail
5735 Record & Prerecorded Tape Stores Retail
5735a Record & Tape Outlet Stores Retail
5735e Video Tape & Disc Stores Retail
5736 Musical Instrument Stores Retail
5736a Sheet Music Stores Retail
5736b Piano Dealers Retail
5736c Organ Dealers Retail
5812 Restaurants
5812a Restaurants - American
5812b Restaurants - Chinese
5812c Restaurants - Barbecue
5812d Restaurants - Fast Food
5812e Restaurants - Cafeterias
5812f Restaurants - French
5812g Restaurants - German
5812h Restaurants - Greek
5812i Restaurants - Health
5812j Restaurants - Indian & Pakistan
5812k Restaurants - Drive in
5812l Restaurants - Italian
5812m Restaurants - Japanese
5812n Restaurants - Korean & Vietnamese
5812o Restaurants - Mexican
5812p Restaurants - Sandwich Shops
5812q Restaurants - Seafood
5812r Restaurants - Spanish
5812s Restaurants - Steak Houses
5812t Restaurants - Thai
5812u Restaurants - Pizza
5812v Caterers & Related Services
5812w Contract Food Services
5812x Ice Cream & Frozen Custard Stands & Parlors Retail
5812y Coffee & Donut Shops
5812z Concessionaires
5813 Alcoholic Beverage Drinking Places
5813a Bars & Cocktail Lounges
5813b Nightclubs
5813c Discotheques
5912 Drug & Proprietary Stores Retail
5912a Proprietary Stores Retail
5921 Liquor Stores Retail
5921a Wine Retail
5921b Beer & Ale Retail
5932 Used Merchandise Stores Retail

5932a Antique Stores Retail
5932b Used & Rare Book Dealers Retail
5932c Used Clothing Stores Retail
5932d Used Home Furniture & Furnishings Retail
5932e Used Office Furniture Furnishings & Equipment Retail
5932f Used Store Fixtures & Equipment Retail
5932g Pawnbrokers
5932h Used Brick Dealers Retail
5932j Used Building Materials Retail
5932p Used Musical Instruments Retail
5932q Back Issue Magazine Sales
5932r Swap Shops
5932s Used Refrigerators & Freezers Retail
5932u Used Major Household Appliances Retail
5932x Used Carpet & Rug Dealers Retail
5932y Used Electric Motors Retail
5941 Sporting Goods Stores & Bicycle Shops Retail
5941a Bicycles & Bicycle Parts & Accessories Retail
5941b Camping Equipment Stores Retail
5941c Bait Shops Retail
5941d Fishing Equipment Stores Retail
5941e Gun Shops and Gunsmiths Retail
5941f Saddlery & Harness Stores Retail
5941g Tennis Shops Retail
5941h Water & Snow Ski Shops Retail
5941i Bowling Equipment Stores Retail
5941j Golfing Equipment Stores Retail
5941k Diver Equipment & Supplies Stores Retail
5941l Surfboard & Windsurfing Stores Retail
5941mBilliard Supply Stores Retail
5941n Archery Supply Stores Retail
5941o Skate Boards & Equipment Stores Retail
5941p Soccer Equipment & Supplies Retail
5941q Skating Supply Stores Retail
5941r Excercise Equipment Stores Retail
5941s Karate & Martial Arts Supply Stores Retail
5941z Trampoline Equipment & Supplies Retail
5942 Book Stores Retail
5943 Stationery Stores Retail
5943a Office Supply Stores Retail
5943b School Supply Stores Retail
5943c Notary & Corporate Seal Dealers Retail
5943e Rubber Metal & Plastic Stamps Retail
5944 Jewelry Stores Retail
5944a Jewelry Designers & Craftsman Retail
5944b Diamonds Retail

5944z Jewelry Engravers
5945   Hobby Toy & Game Shops Retail
5945a Arts & Crafts Supply Stores Retail
5945b Model & Hobby Supplies Stores Retail
5945c Toy Stores Retail
5945d Game Shops Retail
5945e Video Games Retail
5945f Ceramic Equipment & Supplies Retail
5945x Dolls & Doll Houses & Supplies Retail
5946   Camera & Photographic Supply Stores Retail
5946a Photographic Equipment & Supplies Retail
5947   Gift Novelty & Souvenir Shops Retail
5947a Gift Shops Retail
5947b Greeting Cards Retail
5947c Novelty Shops Retail
5947e Souvenir Shops Retail
5947i Gift Baskets & Parcels Retail
5947u Balloon Shops Novelty & Toy Retail
5948   Luggage & Leather Goods Stores Retail
5949   Sewing Needlework & Piece Goods Stores Retail
5949a Needlework Stores Retail
5949b Fabric Shops Retail
5949c Notions & Sewing Supplies Retail
5949e Yarn Retail
5961   Catalog & Mail Order Houses
5961a Magazine Mail Order Subscription Agents
5962   Automatic Merchandising Machine Operators
5963   Direct Selling Establishments
5983   Fuel Oil Dealers Retail
5984   Bottled Liquefied Petroleum Gas Dealers Retail
5989   Fuel Dealers Retail
5989a Coal & Coke Dealers Retail
5989b Firewood Dealers Retail
5992   Florists Retail
5992a Plant Shops Retail
5993   Tobacco Stores & Stands Retail
5993a Pipes & Smokers Articles Retail
5994   News Dealers & Newsstands Retail
5995   Optical Goods Stores Retail
5999   Miscellaneous Retail Stores
5999a Aquarium Supply Stores Retail
5999b Artificial Flower Stores Retail
5999c Art & Art Supply Stores Retail
5999d Awning & Tent Stores Retail
5999e Trophy & Plaque Stores Retail
5999f Cosmetic Stores Retail

5999g Hearing Aid Stores Retail
5999h Candle Stores Retail
5999i Beauty Supply Dealers Retail
5999j Monument Dealers Retail
5999k Wedding Supplies & Services Retail
5999l Orthopedic Prosthesis & Medical Supply Stores Retail
5999m Pets & Pet Supplies Retail
5999n Stamp & Coin Dealers Retail
5999o Feed & Farm Supply Dealers Retail
5999p Lapidaries & Lapidary Equipment & Supplies Retail
5999q Baby Carriage Dealers Retail
5999r Pictures & Picture Frame Shops Retail
5999s Party Supply Shops Retail
5999t Ice Dealers Retail
5999u Telephone & Telephone Equipment Stores Retail
5999v Typewriters & Typewriter Supply Dealers Retail
5999w Religious Goods Stores Retail
5999x Binoculars & Telescopes Retail
5999y Factory Outlet Stores
5999z Christmas Lights & Decorations Retail
6011   Banks - Federal Reserve
6019   Banks - Central Reserve Depository Institutions
6021   Banks - National Commercial Banks & Trusts Member Frs & Fdic Insured
6022   Banks - State Commercial Banks & Trusts
6022a Banks - State Commercial Banks & Trusts Member Frs & Fdic Insured
6022b Banks - State Commercial Banks & Trusts Fdic Insured Only
6029   Banks - Commercial Banks & Trusts
6029a Banks - Commericial Banks & Trusts Member Frs & Fdic Insured
6029b Commericial Banks & Trusts Fdic Insured Only
6029c Banks - Mutual Savings Banks Member Frs & Fdic Insured
6029d Banks - Mutual Savings Banks Fdic Insured Only
6029e Banks - Mutual Savings Banks
6035   Banks - Savings Institutions Federally Chartered
6035a Banks - Federal Savings & Loan Associations Member Fslic
6035b Banks - Federal Savings & Loan Associations Not Member Fslic
6035c Banks - Federal Savings Banks Member Flsic
6035d Banks - Federal Savings Banks Not Member Flsic or Unknown
6035e Federal Savings Institutions Member Flsic
6036   Savings Instutions Not Federally Chartered
6036a Non-federal Savings & Loan Associations Member Fslic
6036b Non-federal Savings & Loan Associations Not Member Fslic or Unknown
6036c Non-federal Savings Banks Member Fslic
6036d Non-federal Savings Banks Not Member Fslic or Unknown
6036e Non-federal Savings Institutions Member Fslic
6061   Credit Unions Federally Chartered
6062   Credit Unions Not Federally Chartered

6062a Credit Unions
6062b State Credit Unions
6081 Banks - (Foreign) Branches & Agencies
6082 Foreign Trade & International Banking Institutions
6091 Non-deposit Trust Facilities
6091a Non-deposit Trusts Federal Reserve
6091b Non-deposit Trusts Not Fdic
6099 Functions Related to Depository Banking
6099a Safe Deposit Companies
6099b Clearing House Associations
6099d Check Cashing Services
6099e Foreign Currency Exchanges
6099f Money Order Services
6099g Traveler Check Issuance
6099h Currency Exchanges
6111 Federal & Federally Sponsored Credit Unions
6111a Government National Mortgage Association
6111b Rediscounting for Agricultural
6111c Banks - Federal Land
6111e Banks - Import Export
6141 Personal Credit Institutions
6141a non Deposit Individual Loan Banks
6141b Loan & Finance Companies
6141c Installment Sales Finance Companies
6153 Short Term Business Credit Institutions Except Agricultural
6153a Factors
6159 Miscellaneous Business Credit Institutions
6162 Mortgage Bankers & Loan Correspondents
6162b Foreclosure Assistance
6163 Loan Brokers
6211 Security Brokers Dealers & Flotation Companies
6211a Investment Security Companies
6211b Stock & Bond Brokers
6211c Mutual Funds
6211f Oil Land Leases
6211g Investment Management Services
6221 Commodity Contracts Brokers & Dealers
6231 Security & Commodity Exchanges
6231a Stock Exchanges
6282 Investment Advice
6282b Retirement Planning Services
6289 Services Allied with the Exchange of Securities or Commodities
6311 Life Insurance
6321 Health & Accident Insurance
6324 Hospital & Medical Service Plans
6331 Fire Marine & Casualty Insurance

6351 Surety Insurance
6361 Title Insurance
6371 Pension Health & Welfare Funds
6399 Insurance Carriers
6399a Insurance Company Home Offices
6411 Insurance Agents Brokers & Service
6411a Insurance Adjusters
6411b Insurance Consultants
6411c Combined Insurance Law & Loan Offices
6411d Pension Plan Consultants
6512 Operators of Nonresidential Buildings
6512a Office Building Management
6512b Shopping Center Management
6512c Operators of Auditoriums Arenas Halls Stadiums & Athletic Fields
6512z Industrial Developments
6513 Operators of Apartment Buildings
6513e Operators of Retirement Centers
6514 Operators of Dwellings Other than Apartment Buildings
6515 Operators of Residential Mobile Home Sites
6517 Lessors of Railroad Property
6519 Lessors of Real Property
6519a Oil Property Leasing & Management
6531 Real Estate Agents & Managers
6531a Real Estate Appraisers
6531b Real Estate & Property Management Firms
6531c Real Estate Agents
6531d Real Estate Rental Information Services
6531f Real Estate Investments
6531g Condominium & Townhouse Management
6541 Title Abstract Offices
6541a Title Companies
6552 Land Subdividers & Developers Except Cemetaries
6552b Land Companies
6553 Cemetery Subdividers & Developers
6553a Cemeteries & Mausoleums
6553b Pet Cemeteries
6712 Offices of Bank Holding Companies
6719 Offices of Holding Companies
6722 Management Investment Offices Open Ended
6726 Unit Investment Trusts Face Amount Cert & Closed End Mgmt Invesmt off
6726a Management Investment Offices Closed End
6726b Unit Investment Trusts
6726c Face Amount Certificate Offices
6732 Educational Religious & Charitable Trusts
6733 Trusts Except Educational Religious & Charitable
6792 Oil Royalty Traders

6794 Patent Owners & Lessors
6798 Real Estate Investment Trusts
6799 Investors
6799a Commodity Traders
7011 Hotels Motels & Tourist Courts
7011a Hotels
7011b Motels
7011c Resorts
7011d Bed & Breakfast Accommodations
7011f Bungalow & Cottage Lodging
7011j Skiing Centers & Resorts
7011k Tourist Accomodations
7011l Guest Ranches
7021 Rooming & Boarding Houses
7021b Dormitories
7032 Sporting & Recreational Camps
7032c Fishing Camps
7033 Recreational Vehicle Parks & Campsites
7041 Organization Hotels & Lodging House on Membersship Basis
7211 Power Launderies Family & Commercial
7212 Garment Pressing & Agents for Laundries & Drycleaners
7213 Linen Supply
7215 Coin Operated Laundries & Drycleaning
7215a Coin Operated & Self Service Laundries
7215b Coin Operated & Self Service Cleaners
7216 Drycleaning Except Rug Cleaning
7216a Drapery & Curtain Cleaners
7216b Cleaners Wholesale
7217 Carpet & Upholstery Cleaners
7218 Industrial Launderers
7218a Uniform Supply Service
7219 Laundry & Garment Services
7219a Reweaving & Mending Services
7219b Clothing Alterations
7219c Cleaning Storage Remodeling & Repair Services Including Fur
7219d Diaper Services
7219e Seamtress Dressmaking Customer Material
7219f Pillow Cleaning & Renovating
7219g Zipper Repairing
7219h Leather Goods Cleaning Dyeing & Repairing
7221 Photographic Portrait Studios
7231 Beauty Shops & Schools
7231a Beauty Culture Schools
7231b Beauty Salons
7231c Manicure & Pedicure Salons
7231k Cosmetology Salons & Cosmetologists

7231w Beauty Salons Selling Wigs
7241 Barber Shops & Schools
7241a Barber Schools
7241b Barber Shops
7241w Barber Shops Selling Wigs
7251 Shoe Repair Shops & Shoeshine Parlors
7251c Shoe Dyers
7261 Funeral Service & Crematories
7261e Funeral Plans
7291 Tax Return Preparation Service
7299 Miscellaneous Personal Services
7299a Tanning Salons
7299b Formal Wear Services
7299c Costume Rental
7299e Massage Parlors
7299f Clothing Rental Except Formal
7299g Dating Services
7299h Party Planning Services
7299i Health Fitness & Weight Control Consultants & Services
7299j Wake up Service
7299k Escort Services
7299l Consignment Service Resale Shops
7299m Mail Receiving Services
7299n Wedding Chapels
7299o Hot Tubs Baths & Spas
7299p Meat Cutting & Butchering Services
7299q Fashion Stylists & Consultants
7299r Shopping Service Personal
7299s Tattoo Service
7299t Personal Service Bureau
7299u Debt & Credit Counseling Services
7299v Color & Style Consultants
7299w Time & Tempature Services
7299y Bail Bond Services
7299z T Shirt Stores
7311 Advertising Agencies
7311f Motion Picture Advertising
7311g Periodical Advertising
7312 Outdoor Advertising Services
7313 Advertising Representatives - Radio Television & Publishers
7313a Newspaper Advertising Representatives
7313b Magazine Advertising Representatives
7313c Radio & Tv Advertising Representatives
7313d Publishers Representatives
7319 Advertising Services
7319a Advertising Clipping Services

7319e Display Installation Services
7319g Aerial Advertising Services
7319h Transit & Transportation Advertising
7322   Adjustment & Collection Services
7322a Collection Agencies
7322b Adjustment Bureaus
7322c Collection & Credit Reporting Services
7323   Credit Reporting Services
7323a Credit Reporting Services (Business)
7331   Direct Mail Advertising Services
7331a Lettershops & Addressing Services
7331b Mailing List Brokers & Compilers
7334   Photocopying & Duplicating Services
7334b Blueprinting Services
7334c Duplicating Services Except Printing
7334d Photocopy Services
7334e Copying & Duplicating Services
7334f Offset Reproductions
7335   Commercial Photography
7335a Aerial Photographers
7335b Slide & Filmstrip Producers
7336   Commercial Art and Graphic Design
7336a Package Designers
7336b Commercial Artists
7336c Calligraphers
7336k Graphic Services
7336l Advertising Art Layout & Production Services
7336mChart Services
7338   Secretarial & Court Reporting Services
7338a Secretarial Services
7338b Stenographic Services
7338c Resume Services
7338d Word Processing Services
7338e Editorial & Proofreading Services
7342   Disinfecting & Pest Control Services
7342a Exterminating & Fumigating Services
7342b Deodorizing & Disinfecting Services
7342h Insect Control Devices & Services
7342j Mothproofing
7349   Building Cleaning & Maintenance Services
7349a Janitorial Services
7349b Chimney Cleaning & Maintenance Services
7349c Building Maintenance & Repair Services
7349d Industrial Chemical Cleaning Services
7349e Window Cleaning Services
7349r Condominium Maintenance Services

7349t Roof Cleaning
7349v Air & Gas Filter Cleaning Services
7349w Property Maintenance
7349x Venilation System Cleaning
7349y Domestic Help & Maid Services
7352 Medical Equipment Rental & Leasing
7352a Oxygen Therapy Equipment Rental
7352b Hospital Equipment Rental
7353 Heavy Construction Equipment Rental & Leasing
7359 Equipment Rental & Leasing
7359a Floor & Carpet Maintenance Equipment Rental
7359b Furniture Rental
7359c Lawn & Garden Equipment Rental
7359d Party Equipment Rental
7359e Industrial Equipment Rental
7359f Video Equipment & Supplies Rental
7359g Office & Commercial Equipment Rental
7359h Television & Radio Rental Dealers
7359i Video Game Rental
7359j Store & Yard Rental Service
7359k Hot Tubs & Spa Rental
7359l Oil Field Equipment & Supplies Rental
7359m Contractor Equipment Rental
7359n Audio Visual Equipment Rental & Leasing
7359o Major Household Appliance Rental
7359q Sound System & Equipment Rental
7359r Washing Machine Dryer & Ironer Rental
7359s Ladder Rental
7359t Spraying Equipment Rental
7359u Refrigerator & Freezer Rental & Leasing
7359v Musical Instrument Rental
7359x Table Rental
7361 Employment Agencies
7361b Nurse Registries
7361c Executive Recruiters
7361j Labor Contractors
7363 Help Supply Services
7363a Temporary Business Supply Services
7363b Modeling Agencies
7363d Bartending Services
7363e Chauffeur Services
7371 Computer Programming Services
7371a Computer Software Development Services
7371b Custom Computer Programming Services
7372 Software (Computer) Prepackaged
7373 Computer Integrated Systems Design

7374 Computer Processing & Data Preparation & Processing Services
7375 Information Retrieval Services
7376 Computer Facilities Management Services
7377 Computer Rental & Leasing
7378 Computer Maintenance & Repair Services
7378a Computer Peripheral Equipment Repair Services
7378b Computer Service and Repair
7378c Word Processing Equipment Maintenance
7379 Computer Related Services
7379c Computer System Consultants
7379d Computer Graphics Services
7381 Detective Guard & Armored Car Services
7381a Armored Car Services
7381b Detective Agencies
7381c Lie Detection Services
7381d Guard & Patrol Services
7382 Security Systems Services
7382a Fire Protection Services
7383 News Syndicates
7384 Photofinishing Laboratories
7384b Photofinishing Retail
7389 Business Services
7389a Appraisers
7389b Auctioneers & Liquidators
7389c Business Brokers
7389d Draftsmen Services
7389e Mediation & Arbitration Services
7389f Interior Design Services
7389g Export Services
7389h Yacht Brokers
7389i Seminar & Lecture Bureaus
7389j Microfilming Services
7389k Packing & Crating Services Except for Shipping
7389l Trade Show, Party Services & Supplies
7389m Swimming Pool & Hot Tub Services
7389n Telephone Answering & Message Services Exc Beeper
7389o Auto Transporters & Drive Away Services
7389p Process Serving Services
7389q Hotel & Motel Reservations
7389r Translators & Interpreters
7389s Notary Publics
7389t Telemarketing & Telephone Interviewing
7389u Sign Letterers & Painters
7389v Embroidery & Monogram Services
7389w Trading Stamp & Coupon Services & Companies
7389x Water Softening Services

7389y Video & Sound Recording Services
7513   Truck Rental & Leasing Without Driver
7514   Automobile Rental
7515   Automobile Leasing
7519   Utility Trailer &
Recreational Vehicle Rental
7519a Mobile Home Rental
7519f Motor Home Rental & Leasing
7521   Automobile Parking
7521a Automobile Parking Lots & Garages
7521c Automobile Parking Attendant Service
7532   Automobile Top Body & Upholstery Repair & Paint Shops
7532a Automobile Tire & Body Repair Shops
7532b Automobile Upholstery & Top Repair Shops
7532c Automobile Body Repair Shops
7532d Automobile Paint Shops
7532e Truck Painting & Lettering
7532g Automobile Customizing & Conversion Services
7533   Automobile Exhaust System Repair Shops
7534   Automobile Tire Retreading & Repair Shops
7536   Automobile Glass Replacement Shops
7537   Automobile Transmission Repair Shops
7538   Automobile Repair Shops
7538a Truck Repair Shops
7538b Recreational Vehicle Repair Shops
7538c Automobile Machine Shops
7538h Bus Repair & Service
7538u Automobile Engine Rebuilding Repair & Exchange
7538z Automobile Crankshaft Grinding Services
7539   Automobile Repair Shops
7539a Automobile Brake Services
7539b Automobile Electrical Services
7539e Automobile Wheel & Frame Alignment Shops
7539f Automobile Radiator & Gas Tank Repair Shops
7539g Automobile Carburetor Repair Shops
7539j Automobile Shock Absorber & Spring Service
7539y Automobile Emission Control Service
7542   Car & Truck Washes
7542a Truck Washes
7542b Automobile Washing & Waxing
7542c Automobile Steam Cleaning Services
7549   Automobile Services Except Repair & Washing
7549a Automobile Towing & Road Services
7549c Automobile Rustproofing & Undercoating Services
7549d Automobile Oil Change & Lubrication Services Only
7549e Mobile Lubrication Services

7549f Automobile Air Conditioning Sales Installation & Service
7622 Radio, Television & Consumer Electronic Repair Shops
7622a Radio & Television Repair Shops
7622b Video Equipment Repair Shops
7622c Stereo & Hi Fi Repair Shops
7622d Antenna Installation & Repair Shops
7622h Audio Visual Equipment Repair Shops
7623 Refrigeration & Air Conditioning Service & Repair Services
7623a Air Conditioning Repair Services
7623b Refrigeration Repair Services
7623e Air Conditioning Equipment Room Unit Repair Services
7623f Air Conditioning System Cleaning Testing & Balancing Services
7629 Electrical & Electronic Repairs
7629a Electrical Appliance Repair Services
7629b Vacuum Cleaner Repair Services
7629c Clothes Washing Machine & Dryer Repair Services
7629d Lamp & Lighting Fixture Repair & Mounting Shops
7629e Electronic Equipment Repair Shops
7629k Electrical Equipment Repair & Service
7629u Marine Electrical Equipment Repair
7629w Garbage Disposal Equipment Repair & Service
7629y Microwave Oven Repair Service
7631 Watch Clock & Jewelry Repair
7631a Watch & Clock Repair Services
7631b Diamond Setters
7631c Jewelry Repair Services
7641 Furniture Repair & Reupholstery
7641a Furniture - Upholsterers
7641b Home Furniture Repair & Refinishing Services
7641c Office Furniture & Equipment Repair & Refinishing Services
7641d Antique Furniture Restoring & Repair Shops
7641g Caning
7692 Welding Repair
7692d Industrial Welding
7694 Armature Rewinding & Electric Motor Repair Shops
7699 Repair Shops & Related Services
7699a Air Compressor & Pump Repair Shops
7699b Bicycle Repair Shops
7699c Blacksmiths
7699d Industrial Tool Grinders
7699e Lawn Mower Repair & Service
7699f Leather Goods Repair
7699g Locksmiths
7699h Sewer Septic Tank & Drain Cleaning & Repair
7699i Racket Restringing & Repair
7699j Gas & Oil Burner Repair Services

7699k Organ & Piano Tuning & Repair Services
7699l Taxidermists
7699m Carpet & Rug Repairing Services
7699n Doors Door Closers & Checks Repair Services
7699o Bathtubs & Sinks Repair & Refinishing
7699p Tool Repair, Sharpening Services & Contractor Equipment
7699q Doll Repair Services
7699r Gas Appliances Repair Services
7699s Mobile Home Repair Services
7699t Sewing Machine Repair Services
7699u Silverware Cleaning Repairing & Replating
7699v Industrial Balancing Services
7699x Musical Instrument Repair Services
7699y Motorcyle Repair Services
7699z Typewriter Repair Services
7812   Motion Picture & Video Tape Production
7812a Film Motion Picture Producers
7812b Television Program Producers
7812e Television Film Production & Distribution
7819   Motion Picture Production Services
7819a Motion Picture Film & Video Editing
7819c Motion Picture Laboratories
7819d Motion Picture Equipment Supplies & Studio Rental
7822   Motion Picture & Video Tape Distribution
7822a Motion Picture Film Distributors & Exchanges
7822b Television Film & Tape Distribution
7822c Video Tapes (Prerecorded) & Discs Wholesale
7829   Motion Picture Distribution Services
7829a Motion Picture Libraries
7832   Motion Picture Theaters Except Drive in
7833   Drive in Motion Picture Theaters
7841   Video Tape Disk & Film Rental
7841a Motion Picture Film Rental to the General Public
7841b Video Disk & Tape Rental to the General Public
7911   Dance Studios Schools & Halls
7911a Dancing Schools
7911b Ballrooms
7922   Producers Except Motion Pictures & Miscellaneous Theatrical Services
7922a Theater & Sports Ticket Agencies
7922b Theatrical Agents
7922c Theater Equipment & Supplies
7922d Opera Companies
7922f Radio Program Producers
7922g Theatres
7922h Dance Companies
7922m Radio & Television Commercial Producers

7922n Television Program Distributors
7929 Bands, Orchestras, Actors & Other Entertainment Groups
7929a Orchestras & Bands
7929b Entertainers
7929c Singing Telegrams
7929d Musicians
7929e Entertainment & Concert Bureaus
7929f Disc Jockeys
7933 Bowling Centers
7941 Professional Sports Clubs & Promoters
7941a Soccer Clubs
7941b Sports Promoters & Managers
7948 Racing Including Track Operations
7991 Physical Fitness Facilities
7991a Athletic Clubs
7991b Health Clubs & Reducing Salons
7991c Spas
7991d Physical Fitness Clubs
7991e Gymnasiums
7992 Public Golf Courses
7993 Coin Operated Amusement Devices
7996 Amusement Parks
7997 Membership Sports & Recreation Clubs
7997a Bridge Clubs
7997b Golf & Country Clubs
7997c Private Tennis, Badmitton, Squash, Handball & Raquet Ball Clubs
7997e Yacht & Boating Clubs
7999 Amusement & Recreation Services
7999a Astrologers
7999b Manned Balloons
7999c Bicycle & Motorcycle Rentals
7999d Ice Skating Rinks
7999e Miniature Golf Courses
7999f Recreation Centers
7999g Riding Academies & Stables
7999h Boating Instructions
7999i Card Playing Rooms
7999j Roller Skating Rinks
7999k Public Tennis & Racquetball Courts
7999l Swimming Pool Facilities Except Membership
7999m Boat & Canoe Rental Services
7999n Guide Services
7999o Tennis Instruction
7999p Martial Arts & Self Defense Instruction
7999q Tourist Attractions
7999r Billiard & Pool Establishments

7999s Recreation Equipment Rental
7999t Diving Instructions
7999u Fairgrounds
7999v Golf Instructions
7999w Knitting Instructions
7999x Swimming Instructions
7999z Fishing Lakes & Parties
8011   Doctors of Medicine - Clinics & Offices
8011a Administrative Physicians & Surgeons
8011c Research Physicians
8011e Physicians & Surgeons
8011i Intern Physicians & Surgeons 1st Year Resident
8011o Office Based Physicians & Surgeons
8011r Resident Physicians & Surgeons
8011s Full Time Hosipital Staff Physicians & Surgeons
8011t Medical Teaching Physicians & Surgeons
8011v Retired Physicians & Surgeons
8021   Dentists - Clinics and Offices
8021a Dental Groups & Clinics
8021b Dentists Group Corporate & Insurance Plans & Practice
8021c Oral Surgeons
8021e Endodontists
8021g Orthodontists
8021h Pedodontists
8021i Periodontists
8021j Prosthodontists
8031   Osteopathy (Doctors Of)
8031b Osteopathic Clinics
8041   Chiropractors Clinics & Offices
8042   Optometrists - Clinics and Offices
8042a Pediatric Optometrists
8042b Contact Lenses Optometrists
8042c Geriatric Optometrists
8042d Low Vision Optometrists
8042e Visual Training Optometrists
8042f Optometrists Group & Corporate Practice
8043   Podiatrists & Chiropodists - Clinics and Offices
8049   Health Practitioners - Clinics and Offices
8049b Psychologists
8049c Acupuncturists
8049d Biofeedback Therapy & Training
8049e Naturopaths
8049f Hypnotists
8049g Dietitians
8049h Drugless Practitioners
8049i Hypnotherapy

8049j Occupational Therapists
8049k Paramedics
8049l Parapsychologists
8049m Naprapaths
8049n Reflexologists
8049o Holostic Practitioners
8049p Psychiatric Social Workers
8049u Dental Hygienists
8049w Midwives
8051   Skilled Nursing Care Facilities
8052   Intermediate Care Facilities
8059   Nursing & Personal Care Facilities
8059a Nursing & Rest Home Boarding Care Facilities
8059b Convalescent Homes
8059d Health Facilities
8059f Hospices
8059g Adult Health Care Facilities
8062   Hospitals - General Medical & Surgical
8062a State Hospitals
8062b County Hospitals
8062c City Hospitals
8062e Government District or Authority Hospitals
8062f Church Operated Hospitals
8062g non Profit Hospitals Not Government
8062o Veterans Administration Hospitals
8062p Ama Approved Residency Hospitals
8062q Hospital Affiliated with Ama Residency
8062r Hospital W/professional Nursing School W/ama Residency
8062s Schools - Hospitals with Professional Nursing Affiliation
8062t Schools - Hospitals with Nursing Internship
8062u Medical Schools with Hospital Affiliation
8062v Hospitals with Professional Nursing School
8063   Psychiatric Hospitals
8069   Specialty Hospitals Except Psychiatric
8069a Sanitariums
8071   Medical & X-ray Laboratories
8071a Medical Laboratories
8071b Medical X-ray Laboratories
8071c Dental X-ray Laboratories
8072   Dental Laboratories
8082   Home Health Care Services
8092   Kidney Dialysis Centers
8093   Specialty Outpatient Facilities
8093a Birth Control & Family Planning Centers
8093b Health & Welfare Clinics
8093c Smoking Information & Treatment Centers

8093d Mental Health & Psychiatric Clinics
8093e Physical & Occupational Therapy & Rehabilitation Services
8093f Alcohol Information & Treatment Centers
8093g Drug Abuse Information & Treatment Centers
8093t Medical Groups & Clinics
8099 Health & Allied Services
8099a Blood Banks
8099c Physician & Surgeon Information & Referral Services
8099d Hmo (Health Maintenance Organizations)
8099e Childbirth Information Services & Preparation Classes
8099g Nursing Home Services
8099h Denture Fabrication & Repair Services
8099j Colonic Irrigation Services
8099k Poison Control Centers
8099l Sperm Banks
8111 Attorneys & Legal Services
8111a Copyright, Patent & Trademark Attorneys
8111e Divorce Assistance
8111f Legal Clinics
8111mAttorney & Lawyer Service Bureaus
8111z Legal Services
8211 Elementary & Secondary Schools
8211a Catholic Elementary Schools
8211b Catholic Junior High Schools
8211c Catholic Senior High Schools
8211d Catholic Combined Elementary & Secondary Schools
8211e Catholic Vocational & Technical Schools
8211f Catholic Special Education Schools
8211g Catholic Schools
8211h Private Elementary Schools
8211i Private Junior High Schools
8211j Private Senior High Schools
8211k Private Combined Elementary & Secondary Schools
8211l Private Vocational & Technical Schools
8211mPrivate Special Education Schools
8211n Private Schools
8211o Public Elementary Schools
8211p Public Junior High Schools
8211q Public Senior High Schools
8211r Public Combined Elementry & Secndry Schools
8211s Public Vocational & Technical Schools
8211t Public Special Education Schools
8211u Public Adult Education Schools
8211v Public Schools
8211w Public School Districts
8211y Private & Parochial Schools

8211z Religious & Parochial Schools
8221 Colleges Universities & Professional Schools
8222 Junior Colleges & Technical Institutes
8231 Libraries
8231a Public Libraries
8231b Special Libraries
8231c College & University Libraries
8231d Junior College Libraries
8231e Law Libraries
8231f Medical Libraries
8231g Military Post Libraries
8231h Government Libraries
8231i Religious Libraries
8243 Data Processing Schools
8244 Business & Secretarial Schools
8244b Business & Vocational Schools
8244c Business Only Educational Services
8249 Vocational Schools
8249a Commercial Art & Photography Schools
8249b Medical & Dental Assistant Schools
8249c Practical Nurse Training Schools
8249d Real Estate & Insurance Schools
8249e Industrial Technical & Trade Schools
8249f Correspondence Schools
8249g Aviation Schools Excluding Flying Instruction
8299 Schools & Educational Services
8299a Flight Schools
8299b Automobile Driving Schools
8299c Dressmaking & Sewing Schools
8299d Language Schools
8299e Modeling & Charm Schools
8299f Music & Fine Art Schools
8299j Art Schools
8299k Bible Study & Schools
8299m Personal Development Schools
8299r School Information & Referral Services
8299s General Interest Schools
8299t Baton Twirling Schools
8299u Cooking Schools
8299v Drama Schools
8299w Public Speaking & Speech Schools
8299x Motivational & Self Improvement Schools
8299y Craft Schools
8299z Schools - Special Academic Education
8322 Individual & Family Social Services
8322a Family & Marriage Counselors

8322b Social Workers
8322c Youth Organizations & Centers
8322d Senior Citizen Organizations
8322e Social Services & Welfare Organizations
8322f Child Abuse Information & Treatment Centers
8322g Suicide Prevention Services
8322h Child & Parental Guidance Institutions
8322m Missions
8322n Social Settlements
8322p Homemaker Services
8322q Adult Day Care Centers
8331 Job Training & Vocational Rehabilitation Services
8331c Career & Vocational Counseling
8331d Apprenticeship Training Programs
8331e Employment Training Services
8351 Child Day Care Services
8361 Residential Care
8361c Homes for the Blind
8361d Adult Residential Care Homes
8361f Retirement Communities & Homes
8399 Social Services
8399b Fund Raising Services
8399z National Association Headquarters
8412 Art Galleries & Museums
8412a Art Galleries
8422 Arboreta & Botanical or Zoological Gardens
8422a Animal & Reptile Exhibits
8422b Zoos
8611 Business Associations
8611a Chambers of Commerce
8611b Junior Chambers of Commerce
8611c Business & Trade Organizations
8621 Professional Membership Organizations
8631 Labor Unions & Similiar Labor Organizations
8641 Civic, Social & Fraternal Associations
8641a Military & Veterans Organizations
8641b Fraternaties and Sororities
8641c Environmental Protection Organizations
8641d Youth Clubs
8641f Educational Organizations
8651 Political Organizations
8661 Religious Organizations & Leaders
8661a Churches, Convents & Monasteries
8661b Apostolic Churches
8661c Assembly of God Churches
8661d Baptist Churches

8661e Seventh Day Adventist Churches
8661f Buddhist Temples
8661g Churches of the Brethern
8661h Christian & Reformed Churches
8661i Jewish Synagogues
8661j Christian Reformed Churches
8661k Churches - Christian Science
8661l Churches of Christ
8661m Churches of God
8661n Covenant & Evangelical Churches
8661o Mormon Churches
8661p Episcopal Churches
8661q Lutheran Churches
8661r Mennonite Churches
8661s Methodist Churches
8661t Churches of the Nazarene
8661u Pentecostal Churches
8661v Presbyterian Churches
8661w Catholic Churches
8661x Reformed Churches
8661y Greek Orthodox Churches
8661z Catholic Diocesan Offices
8699 Membership Organizations
8699b Christian Science Reading Room
8699c Womens Organizations & Services
8711 Engineering Services
8711b Structural Engineering Services
8711c Industrial Engineering & Design Services
8711d Foundation Engineering
8711e Civil Engineers
8711f Energy Conservation Engineers & Engineering Services
8711g Geotechnical Engineering Services
8711h Professional Engineering Services
8711i Acoustical Engineering Services
8711j Electrical & Electronic Engineering Services
8711k Heating, Air Conditioning & Ventilating Engineering Services
8711l Mechanical Engineering Services
8711m Environmental Engineering Services
8711n Mining Engineering Services
8711o Marine Engineers & Engineering Services
8711p Fire Protection Engineers & Engineering Services
8711q Sanitary Engineering Services
8711r Chemical Engineering Services
8711v Land Planning Engineering Services
8711w Petroleum Engineering Services
8712 Architectural Services

8712b Naval Architects
8712c Architect & Builder Services
8712d Architectual Design Services
8712e Engineering & Architectural Services
8713 Surveying Services
8721 Accounting, Auditing & Bookkeeping Services
8721a Accounting Services
8721b Calculating, Statistical & Payroll Services
8721c Bookkeeping Services
8731 Commercial Physical & Biological Research
8731a Electronic Research & Development
8731b Experimental Work
8732 Commercial Economic Sociological & Educational Research
8732a Market Research Services
8733 Noncommercial Research Organizations
8733a Educational Research Foundations
8733b Bacteriologists
8734 Testing Laboratories
8734a Percolation Testing Laboratories
8734d Industrial X-ray Laboratories
8741 Management Services
8741b Inventory Management Services
8741d Sales Management Services
8741e Hotel & Motel Management
8741f Marketing Management Services & Programs
8741g Product Development & Marketing Management Services
8741i Restaurant & Food Service Management Services
8742 Management Consulting Services
8742f Employee & Human Resources Management Consulting
8742h Industrial and Labor Relations Consultants
8742k Marketing Consultants
8743 Public Relations Services
8743c Lobbyists
8744 Facilities Support Management Services
8748 Business Consulting Services
8748a City & Town Planners
8748b Energy Conservation Consultants
8748c Interpersonal Business Communication Consultants
8748d Educational Consultants
8748e Safety Consultants
8748f Electronic Consultants
8748g Petroleum Consultants
8748h Consultants - Mining
8748i Economic Consultants
8748j Hospital Consultants
8748k Acoustical Consultants

8748l Engineering Consulting Services
8748m Building Construction Consultants
8748n Lighting Consultants
8748o Real Estate Consultants
8748p Financial & Financing Consulting Services
8748q Industrial Consultants
8748r Parking & Traffic Consulting Services
8748s Food & Beverage Consultants
8748t Foreign Trade Consultants
8748u Industrial Hygiene Consultants
8811   Private Households
8999   Services
8999a Actuarial Services
8999b Chemists & Scientists
8999c Information Bureaus
8999f Composers & Musical Arrangers
8999g Geophysicists
8999h Geologists
8999i Archaeologists
8999j License Services
8999k Artists & Artists Studios
8999l Sculptors
8999o Professional Talent Management
8999p Art Restoration Services
8999q Eviction Services
8999w Noncommericial Scientific Consulting Services
9111   Executive Offices
9111a City Halls - City & Town Management Offices
9111b County Supervisor & Executive Offices
9111y County Seats - County Government Offices
9111z Local Government Executive Offices
9121   Legislative Bodies
9131   Executive and Legislative Offices Combined
9199   General Government
9199a General Federal Government Offices
9199b General State Government Offices
9211   Courts
9211a Justices of the Peace
9221   Police Protection
9221a City Marshalls
9221b Constables
9221c Sheriffs
9222   Legal Counsel & Prosecution
9223   Correctional Institutions
9224   Fire Protection
9224a Volunteer Fire Departments

9224x Volunteer Rescue Services
9229　Public Order & Safety
9311　Public Finance, Taxation & Monetary Policy
9411　Adminstration of Educational Programs
9411a Bureau of Indian Affairs & Schools
9431　Administration of Public Health Programs
9441　Administration of Social, Human Resource & Income Maintenance
　　　　Programs
9451　Administration of Veterans Affairs Except Health & Insurance
9511　Air, Water Resource & Solid Waste Management
9511a Air Pollution Control Agencies
9511b Water Pollution Control Agencies
9512　Land, Mineral, Wildlife, & Forest Conservation
9531　Administration of Housing Programs
9531a Housing Authorities
9532　Administration of Urban Planning & Rural Development
9611　Administration of General Economic Programs
9621　Regulation & Administration of Transportation Programs
9631　Regulation & Administration of Communications & Utilities
9641　Regulation of Agricultural Marketing & Commodities
9641a County Agricultural Agents
9651　Regulation, Licensing & Inspection of Misc Commercial Sectors
9661　Space Research & Technology
9711　National Security
9711a Armed Forces Recruiting
9721　International Affairs
9721a Consulates & Embassies
9999　Nonclassifiable Establishments

List of Government Acronyms

ACH Automated Clearing House
ACMS Advanced Cost Managemetn System
ACO Administrative Contracting Officer
ACRS Accelerated Cost Recovery System
ADP Automated Data Processing
ADPE Automated Data Processing Equipment
AFAA Air Force Audit Agency
AID Agency for International Development
AMIS Agency Management Information System
ANSI American National Standards Institute
ASA Assistant Secretary for Administration
ASCII American Standard Code for Information Exchange
ASPA Armed Services Procurement Act
ASPM Armed Services Pricing Manual
ASPR Armed Services Procurement Regulation
BAFO Best and Final Offer
BATF Bureau of Alcohol, Tobacco and Firearms
BCA Board of Contract Appeals
BLM Bureau of Land Management
BLS Bureau of Labor Statistics
BOA Basic Ordering Agreement
BPCR Breakout Procurement Center Representatives
BPO Bargain Purchase Option
CAAC Civilian Agency Acquisition Council
CACO Corporate Administrative Contracting Officer
CAGE Commercial and Government Entity Code
CAO Contract Administration Office
CAS Cost Accounting Standard
CCDR Contract Cost Data Report
CFR Code of Federal Regulations
CFSR Contract Funds Status Report
CICA Competition in Contracting Act
CIPR Contractor Insurance/Pension Review
CMR Commercial Market Representatives

CO   Contracting Officer
COC   Certificate of Competency
COE   Corps of Engineers
COTR   Contracting Officer's Technical Representative
CPAF   Cost Plus Award Fee
CPCM   Certified Professional Contract Manager
CPFF   Cost Plus Fixed Fee
CPIF   Cost Plus Incentive Fee
CPR   Cost Performance Report
CPSC   Consumer Products Safety Commission
CPSR   Contract Procurement System Review
CR/DR   Clarification Requests/Deficiency Response
CRAG   Contractor Risk Assessment Guide
CSRA   Civil Service Reform Act
CSSR   Cost/Schedule Status Report
DAC   Defense Acquisition Circular
DAR   Defense Acquisition Regulation
DARC   Defense Acquisition Regulatory Council
DCAA   Defense Contract Audit Agency
DCAI   Defense Contract Audit Institute
DCMC   Defense Contract Management Command
DCMD   Defense Contract Management District
DEA   Drug Enforcement Agency
DESC   Defense Electronic Supply Center
DFAS   Defense Finance and Accounting Service
DIA   Defense Intelligence Agency
DISA   Data Interchange Standards Association
DLA   Defense Logistics Agency
DoD   Department of Defense
DODD   Department of Defense Directive
DODI   Department of Defense Instruction
DOE   Department of Energy
DOJ   Department of Justice
DOL   Department of Labor
DOT   Department of Transportation
DPA   Defense Production Act
DSTU   Draft Standard for Trial Use
DTIC   Defense Technical Information Center
EAC   Estimate at Completion (cost)
EC   Electronic Commerce
ECPN   Electronic Commerce Processing Node
EDI   Electronic Data Interchange
EEOC   Equal Employment Opportunity Commission
EFT   Electronic Funds Transfer
EOQ   Economic Order Quantity
EPA   Environmental Protection Agency

FAA   Federal Aviation Administration
FAC   Federal Acquisition Circular
FAOC   Full and Open Competition
FAR   Federal Acquisition Regulation
FARC   Federal Acquisition Regulatory Council
FBI   Federal Bureau of Investigation
FCA   Farm Credit Administration
FCC   Federal Communication Commission
FDA   Food and Drug Administration
FDIC   Federal Deposit Insurance Corporation
FEMA   Federal Emergency Management Agency
FERC   Federal Energy Regulatory Commission
FFP   Firm Fixed Price
FHA   Federal Highway Administration
FHA   Federal Housing Administration
FICA   Federal Insurance Contributions Act
FIFO   First In, First Out (inventory method)
FIPS   Federal Information Processing Standards
FLRA   Federal Labor Relations Authority
FLSA   Fair Labor Standards Act
FMC   Federal Maritime Commission
FMIS   Field Management Information System
FMS   Foreign Military Sales
FMV   Fair Market Value
FNMA   Federal Natinoal Mortgage Association
FOB   Free on Board
FOIA   Freedom of Information Act
FPASA   Federal Property and Administrative Services Act
FPDC   Federal Procurement Data Center
FPEPA   Fixed Price with Economic Price Adjustment
FPI   Fixed Price Incentive (contract)
FPMR   Federal Property Management Regulation
FPR   Fixed Price Redeterminable (contract)
FPRA   Forward Pricing Rate Agreement
FR   Federal Register
FRA   Federal Railway Administration
FRS   Federal Reserve System
FSC   Federal Service Codes
FSG   Federal Stock Groups
FSS   Federal Supply Service
FTE   Full Time Equivalent (employee)
FUTA   Federal Unemployment Tax Act
G&A   General and Administrative
GAO   General Accounting Office
GASB   Government Accounting Standards Board
GBL   Government Bill of Lading

GFE   Government Furnished Equipment
GNMA Government National Mortgage Administration
GOCO Government Owned, Contractor Operated
GPO   Government Printing Office
GSA   General Services Administration
GSAR   General Services Administration Acquisition Regulation
HCFA Health Care Financing Administration
HHS   Department of Health and Human Services
HRSA Health Resources and Services Administration
HTML Hyper Text Markup Language
HUD   Housing and Urban Development
ICC   Interstate Commerce Commission
ICQ   Internal Control Questionnaire
IDIQ   Indefinite Delivery, Indefinite Quantity (contract)
IFB   Invitation for Bids
IRC   Internal Revenue Code
IRS   Internal Revenue Service
ITA   International Trade Administration
ITC   International Trade Commission
JTR   Joint Travel Regulation
LIFO   Last In, First Out (inventory method)
LSA   Labor Surplus Area
MAAR Mandatory Annual Audit Requirement
MBDA Minority Business Development Agency
MRP   Material Requirements Planning
NASA National Aeronautics and Space Administration
NCMA National Contract Management Association
NGB   National Guard Bureau
NIH   National Institutes of Health
NIST   National Institute of Standards and Technology
NLRB National Labor Relations Board
NOAA National Oceanic and Atmospheric Administration
NRC   Nuclear Regulatory Commission
NSF   National Science Foundation
NTIS   National Technical Information Service
OAGM Office of Acquisition and Grant Management
OFPP Office of Federal Procurement Policy
OIRM Office of Information Resources Management
OMB   Office of Management and Budget
ONR   Office of Naval Research
OPM   Office of Personnel Management
OSHA Occupational Safety and Health Administration
PACO Principal Administrative Contracting Officer
PAO   Procurement Assistance Office
PASS Procurement Automated Source System
PBIS   Performance Based Incentive System

PBS   Public Buildings Service
PCO   Procuring Contracting Officer
PCR   Procurement Center Representatives
PD   Purchase Descriptions
PHS   Public Health Service
PM   Program/Project Manager
PO   Purchase Order
PRS   Performance Requirement Summary
PTO   Patent and Trademark Office
QA   Quality Assurance
QAE   Quality Assurace Evaluator
QBL   Qualified Bidders List
QC   Quality Control
QML   Qualified Manufacturers List
QPL   Qualified Products List
R&D   Research and Development
RFP   Request for Proposals
RFQ   Request for Quotations
RTC   Resolution Trust Corporation
SBA   Small Business Administration
SBIR   Small Business Innovative Research
SCA   Service Contract Act
SDB   Small Disadvantaged Business
SEC   Securities and Exchange Commission
SF   Standard Form
SGML   Standard Generalized Markup Language
SIC   Standard Industrial Classification
SOW   Statement of Work
SSA   Social Security Administration
TCO   Terminating Contracting Officer
TCPR   Traditional Procurement Center Representative
TINA   Truth in Negotiations Act
T&M   Time and Materials (contract)
TOP   Trade Opportunities Program
TQM   Total Quality Management
TSC   Technical Service Center
UCF   Uniform Contract Format
USA   United States Army
USAF   United States Air Force
USC   United States Code
USCG   United States Cost Guard
USDA   United States Department of Agriculture
USGS   United States Geological Survey
USIA   United States Informatin Agency
USMC   United States Marine Corps
USN   United States Navy

USPS United States Postal Service
VA   Vetrans Adminstration
VAN   Value-Added Network
VAS   Value-Added Service
WBS   Work Breakdown Structure

Government Contracting Definitions

Acceptance	The act of accepting an offer. The act of an authorized representative of the Government by which the Government, for itself or as agent of another, assumes ownership of existing identified supplies tendered, or approves specific services rendered as partial or complete performance of the contract.
Acquisition	The acquiring by contract, with appropriated funds, of supplies or services by and for the use of the Federal Government through purchase or lease, whether the supplies or services are already in existence or must be created, developed, demonstrated, and evaluated. Acquisition begins at the point when agency needs are established and includes the description of requirements to satisfy agency needs, solicitation and selection of sources, award of contracts, contract financing, contract performance, contract administration, and those technical and management functions directly related to the process of fulfilling agency needs by contract.
Acquisition Plan	A plan for an acquisition that serves as the basis for initiating the individual contracting actions necessary to acquire a system or support a program.

Acquisition Planning	The process by which the efforts of all personnel responsible for an acquisition are coordinated and integrated through a comprehensive plan, for fulfilling the agency need in a timely manner an at a reasonable cost; includes development of an overall strategy for managing the acquisition.
Actual Cost	An amount determined on the basis of cost incurred as distinguished from forecasted cost.
Administrative Change	A unilateral contract change, in writing, that does not affect the substantive rights of the parties.
Administrative Contracting Officer	A contracting officer having responsibility for the administration of one or more particular contracts. In some cases the term is used to identify a contracting officer who specializes in performing contract administration functions.
Administrative Law	Rules, regulations, and decisions made by instrumentalities of the Federal Government that have the force and effect of law.
Advance Agreement	An agreement negotiated in advance of the incurrence of a particular cost by a contractor specifying how that cost will be treated for purposes of determining its allowability (and thus its allocability) to Government contracts. An advance agreement may be negotiated before or during a contract (but before the incurrence of the subject cost), and must be in writing. For a given contractor, advance agreements may be specific to a particular contract, a group of contracts, or all the contracts of a contracting office, an agency or several agencies
Advance Payments	Advances of money by the Government to a contractor before, in anticipation of, and for the purpose of complete performance under one or more contracts. They are expected

to be liquidated from payments due to the contractor incident to performance of the contracts. Since they are not measured by performance, they differ from partial, progress, or other payments based on the performance or partial performance of a contract.

Affiliates

Business concerns, organizations, or individuals are affiliates of each other if, directly or indirectly, (a) either one has the power to control the other, or (b) a third party controls or has the power to control both. Indicia of control include, but are not limited to, interlocking management or ownership, identity of interests among family members, shared facilities and equipment, common use of employees, or a business entity organized following the debarment, suspension or proposed debarment of a contractor which has the same or similar management, ownership, or principal employees as the contract or that was debarred, suspended or proposed for debarment. A similar, although more detailed, definition has been formulated by the Small Business Administration for use in applying the small business size standards under the SBA's 8(a) program.

Affirmative Action Program

A contractor's program that complies with Department of Labor regulations to assure equal opportunity in employment to minorities and women.

Agency

One party, known as the principal, appoints another party, known as an agent, to enter into a business or contractual relationship with a third party. In Governmental contracting, the: Government is the principal, Contracting Officer (CO) is the agent and the contractor is the third party.

Agency Supplements

Regulations issued by individual Federal Government agencies for the purpose of implementing or supplementing the basic Federal Acquisition Regulation. An example is the Department of Defense Federal Acquisition Regulation Supplement (DFARS).

Agreement	Negotiated understandings on terms and conditions that will be incorporated in forthcoming contracts between the two parties. By definition, an agreement does not contain all the elements necessary to be considered a contract.
Allocable Cost	A cost is allocable to a Government contract if it: Is incurred specifically for the contract; Benefits both the contract and other work, and can be distributed to them in reasonable proportion tot he benefits received; or Is necessary to the overall operation of the business although a direct relationship to any particular cost objective cannot be shown.
Allowable Cost	A cost which meets the tests of reasonableness and allocability, is in consonance with standards promulgated by the Cost Accounting Standards Board (if applicable), or otherwise conforms to generally accepted accounting principles, specific limitations or exclusions set forth in FAR 31, or agreed-to terms between contractual parties.
Amendment	A change to any information contained in an IFB or RFP. The amendment becomes part of the solicitation and any resulting contract.
Anti-Deficiency Act	A law prohibiting the obligation of money in advance of an appropriation or in excess of the amount of an available appropriation.
Anti-Trust Violation	Practices that eliminate competition or restrain trade, such as collusive bidding, follow-the-leader pricing, rotated low bids, collusive price estimating systems, and sharing of the business.
Any-Quantity Rates	Quoted "per item" rates for goods or services that do not vary according to the quantity ordered.

Appropriation	Authority to obligate public funds that will result in immediate or future outlays.
Armed Services Board of Contract Appeals	The executive branch entity responsible for deciding appeals of contracting officers' decisions with respect to contracts for the acquisition by the Department of Defense of supplies and services, other than those related to automated data processing.
Assignment of Claims	The transfer or making over by the contractor to a bank, trust company, or other financing institution -- as security for a loan to the contractor -- of its right to be paid by the Government for contract performance.
Auction	A negotiation tactic prohibited under FAR 15.610. Prohibited auction techniques include: Indicating to an offeror a cost or price that it must meet to obtain further consideration; Advising an offeror of its price standing relative to another offeror; Otherwise furnishing information about other offerors' prices.
Audit	A review of a company's accounting procedures, accounting practices, books, records, documents, and other evidence related to cost or pricing data or costs claimed to have been incurred or anticipated to be incurred in performing a contract.
Authorization Legislation	A law that permits the establishment or continuation of Federal programs and agencies. Authorizing legislation is normally required before the enactment of budget authority, and such authority is normally provided in a separate appropriations act.

Automated
Clearing
House   A network of financial institutions providing electronic funds
                       transfer services.

Base
Comprehensive
Plan   A concise document containing the plans (either incorporated
                       or by reference) that guide the development of the installation.
                       Such plans include transportation, land-use, community
                       centers, environmental quality, facility development (near and
                       long-term), and utilities. Also, as part of the base
                       comprehensive plan updates, most bases update their existing
                       base maps such as base layout and utilities.

Basic
Agreement   A written instrument of understanding, negotiated between
                       an agency or contracting activity and a contractor, that
                       contains contract clauses applying to future contracts between
                       the parties during its term and contemplates separate future
                       contracts that will incorporate by reference or attachment the
                       required and applicable clauses agreed upon in the basic
                       agreement. A basic agreement is not a contract.

Basic Ordering
Agreement   A written instrument of understanding, negotiated between
                       an agency, contracting activity, or contracting office and a
                       contractor, that contains terms and clauses applying to future
                       contracts between the parties during its term; a description, as
                       specific as practicable, of supplies or services to be provided;
                       and methods for pricing, issuing, and delivering future orders
                       under the basic ordering agreement. A basic ordering
                       agreement is not a contract.

Best and Final
Offer   In competitive negotiations, proposals prepared by offerors in
                       the competitive range following completion of discussions
                       and receipt of a written request for BAFOs from the
                       contracting officer.

Bid	An offer in response to an Invitation for Bids
Bid Guarantee	A form of security assuring that the bidder will not withdraw a bid within the period specified for acceptance and will execute a written contract and furnish required bonds, including any necessary coinsurance or reinsurance agreements, within the time specified in the bid, unless a longer time allowed, after receipt of the specified forms.
Bidder	An offeror who submits a bid in response to an Invitation for Bids
Bill of Materials	A descriptive and quantitative listing of materials, supplies, parts, and components required to produce a designated complete end-item of material or assembly or subassembly. May also show estimated costs or fixed prices.
Board of Contract Appeals	An instrumentality of a Federal department or agency that hears contractor appeals of contracting officer decisions on claims arising under or relating to a contract subject to the Contract Disputes Act.
Bond	A written instrument executed by a bidder or contractor, and a second party, to assure fulfillment of the principal's obligation to a third party (the Government), identified in the bond. If the principal's obligations are not met, the bond assures payment, to the extent stipulated, of any loss sustained by the Government.
Bulk Funding	A system whereby a contracting officer receives authorization from a fiscal and accounting officer to obligate funds on purchase documents against a specified lump sum of funds reserved for the purpose for a specified period of time rather than obtaining individual obligational authority on each purchase document.

Buy American Act	An act requiring that only domestic end products be acquired for public use, except articles, materials, and supplies: For use outside the United States; For which the cost would be unreasonable, as determined in accordance with FAR 25.105; For which the agency head determines that domestic preference would be inconsistent with the public interest; That are not mined, produced, or manufactured in the United States in sufficient and reasonably available commercial quantities, of a satisfactory quality; Purchased specifically for commissary resale
CAGE Code	Commercial and Government Entity Code. Unique five character company identification number issued by the Defense Logistics Service Center to identify DoD contractors.
Certificate of Competency	A certificate issued by the Small Business Administration (SBA) stating that the holder is responsible (with respect to all elements of responsibility, including but not limited to capability, competency, capacity, credit, integrity, perseverance, and tenacity) for the purpose of receiving and performing a specific Government contract.
Change Order	A written order signed by the contracting officer, directing the contractor to make a change that the Changes clause authorizes the contracting officer to order without the contractor's consent. A change order is an example of a unilateral modification.
Civilian Agency Acquisition Council	A council chaired by a representative of the GSA and consisting of members representing twelve civilian agencies, that, along with the Defense Acquisition Regulatory Council (DARC), has responsibility for maintaining the FAR.
Claim	A written demand or written assertion by one of the contracting parties seeking, as a matter of right, the payment

of money in a sum certain, the adjustment or interpretation of contract terms, or other relief arising under or relating to the contract.

Clarification   As used in FAR 15.6, "Contracting by Negotiation: Source Selection", means communication with an offeror for the purpose of eliminating minor irregularities, informalities, or apparent clerical mistakes in the proposal. It is achieved by explanation or substantiation, either in response to Government inquiry or as initiated by the offeror. Unlike discussion, clarification does not give the offeror an opportunity to revise or modify its proposal, except to the extent that correction of apparent clerical mistakes results in a revision.

Classified
Information   Any information or material, regardless of its physical form or characteristics, that is owned by the United States Government, and determined pursuant to Executive Order 12356, April 2, 1982 or prior orders to require protection against unauthorized disclosure, and is so designated.

Clause   A term or condition used in contracts or in both solicitation and contracts, and applying after contract award or both before and after award. Clauses state the rights and obligations of the parties to a contract.

Clean Water
Act (CWA)   The water act that decreed that the waters of the nation should be "fishable/swimmable" (i.e. the waters should be safe enough to swim in and support aquatic life). Regulations under the CWA applies primarily to discharges into navigable bodies of water (i.e. lakes, streams, rivers) and basically excludes groundwater.

Closeout   The process for closing out the contract file following physical completion of a contract.

Code of Federal Regulations	Codification of rules published in the Federal Register by the executive departments and agencies of the Federal Government.
Cognizant Audit Agency	The audit agency having responsibility, as determined under the administrative principles enumerated in FAR 42, for performing contract audits of a contractor. Such audit agencies include the Defense Contract Audit Agency (DCAA) of the Department of the Defense and the Office of the Inspector General (OIG) for each of the various civilian departments.
Collusion	Any consultation, communication, or agreement between two or more offerors or competitors relating to proposed prices, the intention to submit an offer, or the methods or factors used to calculate the prices offered.
Commerce Business Daily	A publication of Government procurement invitations, contract awards, and sales of surplus property. Each edition contains approximately 500 to 1000 notices.
Commercial Item	Any item, other than real property, that is of a type customarily used for nongovernmental purposes and which meets at least one of the following criteria: 1. Has been sold, leased, or licensed to the general public ("general public" means buyers other than the government or affiliates of the offeror, see FAR 15.804 1(b)(2)(v)); 2. Has been offered for sale, lease, or license to the general public; 3. Has evolved from a commercial item described above through advances in technology or performance and, while not yet available in the commercial marketplace, will be available in the commercial marketplace in time to satisfy the government's delivery requirements; or 4. Any item that would satisfy criteria 1-3 above but for modifications customarily available in the commercial marketplace or minor modifications not customarily commercially available made to meet Federal

Government requirements. (An example of the latter could be a Boeing 747 as modified to transport the space shuttle for NASA.)

Commerciality	One of two conditions which must be met if an item is to qualify for the established catalog or market price requirement for the submission of cost or pricing data. A commercial item (which may be either supplies or services) if of a class or kind that is (1) regularly used for other than Government purposes, and (2) sold or traded in the course of conducting normal business operations. (The other condition that the item be sold in substantial quantities to the general public is met when the facts support a reasonable conclusion that the quantities regularly sold to other than affiliates of the seller for end use by other than the Government agencies are sufficient to constitute a real commercial product.)
Competent	An agent for a contracting party who, at the time of agreement to a contract is: Of sound mind; Free of the influence of drugs or alcohol, and Otherwise legally authorized to enter into the agreement on behalf of the party.
Competition In Contracting Act	A public law enacted for the purpose of increasing the number of Government procurements conducted under the principles of full and fair competition, as opposed to contracts that are issued under noncompetitive arrangements such as "sole source" or "set-aside" awards.
Competitive Proposals	A competitive procurement that (1) is initiated by a request for proposals, which sets out the Government's requirements and the criteria for evaluation of offers, (2) contemplates the submission of timely proposals by the maximum number of possible offerors, (3) usually provides discussions with those offerors found to be within the competitive range, and (4) concludes with the award of a contract to the one offeror whose offer is most advantageous to the Government, considering only price and the other factors included in the solicitation.

Competitive Range	All proposals that the CO determines have a reasonable chance of being selected for award, based on cost or price and other factors that were stated in the solicitation. Unless the CO decides to award without discussions, the CO must conduct written or oral discussion with all responsible offerors who submit proposals within the competitive range.
Consideration	Anything of value that changes hands between the parties to a contract.
Constructive Change	During contract performance, an oral or written act or omission by the contracting officer or other authorized Government official, which is of such a nature that it is construed to have the same effect as a written change order.
Contingent Fee	Any commission, percentage, brokerage, or other fee that is contingent upon the success that a person or concern has in securing a Government contract.
Contract	A mutually binding legal relationship obligating the seller to furnish supplies or services and the buyer to pay for them.
Contract Administration Office	An office that performs (a) assigned post-award functions related to the administration of contracts and (b) assigned pre-award functions.
Contract Modification	Any written change in the terms of a contract. Unilateral modifications are signed only by the CO; bilateral by both parties.
Contract Schedule	The complete statement of the requirement in the solicitation, including not only the Statement of Work and Specifications but also the terms and conditions with respect to packaging

and marking, inspection and acceptance, deliveries or performance, contract administration data, and other special contract requirements. The Schedule includes Sections A through H of the Uniform Contract Format.

Contract Type	The name of the compensation arrangement established by the terms and conditions of the contract, such as Firm Fixed Price, Fixed Price Redeterminable, Cost Plus Award Fee, Cost Plus Fixed Fee, or Cost Plus Incentive Fee. Also, the name of the ordering arrangement established by the terms and conditions of an indefinite delivery contract, such as Definite Quantity, Indefinite Quantity, or Requirements.
Contracting	The purchasing, renting, leasing, or otherwise obtaining supplies or services from nonfederal sources.
Contracting Activity	An element of an agency designated by the agency head and delegated broad authority regarding acquisition functions.
Contracting Office	An office that awards or executes a contract for supplies or services and performs post-award functions not assigned to a contract administration office.
Contracting Officer	An agent of the Government with authority to enter into, administer, or terminate contracts and make related determinations and findings.
Contracting Officer's Representative	A Federal employee to whom a Contracting Officer has delegated limited authority in writing to make specified contract-related decisions. Depending on the type of authority delegated, may be referred to as the Contracting Officer's Technical Representative (COTR)

Cost	The amount of money expended in acquiring supplies or services. The total cost of an acquisition includes: The dollar amount paid to the contractor under the terms and conditions of the contract; Any direct costs for acquiring the supplies or services not covered in the contract price; Any cost of ownership not covered in the contract price; The Government's overhead for awarding and administering the contract.
Cost Accounting Standards	Standards for the measurement, assignment, and allocation of costs to contracts with the United States. These standards are established by the Cost Accounting Standards Board and incorporated in Part 30 of the FAR.
Cost Analysis	The review and evaluation of the separate cost elements and proposed profit of an offeror's or contractor's cost of pricing data and the judgmental factors applied in projecting from the data to the estimated costs in order to form an opinion on the degree to which the proposed costs represent what the cost of the contract should be, assuming reasonable economy and efficiency.
Cost Input	The cost, except general and administrative (G&A) expenses, which for contracting purposes is allocable to the production of goods and services during a cost accounting period.
Cost Objective	A function, organizational subdivision, contract, or other work unit for which cost data are desired and for which provision is made to accumulate and measure the cost of processes, products, jobs, capitalized projects, etc.
Cost or Pricing Data	All facts as of the date of price agreement that prudent buyers and sellers would reasonably expect to affect price negotiations significantly. Cost or pricing data are factual, not judgmental, and are therefore verifiable. While they do not indicate the accuracy of the prospective contractor's judgment about estimated future costs or projections, they do include

the data forming the basis for that judgment. Cost or priding data are more than historical accounting data; they are all the facts that can be reasonably expected to contribute to the soundness of estimates of future costs and to the validity of determinations of costs already incurred.

Cost Plus
Award Fee
Contract

A cost-reimbursement contract which provides for a fee consisting of (1) a base amount fixed at inception of the contract and (2) an award amount that the contractor may earn in whole or in part during performance and that is sufficient to provide motivation for excellence in such areas as quality, timeliness, technical ingenuity, and cost effective management. The amount of the award fee to be paid is determined by the Government's judgmental evaluation of the contractor's performance in terms of the criteria stated in the contract. This determination is made unilaterally by the Government and is not subject to the disputes clause.

Cost Plus Fixed
Fee Contract

A cost-reimbursement contract which provides payment to the contractor of a negotiated fee that is fixed at the inception of the contract. The fixed fee does not vary with actual cost, but may be adjusted as a result of changes in the work to be performed under the contract. This contract type permits contracting for efforts that might otherwise present too great a risk to contractors, but it provides the contractor only a minimum incentive to control costs.

Cost Plus Incentive
Fee Contract

A cost-reimbursement contract that provides for the initially negotiated fee to be adjusted later by a formula based on the relationship of total allowable costs to total target costs. This contract type specifies a target cost, a target fee, minimum and maximum fees, and a fee adjustment formula. After contract performance, the fee payable to the contractor is determined in accordance with the formula. The formula provides, within limits, for increases in fee above target fee when total allowable costs are less than target costs, and decreases in fee below target fee when total allowable costs exceed target costs. This increase or decrease is intended to provide an incentive for the contractor to manage the contract effectively. When total allowable cost is greater than or less than the range of costs within which the fee adjustment formula operates, the contractor is paid total allowable costs, plus the minimum or maximum fee.

Cost Reimbursement Contracts | Contracts that provide for payment of allowable incurred costs, to the extent prescribed in the contract. These contracts establish an estimate of total cost for the purpose of obligating funds and establishing a ceiling that the contractor may not exceed without the approval of the contracting officer.

Cure Notice | A notice of intent to terminate a contract for default unless the contractor "cures" the problem within 10 days after receipt of the notice from the contracting officer.

Data Element | The smallest, meaningful piece of information in a business transaction. A data element may condense lengthy descriptive information into a short code. Equivalent to a data field in a paper document; a series of data elements are used to build a data segment. A data element dictionary that defines the data element and, where appropriate, the code is part of ASC X12 standards.

Data Element Dictionary | The publication that lists all of the data elements used within EDI standards.

Debarment | An action taken by a debarring official under FAR 9.406 to exclude a contractor from Government contracting or Government approved subcontracting for a reasonable specified period.

Debriefing | Informing unsuccessful offerors of the basis for the selection decision and contract award. This information includes the

Government's evaluation of the significant weak or deficient factors in the offeror's proposal.

Defective Cost or Pricing Data

Cost or pricing data that are inaccurate, incomplete, or nonconcurrent.

Defense Acquisition Regulatory Council

A council comprised of representatives of the Secretary of Defense, the Army, the Navy, the Air Force, the Defense Logistics Agency, and NASA. Among other responsibilities, this council, along with the Civilian Acquisition Council (CAAC), maintains the FAR.

Defense Contract Audit Agency

The audit agency responsible for carrying out the audit function for contracts with the Department of Defense. The DCAA is probably the best known and most influential of the various Government audit agencies. It has broad authority to perform a variety of contract audits as well as to assist in reviewing and evaluating contract cost, pricing, performance and administration. The DCAA also makes its services available to those civilian departments needing such assistance.

Definite Quantity Contract

A contract which provides for delivery of a definite quantity of specific supplies or services for a fixed period, with deliveries to be scheduled at designated locations upon order.

Delivery Order

An order made pursuant to FAR 52-216-18 against an indefinite delivery contract.

Design Specification	A purchase description that establishes precise measurements, tolerances, materials, in process and finished product tests, quality control, inspection requirements, and other specific details of the deliverable.
Determination And Findings	A special form of written approval by an authorized official that is required by statute or regulation as a prerequisite to taking certain contract actions. The "determination" is a conclusion or decision supported by the "findings". The findings are statements of fact or rationale essential to support the determination and must cover each requirement of the statute or regulation.
Discharge of a Contract	The obligations incurred by the parties when they entered into the agreement are excused, and the parties are no longer bound to perform as promised.
Discussions	Any oral or written communication between the Government and an offeror, whether or not initiated by the Government, that involves information essential for determining the acceptability of a proposal, or provides the offeror an opportunity to revise or modify its proposal.
DUNS Number	Data Universal Numbering System: Unique nine character company identification number issued by Dun & Bradstreet Corporation.
EDIFACT	EDI for Administration, Commerce, and Transportation: An international UN-sponsored EDI standard primarily used in Europe and Asia. An alignment is envisioned between ANSI ASC X12 and EDIFACT EDI standards in the future to create a single global EDI standard.
Electronic Commerce	The paperless exchange of business information, using Electronic Data Interchange, electronic mail, electronic bulletin

boards, electronic funds transfer and other similar technologies.

Electronic
Data
Interchange   A major part of Electronic Commerce, is the computer to computer exchange of business data in a standardized format between Trading Partners.

Electronic
Funds
Transfer   The exchange of payment and remittance information electronically.

Electronic
Mailbox   A holding location for EDI transactions generally provided by a Value Added Network to its Customers. The customers would normally dial-up and connect to their EDI mailboxes and download and upload transactions.

Elements of
a Contract   Elements that must be present in a contract if the contract is to be binding. These include: An offer; Acceptance; Consideration; Execution by competent parties; Legality of purpose; Clear terms and condition.

Emerging
Small Business   A small business concern whose size is no greater than 50 percent of the numerical size standard applicable to the Standard Industrial Classification code assigned to a contracting opportunity.

Environmental
Impact
Statement   A report examining the environmental consequences of a proposed federal action that could significantly affect the quality of the human environment. Established under the National Environmental Policy Act (NEPA), it is a systematic, inter-disciplinary approach which examines various attributes of the environment and determines the quantitative effects on

the environment due to a proposed action. Mitigation measures must be included if possible to reduce the effects identified in the statement

Environmental
Protection
Agency (EPA)

At the federal level, it is the agency of the executive branch tasked to oversee protecting the environment on a national scale. Enforcement programs include air, water, solid waste and hazardous waste. The federal agency is broken down into ten EPA regions each covering a specific area of the United States. Many states have also created a state EPA for enforcing state environmental regulations. The federal EPA may delegate enforcement of federal EPA requirements to the states, if the state has a media compliance/enforcement program that is either as stringent as or more stringent than the federal requirements.

Evaluation
Factors

Factors in selecting an offer for award.

Excusable
Delay

Delay in performing, or failure to perform a contract, arising from causes beyond the control and without the fault or negligence of the contractor.

Executive
Order

An order issued by the President that establishes policies to be followed by executive agencies.

Facilities
Contract

A contract under which Government facilities are provided to a contractor or subcontractor by the Government for use in connection with performing one or more related contracts for supplies or services.

Factfinding

The process of identifying and obtaining information necessary to complete the evaluation of proposals. This may include Factfinding sessions with offerors as provided in FAR 15.808a

Federal Acquisition Network	A computer network capability required by the FEDERAL ACQUISITION STREAMLINING ACT OF 1994. The system is designed to inform the public about federal contracting opportunities, outline the details of government solicitations, permit electronic submission of bids and proposals, facilitate responses to questions about solicitations, enhance the quality of data available about the acquisition process, and be accessible to anyone with access to a personal computer and modem.
Federal Acquisition Regulation	Uniform policies and procedures for acquisition by executive agencies. The FAR is jointly prescribed, prepared, issued and maintained by the Department of Defense, the General Services Administration, and the National Aeronautics and Space Administration.
Federal Acquisition Regulatory Council	A council comprised of the Administrator for Federal Procurement Policy, the Secretary of Defense, the Administrator of National Aeronautics and Space, and the Administrator of General Services. Under the Office of Federal Procurement Policy Act, this council assists in the direction and coordination of Government-wide procurement policy and procurement regulatory activities.
Federal Register	A daily Government publication that informs the public of proposed rules, final rules, and other legal notices issued by Federal agencies.
Federal Specifications	Specifications and standards that have been implemented or use by all Federal Agencies. GSA lists them in the Index of

Federal Specifications, Standards, and Commercial Item Descriptions.

Federal Stock
Class Number   Code developed by the Defense Logistics Agency for use in DoD's supply management program.

Federal Supply
Schedules   Indefinite delivery contracts established by the General Services Administration with commercial firms. The Schedules are a required source for commonly used supplies and services, and provide Federal activities with a simplified process for obtaining such supplies and services at prices associated with volume buying.

Federal Supply
Service   A functional division of the General Services Administration. The FSS is responsible, on a Government-wide basis, for acquiring and maintaining stocks of certain supplies; for acquiring office furniture and fixtures, and certain power and hand tools; for purchasing or leasing motor vehicles; and for establishing and maintaining "schedule" contracts.

Fee or
Profit   Money paid to a contractor over and above total reimbursements for allowable costs.

Firm Fixed
Price
Contract   A contract that establishes a price not subject to any adjustment on the basis of the contractor's cost experience in performing the contract.

First
Operational
Performance
Period   The interval of time during which the contractor is solely responsible for the accomplishment of all activities set forth in the PWS through day-to-day management of the required service. (This period excludes the orientation period and any

interval between award of the contract and commencement of performance)

Fixed Price Contract	A contract that establishes a firm price or, in appropriate cases, an adjustable price. Fixed-price contracts profiling for an adjustable price may include a ceiling price, a target price, or both. Unless otherwise specified in the contract, the ceiling price or target price is subject to adjustment only by operation of contract clauses providing for equitable adjustment or other revision of the contract price under stated circumstances.
Fraud	A felonious act of corruption, or an attempt to cheat the Government or corrupt its agents.
Freedom of Information Act	A public law established for the purpose of providing for the disclosure to the general public of Government information not classified in accordance with national security or other confidentiality requirements.
Full & Open Competition	Acquisitions in which all responsible sources are permitted to compete.
Functional Area Chief (FAC)	The commander or functional director of the organization having responsibility for the actual performance by the contractor of a given service.
Functional Specification	A purchase description that describes the deliverable in terms of performance characteristics and intended use, including those characteristics that at a minimum are necessary to satisfy the intended use.
Gateway	A component of the DoD EC/EDI architecture that series as a link between the DoD contracting activity's Agency Information System and the Network Entry Points.

General
Accounting
Office

An office within the legislative branch that serves as "the watchdog for the Congress." Among other things, the GAO audits agency programs and management and makes recommendations on protests.

General and
Administrative
Expense

Any management, financial, and other expense which is incurred by or allocated to a business unit and which is for the general management and administration of the business unit as a whole. G&A expense does not include those management expenses whose beneficial or casual relationship to cost objectives can be more directly measured by a base other than a cost input base representing the total activity of a business unit during a cost accounting period.

Government
Property

All property owned by or leased to the Government or acquired by the Government under the terms of the contract. It includes both Government-furnished property and property acquired or otherwise provided by the contractor for performing a contract and that the Government has title to.

Government
Furnished
Property

Property in the possession of, or directly acquired by, the Government and subsequently made available to the contractor.

Indefinite
Delivery
Contract

A type of contract used when the exact times and/or quantities of future deliveries are not known at the time of contract award.

Indefinite Quantity Contract	A contract which provides for an indefinite quantity, within stated limits, of specific supplies or services to be furnished during a fixed period, with deliveries to be scheduled by placing orders with the contractors.
Inspection	Examining and testing supplies or services to determine whether they conform to contract requirements.
Invitation for Bids	The solicitation used in Sealed Bidding.
Kickback	Any money, fee, commission, credit, gift, gratuity, thing of value, or compensation of any kind which is provided, directly or indirectly, to any prime contractor, prime contractor employee, subcontractor, or subcontractor employee for the purpose of improperly obtaining or rewarding favorable treatment in connection with a prime contract or in connection with a subcontract relating to a prime contract.
Labor Hour Contract	A variation of the time-and-materials contract, differing only in that materials are not supplied by the contractor.
Labor Surplus Area Concern	A concern that together with its first tier subcontractors will perform substantially in labor surplus areas.
Letter Contract	A written preliminary contractual instrument that authorizes the contractor to begin immediately manufacturing supplies or performing services.
Limitation of Cost Clause	A clause prescribed for inclusion in cost-reimbursement type contracts that establishes requirements for notifying the Government a) at any point at which the contractor has reason to believe that the total cost for performance of the contract

will be either greater or substantially less than had been previously estimated, or b) when incurred costs as of a given date plus costs expected to be incurred over the subsequent 60-day period are expected to exceed 75% of the contract target cost. The notification provision is designed to allow the Government an opportunity to assess the contract progress and to issue a stop-work order if it decides not to continue. The notification to be provided must be in writing. Failure to comply with this clause is one of the most common bars to recovery of cost overruns on cost-reimbursement type contracts.

Loan
Guarantees

Guarantees made by Federal Reserve banks, on behalf of designated guaranteeing agencies, to enable contractors to obtain financing from private sources under contracts for the acquisition of supplies or services for the national defense. See also: chapters on the SBA

Market
Research

Collecting and analyzing information about the entire market available to satisfy minimum agency needs to arrive at the most suitable approach to acquiring, distributing and supporting supplies and services.

Material Safety
Data Sheets
(MSDS)

Forms that contain information of the manufacturer, physical properties, hazards, and chemical composition of a product.

Method of
Procurement

The process employed for soliciting offers, evaluating offers, and awarding a contract. In Federal contracting, contracting officers use one of the following methods for any given acquisition: Small Purchase; Sealed Bidding; Negotiation; Two-Step Sealed Bidding.

Military
Specifications

Specifications and standards maintained by the Department of Defense and published in the DoD Index of Specifications and Standards.

Negotiation	A bargaining process between two or more parties seeking to reach a mutually satisfactory agreement or settlement on a matter of common concern. Also, a method of procurement prescribed in Part 15 of the FAR that includes the receipt of proposals from offerors, permits bargaining, and usually affords offerors an opportunity to revise their offers before award of a contract. Bargaining -- in the sense of discussion, persuasion, alteration of initial assumptions and position, and give-and-take -- may apply to price, schedule, technical requirements, type of contract, or other terms of a proposed contract.
Nonpersonal Services Contract	A contract under which the personnel rendering the services are not subject, either by the contract's terms or by the manner of its administration, to the supervision and control that usually prevails in relationships between the Government and its employees.
Novation Agreement	A legal instrument executed by (a) the contractor (transferor), (b) the successor in interest (transferee), and (c) the Government by which, among other things, the transferor guarantees performance of the contract, the transferee assumes all obligations under the contract, and the Government recognizes the transfer of the contract and related assets.
Obligation of Funds	Legally binding commitments, such as contract awards, made by Federal agencies during a given period that will require outlays during the same or some future period.
Offer	A legally binding promise, made by one party to another, to enter into a contractual agreement, if the offer is accepted. In sealed bidding, offers made in response to Invitations for Bids are called "Bids." In negotiated acquisitions, offers made in

response to a Request for Proposals (RFP) are called "proposals".

Option | A unilateral right in a contract by which, for a specified time, the Government may elect to purchase additional supplies or services called for by the contract, or may elect to extend the term of the contract.

Outlays | Payments by a Federal department or agency.

Partial Payments | Payments for items received and accepted by the Government when the contractor has shipped part of the order. Partial payments are generally treated as a method of payment and not as a method of contract financing.

Performance Requirement (PR) | The point that divides acceptable and unacceptable performance of a task according to the PRS and the Inspection of Services clause. In the case of surveillance by random sampling, the PR is the maximum number of defectives in the random sample chosen that may occur before the government will effect the price computation system according to the PRS and the Inspection of Services clause. When the method of surveillance is other than random sampling, the PR is the number of defectives or maximum percent defective in the lot before the government will effect the price computation system according to the PRS and the Inspection of Services clause.

Performance Requirements Summary (PRS) | A listing of the service outputs under the contract that are to be evaluated by the government QAE on a regular basis to assure contract performance standards are met by the contractor, the surveillance methods to be used for these outputs, and the PR of the listed outputs.

Procurement
Automated
Source System   The Small Business Administration's PASS is a data base of
                       over 200,000 companies that are interested in doing business
                       with the U.S. Federal Government or with large Government
                       Prime Contractors. You can find out more about PASS from
                       1-800-231-7277.

Payment
Bond   A bond that assures payments as required by law to all
                       persons supplying labor or material in the prosecution of the
                       work provided for in the contract.

Performance
Bond   A bond that secures performance and fulfillment of the
                       contractor's obligations under the contract.

Performance
Specification   A purchase description that describes the deliverable in terms
                       of desired operational characteristics. Performance
                       specifications tend to be more restrictive than functional
                       specifications, in terms of limiting alternatives that the
                       Government will consider and defining separate performance
                       standards for each such alternative.

Personal Service
Contract   A contract that, by its express terms or as administered, makes
                       the contractor personnel appear, in effect, as Government
                       employees.

Pre-award
Survey   An evaluation by a surveying activity of a prospective
                       contractor's capability to perform a proposed contract.

Prebid/Proposal
Conference   A meeting held with prospective offerors before bid opening
                       or before the closing date for submission of proposals.
                       Generally, the purpose of such meetings is to brief the offerors
                       and explain complicated specifications and requirements. A

	site-visit is often included that allows the offerors to physically examine the facilities where the work is to be performed.
Price	A monetary amount given, received, or asked for in exchange for supplies or services. Cost plus any fee or profit applicable to the contract type.
Procurement Automated Source System	A database maintained by the Small Business Administration (SBA) that lists the capabilities of contractors certified under the SBA's 8(a) program for the benefit of Government agencies and larger contractors who wish to utilize such 8(a) firms.
Procurement Technology Assistance Centers (PTAC)	Are under contract through DLA on behalf of DoD and federal civil agencies to provide procurement assistance to the private sector.
Prompt Payment Act	A law enacted in order to ensure that companies transacting business with the Government are paid in a timely manner. With certain exceptions, the Act requires that the Government make payment within 30 days from the date of submission of a properly prepared invoice by a contractor. For amounts not paid within the required period, the Government is obligated to pay interest at a rate established by the Secretary of the Treasury. At the time of original enactment, the law provided for a 15-day grace period in addition to the basic 30-day period; this provision was subsequently repealed due to perceived abuse by the Government.
Protest	A written objection by an interested party to a solicitation by an agency for offers for a proposed contract for the acquisition of supplies or services or a written objection by an interested party to a proposed award or the award of such a contract.

Provision	A term or condition used only in solicitations and applying only before contract award. Provisions provide information to prospective offerors on such matters as: Preparing and submitting offers, the evaluation of offers and the offeror's right to protest award.
Progress Payments	Payments made under a fixed price contract on the basis either of costs incurred by the contractor as work progresses under the contract or on physical progress in accomplishing the work.
Purchase Order	An offer by the Government to buy certain supplies or nonpersonal services and construction from commercial sources, upon specified terms and conditions, the aggregate amount of which does not exceed the small purchase limit.
Purchase Request	A requisition prepared by a requiring activity that describes the supplies or services to be acquired; certifies the availability of funds for the acquisition, and includes other information, clearances, and approvals necessary for the CO to initiate the acquisition.
Qualified Bidders List	A list of bidders who have had their products examined and tested and who have satisfied all applicable qualification requirements for that produce or have otherwise satisfied all applicable qualification requirements.
Qualified Manufacturers List	A list of manufacturers who have had their products examined and tested and who have satisfied all applicable qualification requirements for that product.
Qualified Products List	A list of products which have been examined, tested, and have satisfied all applicable qualification requirements.

Quality Assurance (QA)	A planned and systematic pattern of all actions necessary to provide confidence to the government that adequate technical requirements are established; products and services conform to established technical requirements; and satisfactory performance is achieved. For the purpose of this document, Quality Assurance refers to actions by the government.
Quality Assurance Evaluator (QAE)	A functionally qualified government person responsible for surveillance of contractor performance.
Quality _Assurance Surveillance Plan (QASP)	An organized written document used for quality assurance surveillance. The document contains specific methods to perform surveillance of the contractor.
Quality Control	Those actions taken by a contractor to control the production of outputs to ensure that they conform to the contract requirements.
Quality Control Plan (QCP)	Those actions taken by a contractor to control the production of goods or services so that they meet the requirements of the PWS.
Request for Proposals	The solicitation in negotiated acquisitions
Request for Quotations	A document used in soliciting quotations. RFQs are used when the Government does not intend to award a contract on the basis of the solicitation but wishes to obtain price, delivery, or other market information as the basis for preparing a purchase order or for planning purposes. Based on the information received by the CO, a purchase may be made.

Requirements Contract	A contract which provides for filling all actual purchase requirements of designated Government activities for specific supplies or services during a specified contract period, with deliveries to be scheduled by placing orders with the contractor.
Responsible Offeror	An offeror that meets the general and any special standards established under FAR 9.104. To be determined responsible under the general standards, a prospective contractor must: Have adequate financial resources to perform the contract, or the ability to obtain them; Be able to comply with the required or proposed delivery or performance schedule, taking into consideration all existing commercial and Governmental business commitments; Have a satisfactory performance record; Have a satisfactory record of integrity and business ethics; Have the necessary organization, experience, accounting and operational controls, and technical skills, or the ability to obtain them; Have the necessary production, construction, and technical equipment and facilities, or the ability to obtain them; and be otherwise qualified and eligible to receive an award under applicable laws and regulations.
Sealed Bidding	A method of procurement prescribed in Part 14 of the FAR that employs competitive bids, public opening of bids, and awards. Under this method: The CO issues an Invitation for Bids; Offerors submit sealed bids; The bids are publicly opened; Award is made to the responsible bidder whose bid, conforming to the invitation for bids, will be the most advantageous to the Government, considering only price and the price-related factors included in the invitation.
Service Contract	A contract that directly engages the time and effort of a contractor whose primary purpose is to perform an identifiable task rather than to furnish an end item of supply.

Set-aside	An acquisition reserved exclusively for offerors who fit into a specified category. Set-asides are commonly established for small business, businesses in labor surplus areas and SBA 8(a) concerns.
SF-129	Solicitation Mailing List Application: A standard form used by the Federal Government to collect information about contractors and to add them to solicitation mailing lists. Information is collected by individual procurement offices. In most cases, the SF-129 form is being superseded by the EDI 838 contractor registration process.
SIC Code	A code representing a category within the Standard Industrial Classification System administered by the Statistical Policy Division of the U.S. Office of Management and Budget. The system was established to classify all industries in the U.S. economy. A two-digit code designates each major industry group, which is coupled with a second two-digit code representing subcategories.
Size Standards	Measures established by the Small Business Administration for the purpose of determining whether a business qualifies as a small business for purposes of implementing the socioeconomic programs enumerated in Part 19 of the Federal Acquisition Regulation. SBA size standards establish ceilings on either number of employees or the amount of annual revenue for each industry code contained in the Standard Industrial Classification Manual published by the Government.
Small Business Administration	The Government agency that has primary responsibility for the advancement of small business. The SBA serves as a small business advocate through its many programs designed to assist small businesses in areas such as training, financing, and the identification of opportunities.
Small Business	A business that is independently owned and operated, is not dominant in its field of operation in which it is bidding on

government contracts, and has no more than 500 employees (Federal Acquisition Regulation, Part 19).

Small Business
Development
Center (SBDC)   Located at universities and colleges throughout the United States to provide assistance to small businesses in management, training, counseling and research. SBDCs are a cooperative effort of the Small Business Association, state and local governments, and professional and trade associations. Click here for the LOUISIANA SBDC Network

Small Purchase   The acquisition of supplies, nonpersonal services, and construction in the amount of $25,000 or less through the "simplified procedures" prescribed in Part 13 of the FAR.

Sole Source
Acquisition   A contract for the purchase of supplies or services that is entered into or proposed to be entered into by an agency after soliciting and negotiating with only one source.

Solicitation   A document requesting or inviting offerors to submit offers. Solicitations basically consist of a draft contract and provisions on preparing and submitting offers.

Source
Selection   The process of soliciting and evaluating offers for award. Formal source selections usually involve the Establishment of a group to evaluate proposals; Naming of a Source Selection Authority, who might be the CO, the requiring activity manager, or a higher level agency official, depending on the size and importance of the acquisition; Preparation of a written source selection plan.

Specification   A description of the technical requirements for a material, product, or service that includes the criteria for determining whether the requirements are met.

Standard   A document that establishes engineering and technical limitations and applications of items, materials, processes, methods, designs, and engineering practices; includes any related criteria deemed essential to achieve the highest practical degree of uniformity in materials or products, or the interchangeablitiy of parts used in those products.

Statement of Work	The complete description of work to be performed under the contract, encompassing all specifications and standards established or referenced in the contract. The SOW constitutes Part C of the Uniform Contract Format.
Statute	A law enacted by the legislative branch of Government and signed by the President
Stop Work Order	Under the clause at FAR 52.212-13, a written order to the contractor from the CO requiring the contractor to stop all, or any part, of the work called for by the contract for a period of 90 days after the order is delivered to the contractor, and for any further period to which the parties may agree.
Subcontract	Any contract entered into by a subcontractor to furnish supplies or services for performance of a prime contract or a subcontract. It includes, but is not limited to, purchase orders, and changes and modifications to purchase orders.
Subcontractor	Any supplier, distributor, vendor, or firm that furnishes supplies or services to or for a prime contractor or another subcontractor.
Suspension	An action taken by a suspending official under FAR 9.407 to disqualify a contractor temporarily from Government contracting and Government-approved subcontracting.
Taxpayer Identifying Number (TIN)	A numbering system developed by the Internal Revenue Service (IRS) and is required by the Code of Federal Regulation, subsection 301.6109.1. The TIN consists of two types of identifying numbers: social security numbers and

employer identification numbers. For information on obtaining a TIN, call the IRS at 1-800-829-1040.

Technical
Analysis

The examination and evaluation by personnel having specialized knowledge, skills, experience, or capability in engineering, science, or management of proposed quantities and kinds of materials, labor, processes, special tooling, facilities, and associated factors set forth in a proposal in order to determine and report on the need for and reasonableness of the proposed resources assuming reasonable economy and efficiency.

Technical
Factors

Factors other than price-related used in evaluating offers for award. Examples include technical excellence, management capability, personnel qualifications, prior experience and past performance.

Termination
Contracting
Officer

A contracting officer having responsibility for settling one or more particular contracts. In some cases the term is used to identify a contracting officer who specializes in the settlement of terminated contracts.

Termination for
Convenience

The termination of a contract by the Government for reasons other than nonperformance or default when the Government deems it to be in its interest to do so. A termination for convenience is a unilateral contract action undertaken by the Government under the provisions appearing at FAR 49 and the various termination for convenience contract clauses. In a termination for convenience action, the contractor generally is entitled to negotiate a settlement agreement for the purpose of providing an equitable recovery of costs reasonably incurred by the contractor in anticipation of fulfilling the contract, and a reasonable profit thereon.

Termination for Default	The termination of a contract by the Government for failure to perform the contract in accordance with its requirements. A termination for default is a unilateral contract action undertaken by the Government under the provisions appearing at FAR 49 (and especially FAR 49.4). In a termination for default action, the contractor generally is not entitled to any payment for undelivered items, and may be liable to the Government for the repayment of progress payments or advances, liquidated or other damages, and the excess cost of acquiring the undelivered items from another source.
Time and Materials Contract	A type of contract that provides for acquiring supplies or services on the basis of direct labor hours at specified fixed hourly rates that include wages, overhead, general and administrative expenses, and profit, as well as materials at cost
Trading Partners	Commercial entities that do business with each other using EDI.
Truth In Negotiations Act (TINA)	A public law enacted for the purpose of providing for full and fair disclosure by contractors in the conduct of negotiations with the Government. The most significant provision included in TINA is the requirement that contractors submit certified cost and pricing data for negotiated procurements above a defined threshold.
Two-step Sealed Bid	A method of procurement prescribed in section 14.5 of the FAR. The two steps are as follows: The CO issues a request for technical proposals. Technical proposals received are evaluated, and, if necessary, discussed. Sealed bids are

solicited from only those sources that submitted acceptable technical proposals under step one.

Value Added
Network

Generally commercial entities that transmit, receive and store EDI transactions on behalf of their customers. VANs may also provide additional services known as Value Added Services. Also known as third party networks.

Value Added
Service

A Value Added Service may be a separate commercial organization (also known as an EDI service bureau) that provides EDI-related services, or a VAN that provides extra fee-based services beyond standard VAN services to its customers. Such services may range from translation to "EDI-to-FAX" services to complete EDI-integrated business systems.

Walsh-Healy
Act

A public law designed to prevent the practice of "bid brokering", i.e., the practice of buying items and then reselling them to the Government without the adding of any value to the item by the reseller. The Act provides that contracts subject to its provisions (generally contracts over $10,000) may be awarded only to "manufacturers" or "regular dealers", as defined.

Government Links

Most Useful

The Small Business Administration (SBA Online):
http://www.sba.gov/

General Services Administration (GSA):
http://www.gsa.gov/

Central Contractor Registration: Very Important! All contractors must be registered with CCR. There is no cost and it is good business to have your company listed for subcontracting opportunities. http://www.ccr.gov/

GAO

GAO Bid Protest Regulations:
http://www.gao.gov/decisions/bidpro/new.reg/highlite.htm

GAO Bid Protest Decisions:
http://www.gao.gov/decisions/bidpro/bidpro.htm

Decisions of the Comptroller General provides decisions from 1993 to present which are listed in broad categories including acquisitions and bid protests:
http://www.gao.gov/decisions/decision.htm

FAR, FAR Supplements and Other Regulatory Resources

This Federal Acquisition Regulation (FAR) site contains the 1997 reprint edition, and archived versions from FAC 90-34 (1995 to present):
http://www.arnet.gov/far/

Code of Federal Regulations:
http://www.gpoaccess.gov/cfr/index.html

Defense FAR Supplement (DFARS):
http://www.acq.osd.mil/dpap/dars/dfars/index.htm

The Air Force FAR Supplement
http://farsite.hill.af.mil/

Environmental Protection Agency Acquisition Regulation (EPAAR):
http://www.epa.gov/oamrfp12/ptod/

More Sites

Defense Technical Information Center (DTIC):
http://www.dtic.mil/

Qui Tam Information Center: "The Qui Tam Information Center is a site for attorneys and whistleblowers to gain information and help in pursuing qui tam actions under the Federal Civil False Claims Act:"
http://www.quitam.com

 The ABA Public Contract Law Section contains the Public Contract Law Journal:
http://www.abanet.org/contract/

DCAA Field Memos:
http://www.dcaa.mil.

The CCH:
http://www.cch.com/

Grants Listed By Government Agency

MOST USEFUL SITE - Grants
http://www.grants.gov

Department of Defense (DOS) - Grants
http://www.defenselink.mil/other_info/nonprft.html

Department of Transportation (DOT) - Grants
http://www.dot.gov/ost/m60/grant/grelate.htm

Health Resources and Services Administration (NRSA) - Grants
http://www.hrsa.gov./grants/

National Institutes of Health (NIH) - Grants
http://grants.nih.gov/grants/oer.htm

National Institute of Standards and Technology (NIST) - Grants
http://www.nist.gov/public_affairs/grants.htm

National Library of Medicine (NLM) - Grants
http://www.nlm.nih.gov/ep/extramural.html

National Oceanic and Atmospheric Administration (NOAA) - Grants
http://www.rdc.noaa.gov/~grants/

National Science Foundation (NSF) - Grants
http://www.nsf.gov/funding/

U.S. Geological Survey (USGS) - Grants
http://www.usgs.gov/contracts/grants/

U.S. Institute of Peace - Grants
http://www.usip.org/grants.html

Government Grants Listed By Topic

Education Technology - Grants
http://www.ed.gov/Technology/tec-guid.html

Health – Grants
http://www.health.gov/statelocal/comp_grants.html

Public Health – Grants
http://www.sph.emory.edu/PHIL/grants.html

Water Quality – Grants
http://www.nal.usda.gov/wqic/funding.html

Other Government Grant Related Links

The Catalog of Federal Domestic Assistance: A government-wide compendium of Federal programs, projects, services, and activities. Financial and non-financial assistance programs administered by the U.S. government.
http://www.cfda.gov/

Links to sites containing information of interest to researchers in all fields of science and technology.
http://www.cs.virginia.edu/research/sponsors.html

SBIR National Home Page: SBIR agency program links, conference calendar, state and regional SBIR newsletters, and SBIR/STTR solicitation date finder.
http://www.zyn.com/sbir/#agprog

82009590R00157

Made in the USA
Columbia, SC
28 November 2017